MW01010390

The Ethical Implications of Shakespeare in Performance and Appropriation

The Ethical Implications of Shakespeare in Performance and Appropriation

Edited by Louise Geddes, Kathryn Vomero Santos and Geoffrey Way

EDINBURGH
University Press

Edinburgh University Press is one of the leading university presses in the UK. We publish academic books and journals in our selected subject areas across the humanities and social sciences, combining cutting-edge scholarship with high editorial and production values to produce academic works of lasting importance. For more information visit our website: edinburghuniversitypress.com

© editorial matter and organisation Louise Geddes, Kathryn Vomero Santos and Geoffrey Way 2024
© the chapters their several authors 2024

Edinburgh University Press Ltd
13 Infirmary Street
Edinburgh EH1 1LT

Typeset in 11/13 Bembo Std by
IDSUK (DataConnection) Ltd,

A CIP record for this book is available from the British Library

ISBN 978 1 3995 2491 9 (hardback)
ISBN 978 1 3995 2493 3 (webready PDF)
ISBN 978 1 3995 2494 0 (epub)

The right of Louise Geddes, Kathryn Vomero Santos and Geoffrey Way to be identified as the editor of this work has been asserted in accordance with the Copyright, Designs and Patents Act 1988, and the Copyright and Related Rights Regulations 2003 (SI No. 2498).

Contents

Figures

Acknowledgements

This collection began with an observation that led to a question: why have Shakespearean performance studies and adaptation/appropriation studies not been in dialogue with each other? We are thankful for the overlapping conversations with brilliant colleagues in both fields that helped to bring this book into focus. We are particularly grateful to the authors who took the next step in the conversation and trusted us with their work. Their enthusiastic responses to our call demonstrate the importance of creating a space for such productive intersections.

When we issued the call for abstracts in late 2019, we certainly could not have anticipated what the following years would bring, so we are especially appreciative of the fact that the authors featured here undertook the work of writing and revising these essays during a global pandemic when time and energy were in short supply. We thank Michelle Houston for her early enthusiasm for this project, Emily Sharp for giving it a home at Edinburgh University Press, and Elizabeth Fraser for shepherding it through production. The essays and framework for this collection have benefited enormously from the thoughtful, compassionate and constructive feedback of our anonymous reviewers. To our respective institutions – Adelphi, Trinity and Arizona State Universities – we extend our gratitude for the time and support given in bringing this project to print.

Finally, we would like to thank those who matter to us most: Mike, Marc, Hannah, Charlotte, Tessa, and the many animals who fill our homes with love.

Contributor Biographies

Editors

Louise Geddes is Professor of English at Adelphi University, New York. She is the author of *Appropriating Shakespeare: A Cultural History of Pyramus and Thisbe* and with Valerie M. Fazel, she has co-authored *The Shakespeare Multiverse: Fandom as Literary Praxis* and co-edited *The Shakespeare User: Creative and Critical Appropriation in Networked Culture* and *Variable Objects: Speculative Shakespeare Appropriation*. She has had articles published in *Shakespeare Bulletin*, *Medieval and Renaissance Drama in England*, *Shakespeare* and *Shakespeare Survey*. She is currently general co-editor of the open access journal, *Borrowers and Lenders: The Journal of Shakespeare Appropriation*.

Kathryn Vomero Santos is Assistant Professor of English and co-director of the Humanities Collective at Trinity University, San Antonio, Texas. She is currently completing a book entitled *Shakespeare in Tongues* for the *Spotlight on Shakespeare* series. Her articles on language, race and empire have been published in journals such as *Shakespeare Quarterly*, *Shakespeare Studies*, *Borrowers and Lenders*, *Philological Quarterly* and *Latino Studies*. With Katherine Gillen and Adrianna M. Santos, she co-founded the Borderlands Shakespeare Colectiva, which has received funding from the Mellon Foundation and the National Endowment for the Humanities. Together, they are editing *The Bard in the Borderlands: An Anthology of Shakespeare Appropriations en La Frontera*.

Geoffrey Way is the Manager of Publishing Futures for the Arizona Center for Medieval and Renaissance Studies and ACMRS Press, where he serves as the Managing Editor for *The Sundial* and *Borrowers and Lenders*. He is co-editor of *Shakespeare and Cultural Appropriation* with Vanessa I. Corredera and L. Monique Pittman. He has also published on Shakespeare, appropriation, digital media, and performance in *Shakespeare Bulletin, Borrowers and Lenders, Journal of Narrative Theory* and *Humanities*, and in several edited collections.

Contributors

Vanessa I. Corredera is an Associate Professor and Chair of English at Andrews University, Berrien Springs, Michigan. Her scholarship examining the intersections of Shakespeare, race and gender in performance, adaptions/appropriations and pop culture includes *Reanimating Shakespeare's Othello in Post-Racial America* (Edinburgh University Press, 2022), articles in *Literature Compass, The Journal of American Studies, Borrowers and Lenders*, and *Shakespeare Quarterly*, and essays in several edited collections. Her work is forthcoming in *The Oxford Handbook of Shakespeare and Race, Shakespeare Bulletin* and *Shakespeare/Play*. She is also co-editor, alongside L. Monique Pittman and Geoffrey Way, of *Shakespeare and Cultural Appropriation* (2023), as well as General Editor of *Borrowers and Lenders: The Journal of Shakespeare and Appropriation*.

Kristin N. Denslow is Associate Professor of English at Andrews University, Berrien Springs, Michigan. Her published articles and book chapters centre on intermedial adaptions of Shakespeare's plays and the appropriation of twentieth- and twenty-first century representational technologies in performance, film and television.

John S. Garrison teaches at Harvard-Westlake School, Los Angeles. His books include *Shakespeare at Peace* (with Kyle Pivetti, 2018), *Shakespeare and the Afterlife* (2019) and *The Pleasures of Memory in Shakespeare's Sonnets* (2023). In 2021, he was named a Guggenheim Fellow.

Yasmine Hachimi (PhD, University of California at Davis) is Public Humanities Postdoctoral Fellow at the Newberry Library's Center for Renaissance Studies. Her book project, *Tudorotica*, traces the eroticisation of England's Tudor queens across centuries and genres, from sixteenth-century letters and plays, to TV shows and fan fiction today. Yasmine is interested in how popular media and images of the premodern period challenge or affirm public understandings of the past, particularly with regards to sexuality and race. She has shared her work and expertise in several venues, including public-facing talks, publications, podcasts and social media outlets. Yasmine is co-curator of *Seeing Race Before Race*, an exhibition at the Newberry Library that explores the roots of race from 1100–1800 (on view Fall 2023), and she is currently exploring the affordances and limitations of colour-conscious casting in period dramas.

Andrew James Hartley is Emeritus Robinson Professor of Shakespeare at the University of North Carolina at Charlotte. He specialises in performance issues, and is the author of books on issues such as dramaturgy, political theatre and performance history. He edited collections on Shakespeare on the university stage, in millennial fiction, and (with Peter Holland) on geek culture. He was editor of *Shakespeare Bulletin* for a decade, and is currently editing *Julius Caesar* for the Arden Fourth Series. As A. J. Hartley (AKA Andrew Hart) he is the bestselling author of twenty-five novels in a variety of genres including mystery, fantasy, sci-fi, thriller, paranormal, children's and young adult. His latest novels are *Hideki Smith, Demon Queller* and a playful time travel adventure called *Burning Shakespeare*.

Chris Klippenstein is a PhD Candidate in the Department of English and Comparative Literature at Columbia University, where she works on early modern drama. Her dissertation makes the case for a more capacious understanding of 'neighbourship' that includes non-human entities, such as fairies and animals. In 2023, Chris was a speaker on the NextGenPlen panel hosted by the Shakespeare Association of America. Her performance reviews have been published in a 'Shakespeare, Race, and Nation' special edition of *Shakespeare* and in *Shakespeare Bulletin*.

Oliver Knabe is Assistant Professor of German at the University of Dayton, Ohio. His research examines social justice issues in German cinema, literature and popular culture since 1945 with a particular focus on the realm of sports. He co-edited the 2022 volume *Football Nation: The Playing Fields of German Culture, History, and Society* and is further publishing on East German football films with the DEFA Film Library and in *Colloquia Germanica*. His newest book project explores the game of football as a space for social (in)justice in the context of German media, film and literature. It analyses football as a cultural phenomenon that shapes German responses to issues of sexism, racism, heteronormativity, class inequalities, as well as authoritarian rule.

Matt Kozusko is Professor of English at Ursinus College, Collegeville, Pennsylvania, where he teaches Shakespeare and early modern drama. His principal research interest is in Shakespeare and questions of performance, theatre history and appropriation. He is editor of *The Two Gentlemen of Verona* (2014) and multiple essay collections. His scholarship has appeared in *Shakespeare Survey, Early Theatre, Shakespeare Bulletin, Borrowers and Lenders* and numerous collections. He is series editor for *Shakespeare and the Stage*.

Kendra Preston Leonard is a musicologist and music theorist whose work focuses on women and music in the twentieth and twenty-first centuries; and music and media, particularly adaptations of Shakespeare. Her work has appeared in *Cerae, This Rough Magic, Borrowers and Lenders* and *Early Modern Studies Journal*, among other venues.

Kirsten N. Mendoza is Assistant Professor of English and Associate Director of the Human Rights Studies Program at the University of Dayton, Ohio. Her first book project, *A Politics of Touch: The Racialization of Consent in Early Modern English Literature*, examines the conceptual ties that link shifting sixteenth- and seventeenth-century discourses on self-possession and sexual consent with England's colonial endeavours, involvement in the slave trade and global mercantile pursuits. She was the recipient of an ACLS Dissertation Completion Fellowship and of the 2022 MRDS Stevens Award for Best New Essay in Early Drama Studies. Her work has appeared in journals and collections, such as *Renaissance Drama, Shakespeare Bulletin, Race and Affect in Early Modern English Literature* and *Teaching Social Justice Through Shakespeare: Why Renaissance Literature Matters Now*.

Niamh J. O'Leary is Associate Professor of English at Xavier University in Cincinnati. She co-edited, with Christina Luckyj, *The Politics of Female Alliance in Early Modern England* (2017). Her articles on early modern theatre, performance and film have appeared in *Comparative Drama, CEA Forum, Upstart Crow, Early Modern Studies Journal, Scene, Shakespeare Bulletin, Shakespeare Newsletter* and *The Shakespearean International Yearbook*. She is working on a book about Shakespeare in Cincinnati.

L. Monique Pittman is Professor of English and Director of the J. N. Andrews Honors Program at Andrews University, Berrien Springs, Michigan. Her recent articles (*Shakespeare Survey, Shakespeare Bulletin, Borrowers and Lenders, Adaptation*) and previous monograph (*Authorizing Shakespeare on Film and Television*, 2011) examine how constructions of Shakespearean authority shape the portrayal of gender, class and racial identities. Her book, *Shakespeare's Contested Nations* (2022), explores multicultural Britain and Shakespearean historiography in performance.

Saiham Sharif is a PhD student at the University of California, Irvine. His work focuses on race in early modern literature as well as on the reception of Shakespeare among contemporary writers of colour. His work has appeared in the journal *Pedagogy*.

Nora J. Williams is the Associate Dean for Access and Participation at BIMM University. She works in practice-as-research, particularly at the intersection of early modern drama, physical theatre and feminist criticism. Her first book, *Canonical Misogyny: Shakespeare and Dramaturgies of Sexual Violence*, is currently under contract with Edinburgh University Press.

Introduction: Performing the Promise of Shakespeare

Louise Geddes, Kathryn Vomero Santos and Geoffrey Way

In 2007, the satirical news website *The Onion* published a piece with the headline 'Unconventional Director Sets Shakespeare Play In Time, Place Shakespeare Intended'.[1] The article goes on to explain that in the Morristown Community Players' rendition of *The Merchant of Venice*:

> everything in the production will be adapted to the unconventional setting. Swords will replace guns, ducats will be used instead of the American dollar or Japanese yen, and costumes, such as Shylock's customary pinstripe suit, general's uniform, or nudity, will be replaced by garb of the kind worn by Jewish moneylenders of the Italian Renaissance.[2]

The Onion's joke is that the Morristown Players offer an unorthodox staging by returning Shakespeare's play to its 'intended' form. The article satirises the theatrical traditions that, through continuous modernisation, implicitly promise to fulfil Shakespeare's presumed universality by applying his works ad nauseam to contemporary culture and diverse historical contexts. As the article playfully suggests, in the twenty-first century, returning Shakespeare to Shakespeare is radical. Happily reading too deeply, we would argue that *The Onion* shares our view that any use of Shakespeare – even one steeped in original practices – is both an appropriation and a performance of what is later identified as 'the text'. The Morristown Players' production further implies that consumers of Shakespeare are so accustomed to the application of new contexts that *not* adapting his works stands out as a performance choice. The framing of original practices as appropriation draws attention to this collection's project of putting two separated disciplines into conversation as a means of considering what is promised when Shakespeare is performed or adapted. *The Ethical Implications of Shakespeare in Performance and Appropriation*, therefore, considers not only the choices made by artists when they reach the intersection of Shakespeare and their performative cultural adaptations, but also our obligations as critics when we examine these crossover points.

From a theoretical standpoint, Shakespeare performance studies and adaptation and appropriation studies are, at the very least, fields with significant overlap. The oscillation of Shakespeare between page and stage – or through screen, novel, song or poem – is a process that depends on a complex negotiation between what Shakespeare is perceived to be and what it is imagined that he can offer to contemporary audiences. This principle, then, makes most appropriations performative as they reproduce and proffer an imagined Shakespeare to a potential audience. Such interactions are informed both by the human agents who bring their own understanding of Shakespeare's ontological capaciousness to the process, and by non-human agents, such as the technology or genres that are used to reproduce Shakespeare and that demarcate the limits as to what Shakespeare can represent in any given framework. Both appropriation and performance, therefore, navigate a vast network of meanings and limitations (material and immaterial), making choices at every intersection to shape the final product that is then accepted as Shakespeare. Implicit within this process is the illocutionary exchange that J. L. Austin famously theorised when he explained that a promise fulfils a 'code of procedure'[3] in which an utterance performs an idea or offers a social commitment or linguistic exchange that is subsequently accepted on the extended terms. This process of exchange, aptly defined by Austin as a 'performative utterance' or a 'performative' for short,[4] underwrites the procedures of theatre or adaptation, in which Shakespeare, a thing as amorphous and immaterial as speech itself, is extended like a promise, a transaction between artist and audience. Shakespearean appropriation, therefore, relies on the codification of Shakespeare through an Austinian perlocutionary praxis, in which the text represented performs, becoming a signifier for something agreed upon as valuable: in this case, occurring across media, but nonetheless accepted as a 'lingua franca' for modes of cultural or social exchange. Shakespeare is, in a sense, applied (or as Fazel and Geddes have argued elsewhere, used),[5] and this application of Shakespeare as a performative raises questions of how and why it is deployed in this manner.

Exploring, realising and critiquing the idea of 'making Shakespeare fit' for new cultural moments and new audiences has long been a driving force behind both Shakespearean performance scholarship and the study of Shakespearean appropriation.[6] When we consider some of the questions and concerns that continue to animate both fields, it quickly becomes evident how the decision-making processes that have become commonplace in Shakespearean performance are recognisably similar to the types of choices that shape Shakespearean adaptations or appropriations; questions such as setting, perspective and use of language all impact what is commonly defined as an interpretation. This collection, then, takes seriously *The Onion*'s premise that Shakespeare is subject to so many interpretive decisions and recontextualisations that many of these choices are frequently rendered invisible. To belabour *The Onion*'s point a little more, we suggest that recognising the conflation between adaptation and performance affirms Diana Henderson's claim that any Shakespeare appropriation is inherently collaborative.[7] This collection responds to the collaborative nature of the process of making Shakespeare by exploring how the decisions involved are informed by affective, cultural or ideological pressures. Drawing the fields of performance and appropriation studies into conversation with one another, this book contends, not only renders these overlapping processes visible in new ways, but also raises questions about how to cultivate a scholarly practice that pauses at critical junctures to consider the ethical implications of decisions based on cultural contexts, media and the perceived value(s) of Shakespeare.

Performance has the capacity to encompass adaptation and appropriation studies because it is Shakespeare's chosen medium. Shakespeare, as we know, wrote primarily for the stage and never retained proprietary rights over his materials. With the exception of early quarto printings of some plays, the Shakespeare play as a literary text did not fully exist until John Heminges and Henry Condell collated the scripts into a collected works for publication in 1623. It is appealing to think that Shakespeare, the borrower and lender that he was, would be entirely comfortable with the continued adjustments of his texts for the stage and supportive of rewriting them for profit and new media platforms. This, perhaps, gives licence for practitioners to freely spread his works across media. Shakespeare exists over a wide range of platforms, from digital to film to social media, and so in the twenty-first century, there is no guarantee that audiences will experience him primarily as a stage writer. Indeed, our experience as students, educators and scholars tells us that Shakespeare is encountered first and foremost in the literature classroom, ostensibly marking him up as a literary author whose text is fixed on the page. We therefore cannot assume that theatre remains the natural setting for Shakespeare without reverting to antiquated and perhaps troubling notions of what Shakespeare represents, a topic that Chris Klippenstein explores in her analysis of accents and original practices in this volume. Moreover, as it becomes increasingly transmedial, the idea of performance is expanded to accommodate appropriative acts that stretch across various media. Today's theatre is so profoundly different from theatre as we imagine Shakespeare would have known it that we cannot treat modern performance as ground zero for Shakespeare either.[8] Every encounter with Shakespeare, in other words, is the product of some form of remediation, adaptation or appropriation[9] that performs, as W. B. Worthen notes, a version of what we want Shakespeare to be.[10]

To understand Shakespeare as a product of a continuously remediative process, then, creates a spectrum of use in which theatre and appropriation frequently overlap. The productive tension that emerges from the critical connections between the study of Shakespeare in performance and Shakespeare as adaptation or appropriation is the driving force of this book. Although, in 2009, M. J. Kidnie described the unsettled nature of the Shakespearean text as it moves across both performance and appropriation as a 'problem', inviting a comparative approach, the continued severance of these disciplines over a decade later means that the field has overlooked the productive commonality that these approaches share.[11] Both performance studies and appropriation theory are preoccupied with questions of authority, authenticity and representation. While it was once necessary to separate these fields and build discrete practices because of how they draw our attention to the consequences of the materialist processes by which we attribute meaning to Shakespeare, there is much to be gained by leading them back into communication with one another.

Of course, as Kirsten N. Mendoza and Oliver Knabe illustrate in their contribution to this collection, medium still matters. A novel, a web episode or a rap album can perform ideas latent in Shakespeare – or, just as importantly, ideas attributed to Shakespeare, or presented within a Shakespearean framework – in ways that theatre perhaps cannot, and the immersive experience of the playhouse cannot always be replicated on other platforms. However, the inadvertent result of trying to define these fields is an expansion of the problem that William N. West notes characterises Shakespeare performance studies: that is, the practice of 'setting the approaches of performance studies and theatre history against one another'.[12] The result is the loss of a productive cross-fertilisation. According to West, many theatre studies critics either dig deep into a theoretical approach or present theatrical history as some kind of cabinet of curiosities, assuming that a production's embeddedness in history is disconnected from the theoretical discussions that consider theatrical performance as a work in progress.

Similarly, Andrew James Hartley's observation that 'we have been too quick to assume that historical difference demands a rejection of all that is familiar' has been played out in critical practice.[13] The result for Shakespeare studies is fractures within the discipline that allow materialist conditions of reproduction to designate one text as adaptation and another as performance. Resisting a consideration of these forms as part of the same practice of use undermines our capacities to apply more diverse critical methodologies to the many Shakespearean objects that the field encounters. Instead, to imagine a spectrum that begins with the most literal representation of a text and ends with appropriation at its most opaque invites questions of why one medium works over another and facilitates a consideration of what limitations theatrical, cinematic or musical traditions impart on Shakespeare. Drawing together these sub-disciplines crucially returns us to cultural materialist questions of how economics, race, nationhood, religion, sexuality and gender might be at play within these Shakespearean applications. The chapters in this book collectively advance an argument for the interdependence of terms such as appropriation and performance and suggest that this co-dependency is valuable precisely because of the concerns these labels raise about platform, historical specificity and cultural context. These fields practise similar critical methodologies, all of which centre on the idea of choice and the autonomy of the artist, scholar and their audiences to decide what is prioritised and what is not.

Over the past two decades, there has been significant scholarly thought dedicated to parsing out the distinction between adaptation and appropriation, particularly as they relate to degrees of proximity to Shakespeare, and these debates inform this book's larger project. When discussing the distinction between adaptation and appropriation, it is clear that intention matters. Christy Desmet and Sujata Iyengar have attributed the fragmentation of discourses around Shakespeare to the seismic shifts in media consumption and archaeology that have occurred in the past thirty years and suggest how different practices needed to be refined to reflect the medium through which Shakespeare is being remade. The distinction that they make between adaptation and appropriation might easily be expanded to allow reflection upon the way in which performance has been siloed from these conversations. Desmet and Iyengar explain:

To some extent, the distinction between these terms depends on a historical contingency: adaptation became prominent because of its use in film studies, appropriation because of its association not only with cultural materialist Shakespeare studies of the 1980s but also with ongoing studies of art, collecting, and the internet in a global context. The terms originate within different cultural spheres and are influenced by the praxis and attendant discourse from these spheres.[14]

Desmet and Iyengar here evoke West's notation of the impasse in theatre studies as it tries to navigate between historical and theoretical approaches. For Desmet and Iyengar, the division between the terms was previously necessary to annotate the separation of how we talk about media as distinct from a text's cultural histories, even when they went hand in hand. Certainly, adaptation offers more flexibility as Shakespeare mutates across film, novels, art and other media, but to acknowledge that these are dependent on the materiality of praxis (and their attendant discourses) adds theatrical practice back into this hazy space that we term adaptation.

Desmet and Iyengar have been rigorous in their attempt to parse out the distinction between these fields and trace the intellectual history that has led to these separations. They also, however, look ahead to the fluidity that this collection aims to create, and suggest that 'the difference between adaptation and appropriation, from a theoretical and historical perspective, proves to be a difference in degree rather than kind' that results from 'a constant shifting in perspective that corresponds to equally dynamic shifts in motive, whether of producers, consumers, or institutional regulators of Shakespeare's cultural capital'.[15] For Desmet and Iyengar, then, more is to be gained from embracing the agential flexibility of what constitutes a Shakespeare adaptation or appropriation than resisting it. Although they claim that user subjectivity is the driving force behind the application of separate terms (and perhaps, too, separate practices), their ultimate shrug – that scholars may select their own terminology or choose 'what you will'[16] – not only speaks more to the awareness of the interconnected scholarly practices that uphold these fields, but also opens the door to the proposition that across the fields of appropriation (or adaptation) and performance studies adaptors, artists and scholars make choices that are uncritically assumed to be Shakespearean and thereby rendered invisible.

The chapters in this book strive to reclaim that space of visibility and interrogate how the choices made are both impacted by and themselves impact Shakespeare's cultural heritage. When one performs Shakespeare in any capacity – and perhaps more importantly, when one studies these uses – decisions are made to privilege one expression over another, which is, on all interpretive levels, a culturally materialist act with implications for the continued dissemination and authority of Shakespeare. This collection, therefore, aims to foreground the ethical questions that arise when considerations of fidelity are discarded in favour of a spectrum of use that puts performance and appropriation on equal footing as collaborative acts. Critics, as these chapters demonstrate, sit at a juncture and witness how Shakespeare is applied to – or expressed through – a medium at a particular point in place or time and, as a result, are empowered to make choices about what gets identified as Shakespeare and what is overlaid onto him. Accepting Alexa Alice Joubin and Elizabeth Rivlin's proposal that ethical scholars should treat every text as representative of a person or a community means that adaptation and performance scholarship should view new performance and adaptive texts as affective objects, informed by a variety of pressures across culture, time and media.[17] As a result, this collection strives to trace that praxis and understand the decision-making processes that lead to the creation of new Shakespeare texts.

Examining the ethics of the Shakespearean promise is a practice that has little interest in proximity to Shakespeare. It neither moves away from Shakespeare, as appropriation does, nor points directly back at him, as is the case with performance. Rather, it engages more directly with the networks that culminate in the connection(s) with Shakespeare. West describes performance as 'less an event than the management of a rhythm of repetition – a practice of fulfilling an ordinary gesture, word, or phrase with meaning through iteration, spacing, and change' that 'articulates a process that reorients the various voices involved in theatre back towards the idea of reproducing Shakespeare, inviting critics to think about the cultural power of the ways in which a gesture, word, or phrase is represented and potentially changed'.[18] Likewise, Douglas M. Lanier's rhizomatic theory of appropriation, which suggests that we understand 'our shared object of study not as Shakespeare the text but as a vast web of adaptations, allusions and (re)productions that comprises the ever changing cultural phenomenon' that is Shakespeare is an entirely accurate summation of the ways in which appropriation scholarship works and offers the opportunity to unpack these networks before they reach Shakespeare.[19] This vast web, however, to echo Joubin and Rivlin, is primarily made up of human actions with human consequences. Taking either position that is offered by West or Lanier invites a more careful interrogation about what drives these transmedial Shakespeare performances, and perhaps what cultural legacies inform adaptive or appropriative decisions. As Andrew James

Hartley meditates on his multifaceted role as adaptor, director and scholar in this collection's final chapter, he raises questions about ownership and authority as he considers how an artist navigates their obligation to Shakespeare and to their audience. To privilege the unsettled spectrum of what is inherent in Shakespeare and what choices have been made through remediations or representations of Shakespeare, as Kristin N. Denslow and L. Monique Pittman make clear, is an ideologically loaded process that implicates both the media in play and the interpretive capacities of the artists. Prioritising the promises implicit in uses of Shakespeare as he is processed through diverse media and contexts requires a more self-reflective practice of tracking the adaptive process within the rhizome, and invites the scholar to pause along the path, stop at the figurative crossroads, and consider the directions that lie before them. Sometimes, we might discover, what has been omitted is just as important as what has been included.

Approaching adaptive or performative praxis as something that emerges at the intersection of a series of choices suggests that the cultural contexts, affective understanding of Shakespeare, and ideological goals of an application of Shakespeare matter. In an argument evocative of Marvin Carlson's definition of theatre as a ghosted memory machine, Linda Hutcheon suggests that 'we experience adaptations (as adaptations) as palimpsests through our memories of other works that resonate through reception with variation'.[20] As readers, audience members or scholars, we also make choices about reception, and in some cases, what we reproduce or identify as Shakespeare or Shakespearean. The result of this is often the consolidation of a Shakespearean lens that is deeply ideological. To choose to identify anything as Shakespearean is to insert Shakespeare's cultural capital into the discourse, which can often give a framework to palimpsested meanings. The result is that, as Shakespeare itself is affiliated with elite, serious culture, there is perhaps a greater prestige allocated to a trivial object of popular culture because of its embeddedness within this Shakespearean matrix. The application of Shakespeare might also work to ameliorate questionable politics by linking it to the presumed universality of 'The Bard'. Moreover, because of the transient nature of theatre and the increasingly ephemeral presence of digital products that appropriate Shakespeare, there is an important archival aspect to such scholarly work as is presented within this collection. Given the nature of cultural hierarchies, academic work is empowered to validate such ephemera in scholarly journals or books such as this, preserving matter and attaching it to Shakespearean value. The result is that appropriation or performance scholars are themselves engaged in an ethical practice that can have significant effects on how texts are framed as adjacent to, derivative of, or interacting with Shakespeare.

What, then, is an ethical critical practice of appropriation or performance studies? Niamh J. O'Leary explores Joubin and Rivlin's suggestion that the practice of appropriation itself is primarily defined through an understanding of relationships between people and demonstrates how these questions unfold to include the scholars who study these critical junctures. The transaction that is the fulfilment of the promise of Shakespeare is an interaction that encompasses both the creator of art and its audience, and an implicit agreement (or in some cases, disagreement) about how Shakespeare is ideologically constructed and deployed. To capture a process in motion, then, is more expansive than an interrogation of an artefact, and alerts the ethical scholar to the ways in which Shakespeare is constructed, why it is constructed in such a manner, and for whom. An ethical scholarly approach, therefore, explores the way in which Shakespeare is codified and disseminated, examining a circular praxis that leads the researcher from Shakespeare, through the artist, beyond the audience, and then back to Shakespeare. Such an approach reframes 'good' and 'bad' adaptations more performatively as 'successful' or 'unsuccessful', inviting a consideration of the critic's own situatedness in the institutions and discourses of power and authority. Such a methodology then demands a more open acknowledgement, for example, of how racist or anti-racist institutions ethically frame the ways in which remediations or updates are critically assessed.

In taking up these threads, this collection expands Kidnie's 'definitional problem' of Shakespeare that insists that even though 'drama, as distinct from the novel, is generically situated at the intersection of text and performance', it resists 'any ready identification of adaptation with performance'.[21] Matt Kozusko's chapter makes a compelling case for the adaptive nature of theatre and indicates how adaptations of Shakespeare are deeply embedded in performance histories, perpetuating the kind of dramaturgical practices that Nora J. Williams also sees in the staged deployment of Isabella's veil in productions of *Measure for Measure*. Of course, adaptational stage practices are common knowledge to performance theorists, many of whom agree with W. B. Worthen's insistence that 'Shakespeare has become an instrument for exploring the continually contested parameters of performance, the boundaries between writing and doing, between onstage and offstage acting, between literature, theatre, and other technologies of mediated performance.'[22] Kendra Preston

Leonard's chapter in this collection examines music as one of the boundaries of mediated performance, highlighting the extent to which it appropriates what is being seen and influences 'narratives of tragic Jewishness'
in representations of *The Merchant of Venice*.

The question of what is promised through Shakespeare in adaptation or performance, therefore, is not new, although we might argue
that it is urgent. Kim F. Hall's foundational book *Things of Darkness*
demonstrated the value of bringing Black feminist methodologies and
approaches to Shakespeare studies, and, in recent years, the field has
begun to produce and embrace an overdue groundswell of work that
considers what it means to read and experience Shakespeare from a
non-white perspective.[23] Ayanna Thompson's work on race in performance has drawn attention to the ethics of practising Shakespeare
in a multicultural world when she asks whether 'Shakespeare's plays
need to be edited, appropriated, revised, updated, or rewritten to affirm
racial equality and relevance'.[24] To perform Shakespeare, Thompson
suggests, requires adaptation, which runs a spectrum from colour-conscious casting to remediating to changing the framework of the script or
language – a practice Vanessa I. Corredera elsewhere describes as 'adaptive re-vision'.[25] These decisions are profound and complex, something
that O'Leary wrestles with when she suggests that Shakespeare might
be understood as a means of negotiating white gentrification into Black
neighbourhoods of Cincinnati. O'Leary's exploration of what it means
to offer anti-racist artistic reparations when Shakespeare is the medium
implicates Shakespeare, the Cincinnati Shakespeare Company and her
own scholarship because of her intellectual relationship with the company and the local community. In her book, *Reanimating Shakespeare's
Othello in Post-Racial America*, Corredera argues that self-reflective
practices are just as important in performance and appropriation, if
not more so, because they so frequently rest on uncritical assumptions
that Shakespeare's fame as a humanist disqualifies him from also being
racist. Without careful consideration of such assumptions, Corredera
contends, new iterations can inadvertently reproduce 400-year-old stereotypes.[26]

Therefore, if one accepts Joubin and Rivlin's 2014 argument that
adapted and adaptable texts 'act as substitutes and proxies for, and extensions of, people, including audiences, readers, and critics, in our relationship to others', then one must also acknowledge the intersectional praxis
of adaptation and performance.[27] Joubin and Rivlin go on to explain that
for their purposes, an ethical appropriation means 'an obligation, care, or

duty on the part of one actor toward another or others, even or especially when others are encountered in the forms of texts and works'.[28] While we certainly agree that such care *should* be the driving force of adaptation and performance, too often, it quite simply is not. Frequently, as Yasmine Hachimi points out, those creating the adaptation or performance rely on a presumed capaciousness of the text to validate the reading that they wish to promote through Shakespeare. If, as we contend, deploying Shakespeare is an act of choosing what is prioritised – Shakespeare or his contemporary representation across media or culture – then critical practice should take on Joubin and Rivlin's obligation as its primary care.

What is at stake in the shades of difference between performance and appropriation are the values that emerge from minimising the significance of degrees of proximity to Shakespeare. By claiming a more direct kinship to Shakespeare, terms such as adaptation and interpretation connote the ways in which ideas and critiques might benefit from the force of Shakespeare's cultural power at its back. As Corredera's chapter in this collection explicitly states, what matters when appropriators make choices is 'not only *who* can perform Shakespeare, but also *how* they do so'. Inadvertently, then, Shakespeare could become a shorthand for antiquated ideas about race, nationality or gender, just as easily as it can represent progressive and/or groundbreaking new perspectives. As critics, scholars have the capacity to validate or deconstruct diverse readings, deploying the authority of the academy to designate some interpretations as successful and others less so. Exercising such authority, in turn, implicitly or overtly influences other scholarly engagements with Shakespeare. The value of a more self-aware critical practice of adapting Shakespeare is evidenced in John S. Garrison and Saiham Sharif's discussion of Rita Dove's deliberate misquoting of Shakespeare that alters the dynamics of appropriation by improvising over him and affirming the value of a Black woman's voice. By creating a framework that intentionally destabilises the notion that performance and adaptation are disciplinarily incompatible, these essays invite questions about how those who use Shakespeare intervene – or not – with the implicit and explicit assumptions that Shakespeare's prestige engenders. Analysing transmedial uses of Shakespeare at the crossroads of performance and appropriation, this collection contends, demands structures that make visible the ideological and methodological palimpsests that drive critical praxis. We invite critics to take accountability for how we read these choices in light of multiplicitous identities, interlocking forms of oppression, and structures of power.

The chapters in the book are designed to consider not only how stagings of Shakespeare make appropriative decisions that are absorbed into the idea of what Shakespeare represents and are transmitted under the authority of Shakespeare's cultural capital, but also how appropriations stage Shakespearean value. Implicitly and explicitly, these chapters think about dramaturgy as an appropriative practice. Corredera begins a consideration of who has access to Shakespeare and what the Shakespeare text does or does not allow collaborators (fictional and otherwise) to say in her examination of three metatheatrical plays – Derek Walcott's *A Branch of the Blue Nile*, Carlyle Brown's *The African Company Presents Richard III* and Lolita Chakrabarti's *Red Velvet* – that appropriate Shakespeare in order to speak out about racialised practices of gatekeeping within the theatre. Like Garrison and Sharif later, Corredera views appropriation as a means to claim ownership of Shakespeare by talking about him without being yoked to the burden of his words that are recognisably white property. Appropriating Shakespeare, therefore, becomes a response not only to the texts, but also to the stage practices that perpetuate racist practices that would continue to possess Shakespeare as white property.

L. Monique Pittman and Kristin N. Denslow respond to the racialised practices implicit in performing Shakespeare with an analysis of *The Mousetrap*, *Hamlet*'s play-within-a-play, tracking the ways in which it shifts meaning as it moves across productions and media. In comparing two filmed stage productions for the RSC – Simon Godwin's 2016 production, and Gregory Doran's 2008 production – Pittman and Denslow evoke complex questions about the opportunities and limitations of presenting the playlet as a statement of resistance to a digitised surveillance culture. For Pittman and Denslow, the playlet's mutation across media amplifies the ways in which production choices expose institutional privileges and implicit racial bias.

Kendra Preston Leonard's chapter considers how appropriations enable a more careful examination of how identity is performed in accordance with the expectations that an individual's race, gender or religion activate within their society. Leonard's chapter explores the ways in which music both performs and appropriates Jewishness in Michael Radford's 2004 film adaptation of *The Merchant of Venice*. For Leonard, the film's score exposes how antisemitism operates in Shakespeare's Venice and highlights the film's adaptational choices to critique the indifference to Jewish suffering that characterises Shakespeare's play. The music, Leonard contends, performs an aural backdrop that is inherently tragic and expresses a sadness on behalf of the Jewish characters that the play does not necessarily allow for. Leonard, then, by exploring choices that are made on behalf of the under-represented characters, implicitly draws attention to the choices not made in other productions. Similarly, Garrison and Sharif propose that the misappropriation of Shakespeare is a powerful affirmation of autonomy in the work of African American poet Rita Dove. Dove's choice to improvise Shakespeare, they argue, is a deliberate appropriation of Shakespeare's cultural power, affirming the right of the appropriator to put Shakespeare's words in her own mouth and use them as she sees fit. Performing Shakespeare, this suggests, can be embraced for the appropriative act that it is, channelling his cultural currency in order to subvert and undermine it.

The next group of chapters in the collection consider how appropriations can position Shakespeare as a site – both figuratively and literally – upon which discourses of racial identity are played out. Performing Shakespeare in various ways stages racialised identities to varying degrees of success. Kirsten N. Mendoza and Oliver Knabe examine German rapper OG Keemo's 2019 EP *Otello* as a critical revision and appropriation of Shakespeare's play. Inspired by Germany's reticence to reckon with its convoluted racial politics in the early twenty-first century, Mendoza and Knabe suggest that OG Keemo's *Otello* invites its audience to look back at stagings of Black masculinity through the dual lens of Shakespeare and German rap culture.

Next, Chris Klippenstein examines how the cultural appropriation of Shakespeare as an emblem of deep-rooted cultural whiteness, one that might be archaically described as 'Anglo-Saxon', is visible in Appalachia's claim to an accent that is a direct descendant of Shakespeare's English. This supremacist insistence on accent as a marker of uninterrupted lineage with a white past, Klippenstein suggests, implicates modern discourses of staging Shakespeare, particularly when the performance depends on OP, or original pronunciation, as a mark of authenticity. Niamh J. O'Leary then examines an actual location in which Shakespeare is performed, asking how theatre companies might appropriate Black spaces. Like Hartley, O'Leary openly acknowledges the scholar's complicity in these discourses of appropriation and potential reparation when she considers her own relationship to the Cincinnati Shakespeare Company and its role in her assessment of the company's artistic response to moving Shakespeare into a Black neighbourhood in Cincinnati as part of a process of gentrification.

Matt Kozusko's chapter also questions how scholarly and artistic praxis shapes the Shakespearean promise. His work considers how nineteenth-century prompt books of *The Two Gentlemen of Verona* reveal the extent to which Shakespeare is adapted to ameliorate the play's 'broken' ending that silences the women and absolves the men. Using the protean nature of appropriation, Kozusko reframes how critics might think about performance as a form of radical editing that is presumed to speak not to but for Shakespeare, and he examines how the traces of such appropriation are reflected in the textual emendations found in nineteenth-century prompt books. Likewise, Nora J. Williams examines the increasingly popular dramaturgical choice to unveil Isabella in contemporary productions of *Measure for Measure*. Suggesting that dramaturgy is in itself an appropriative gesture, Williams explores the complex networks of assumptions that the performance potentially activates, and suggests that, in the face of rising Islamophobia in the world, the stakes of such practices are especially high.

The final two chapters examine what it means to perform Shakespeare through diverse media and for different audiences. Yasmine Hachimi's work explores how legacies of Shakespeare reinforce gender stereotypes. Hachimi turns to contemporary television to examine the legacy of Anne Boleyn, suggesting that, by virtue of being an ambiguous, sexualised woman, the historical Boleyn has also been subject to a practice of exclusion, and her representation has become male property. Shakespeare stages her as a silent woman, Hachimi suggests, so that men (and women, too) can project agency onto her and implicate her in Henry's abuses of power. The representational vacuum that is at the heart of Anne's presence in Shakespeare's *Henry VIII, or All Is True*, she argues, is reimagined as dangerous sexuality in the early 2000s Showtime television show *The Tudors*. Perpetuating the implicit misogyny that Shakespeare stages through Anne's silence, *The Tudors* can only understand this silence as wanton cunning, and as a result, represents her as a hypersexualised nymph who knowingly tempts the king. In the absence of Anne's voice to articulate her agency, Hachimi proposes, Anne's stagings from Shakespeare to now have repeatedly appropriated her body to speak on her behalf, often through a hypersexualised lens.

The book closes with its most personal chapter, as Andrew James Hartley, known on the *New York Times* bestseller list as Andrew Hart, thinks about his dual role as an appropriator of Shakespeare and a scholar of Shakespeare in performance. Recounting his own processes of adapting *Macbeth* as an audiobook, he asks questions about his obligations as an artist and scholar of Shakespeare and ends the collection on a set of questions that we hope will spur further conversation. He asks whether he owns his novel adaptation of *Macbeth* and suggests that his appropriation is akin to the collaborative process of theatre making that he participates in as part of his pedagogical career. These constant adjustments that Hartley has to make in his relationship to Shakespeare enact the processes that scholars are attempting to trace elsewhere in this book. Together, these chapters demonstrate how ethnographic scholarship sits alongside performance studies and adaptation and appropriation theory as part of a wider discourse that engages not only how artists use Shakespeare, but also how scholars participate in the generation of meaning, a practice replete with its own ideological responsibilities and consequences.

Notes

1. 'Unconventional Director Sets Shakespeare Play In Time, Place Shakespeare Intended', *The Onion*, 2 June 2007, https://www.theonion.com/unconventional-director-sets-shakespeare-play-in-time-1819569151. Accessed 28 February 2023.
2. Ibid.
3. J. L. Austin, *How to Do Things With Words* (Cambridge, MA: Harvard University Press, 1962), 27.
4. Austin, *How to Do Things With Words*, 17.
5. See Valerie M. Fazel and Louise Geddes, *The Shakespeare User: Creative and Critical Appropriations in a Networked Culture* (New York: Palgrave MacMillan, 2017).
6. While adaptation and appropriation are largely interchangeable terms (as is discussed in the introduction, further down), the editors of the book choose appropriation as the preferred term, because of the ways it implies a collaborative agency, rather than a top-down authority that defines Shakespeare as a singular source text.
7. See Diana Henderson, *Collaborations with the Past: Reshaping Shakespeare Across Time and Media* (Ithaca, NY: Cornell University Press, 2006).
8. See W. B. Worthen, '*Hamlet* at Ground Zero: The Wooster Group and the Archive of Performance', *Shakespeare Quarterly* 59, no. 3 (Fall 2008): 303–22.
9. See Fazel and Geddes, *The Shakespeare User*.
10. W. B. Worthen, *Shakespeare and the Authority of Performance* (Cambridge: Cambridge University Press, 1995).
11. Margaret Jane Kidnie, *Shakespeare and the Problem of Adaptation* (London: Routledge, 2009).
12. William N. West, 'Replaying Early Modern Performances', in *New Directions in Renaissance Drama and Performance Studies*, ed. Sarah Werner (New York: Palgrave, 2010), 31.
13. Andrew James Hartley, 'Page and State Again: Rethinking Renaissance Character Phenomenologically', in *New Directions in Renaissance Drama and Performance Studies*, 89.

14. Christy Desmet and Sujata Iyengar, 'Adaptation, appropriation, or what you will', *Shakespeare* 11, no. 1 (2015): 11.
15. Ibid. 16.
16. Ibid. 15.
17. Joubin and Rivlin, 'Introduction', *Shakespeare and the Ethics of Appropriation*, ed. Alexa Alice Joubin and Elizabeth Rivlin (New York: Palgrave Macmillan, 2014), 3.
18. West, 'Replaying Early Modern Performances', 35.
19. Douglas M. Lanier, 'Shakespearean Rhizomatics: Adaptation, Ethics, Value', in *Shakespeare and the Ethics of Appropriation*, 29.
20. Linda Hutcheon, *A Theory of Adaptation*, 2nd ed. (London: Routledge, 2012), 8. See also Marvin Carlson, *The Haunted Stage: Theatre as Memory Machine* (Ann Arbor: University of Michigan Press, 2001).
21. Kidnie, *Shakespeare and the Problem of Adaptation*, 7.
22. W. B. Worthen, *Shakespeare Performance Studies* (Cambridge: Cambridge University Press, 2014), 2.
23. Kim F. Hall, *Things of Darkness: Economies of Race and Gender in Early Modern England* (Ithaca, NY: Cornell University Press, 1995).
24. Ayanna Thompson, *Passing Strange, Shakespeare, Race, and Contemporary America* (New York: Oxford University Press, 2011), 6.
25. Vanessa I. Corredera, *Reanimating Shakespeare's* Othello *in Post-Racial America* (Edinburgh University Press, 2022), 22.
26. Ibid. 4.
27. Joubin and Rivlin, 'Introduction', 3.
28. Ibid.

1

'. . . a thing impossible I should love thee': Shakespearean Performance as White Property

Vanessa I. Corredera

In *The Merry Wives of Windsor* (c. 1597), Fenton laments to Ann Page that he 'cannot get thy father's love' because Master George Page mistrusts Fenton, believing he wants to 'heal' his estate through Page's wealth, elaborating that Fenton's 'riots past' suggest that ''tis a thing impossible / I should love thee but as a *property*' (emphasis added).[1] The *Oxford English Dictionary* uses this line to illustrate and authorise *property*'s meaning as 'A means to an end; a person or thing to be made use of, an instrument or tool', and that is certainly true in context.[2] The idea of property as a tool would only be enhanced by the slant metatheatrical invocation of a theatrical property. But this definition does not fully signal the fact that despite their mutual love and desire for companionship, Ann would nevertheless become Fenton's marital property, a 'thing belonging to a person'.[3] I turn to this instance in *The Merry Wives of Windsor* in order to put pressure on the concept of *property*. Fenton's use of the term demonstrates its nuances, extending beyond its earliest definition as a person's quality or nature. Rather, *property* here raises questions about motivation, authority, use and ownership. Property, therefore, is inextricably tied to power.

Similar questions of motivation, authority, use and power hover over the term *appropriation*, perhaps unsurprisingly, for it is fundamentally tied to the concept of property. Essentially, *appropriation* describes the process of 'making of a thing private property, whether another's or (as now commonly) one's own; taking as one's own or to one's own use'.[4] The act of appropriating thereby depends on ownership, use and access – whether the appropriated object is public or private, whether it belongs to another or is made 'one's own' and therefore available for 'use'. Christy Desmet's definition of *appropriation* emphasises these dynamics when she notes that

'The word "appropriation" implies an exchange, either the theft of something valuable (such as *property* or ideas) or a gift, the allocation of resources for a worthy cause (such as the legislative appropriation of funds for a new school).'[5] An *appropriation*, then, may in its most concrete form reference the specific object or 'property' newly possessed, perhaps stolen, or more positively, the allocated gift. But even if used in this way, the term nevertheless carries with it questions about what demarcates the boundaries of theft, who or what determines value and worth, and who has the power to decide on the (re)allocation of the newly acquired resources.

Clearly, *property* and *appropriation* exist in an intimate relationship, raising similar, vital questions about the terms I keep returning to: use, authority, ownership and power. Here, I excavate this intimate relationship between *property* and *appropriation* in relation to race and Shakespearean performance, continuing Premodern Critical Race scholarship by Arthur Little Jr, Ian Smith, Kim F. Hall and Ayanna Thompson on the implications of Shakespeare as white property.[6] What does the status of Shakespeare as white property mean for Shakespearean performance? What inequitable power dynamics plaguing the Shakespearean stage are made identifiable by recognising Shakespeare's racialised proprietorship and use, Shakespeare as a white supremacist tool? How might performances deemed appropriations engage with, contest and respond to the problem of Shakespeare as white performance property?

To begin answering these questions, I turn to three distinctly metatheatrical plays: Derek Walcott's *A Branch of the Blue Nile* (1986), Carlyle Brown's *The African Company Presents Richard III* (1989) and Lolita Chakrabarti's *Red Velvet* (2012). These plays traverse place and time, from 1980s West Indies to circa 1821 New York City to London in 1825. Yet all three meditate on the role race plays in gatekeeping, inequity and ownership on the historical and contemporary Shakespearean stage; in other words, on Shakespearean performance as white property. More specifically, all three plays consider how Shakespeare as white property delimits who performs Shakespeare and how staging 'authentic' Shakespearean performance becomes defined in opposition to the qualities ascribed to non-white performances. This relentless oppositional stance ultimately extracts an emotional, material and psychological cost by circumscribing not just a person of colour's performance, but also their subjectivity. And significantly, all three plays also offer up a compelling answer to these problems: appropriation. In each play, appropriation takes a different form, whether by turning to the appropriation of the stage by people of colour (appropriation as use), wresting Shakespeare performance practices from white hands to afford him new performance styles (appropriation as product), or launching a metacommentary that joins these two approaches. As such, *appropriation* functions as either/both a transformative product (as in adaptation/appropriation) and/or as a new claim to ownership (as in cultural appropriation), each of which helps dislodge Shakespeare as white property. Ultimately, however, despite their differences, all three plays lean into the idea of appropriation as theft by stressing a fundamental need: wresting the white property that is Shakespearean performance away from white control in order to open up Shakespeare's use and enjoyment to multicultural identities.

Appropriation, Race and Authenticity

What these plays thus suggest is that to create the possibility of racial equity in theatre, the concept of appropriation must always be present, precisely because Shakespeare has been and continues to be white property. Activating and recuperating the most vexing meaning of appropriation, that of theft, Shakespeare must be forced out of, even stolen from, white hands that refuse to let go of their long-standing authority over Shakespeare in/and performance. Authority is key here, for both Shakespearean performance and the societal performance of race reify authority through the concept of authenticity. For instance, as M. J. Kidnie convincingly argues, performance is always inherently tied up with adaptation 'in a reciprocal relation to the Shakespearean "work"'[7] because adaptation functions as the measuring stick for determining what counts as 'authentic' rather than adapted Shakespeare. Though Brandi Wilkins Cantanese uses the term 'fidelity', she too notes how authenticity and performance interweave in the social performance of race. Cantanese explains, 'Race is best understood as a complex synthesis of involuntary and voluntary attributes and affiliations whose significance is performative, produced through our fidelity to them rather than as anterior, interior fact.'[8] In turn, this fidelity 'is structured around the allocation of privilege'.[9] Margo Hendricks incisively brings together the throughline between Kidnie's and Cantanese's analyses, arguing, 'The desire for some authentic Shakespeare, dramatic representations that are "real" to us, for language that speaks to some inherently human element, haunts spectators of Shakespeare's plays – whether theatrically or cinematically performed. The desire for authenticity in performing "race" is even more profoundly framed by this sense of mourning.'[10] Authenticity thus proves central to both Shakespearean and racial performance. Just as the label 'authentic' ascribes privilege to certain types of Shakespearean performance over others, similarly, the faithful racial performance also ascribes privilege to certain racialised performances over others.

What role, then, can appropriation play in challenging this investment in authenticity? Helpful here is Julie Sanders's contention that appropriation signals 'a more decisive journey away from the informing text into a whole new cultural product . . .'[11] Often, this entails 'a more wholesale redrafting, or indeed recrafting . . .'[12] Yet even as Sanders stresses the importance of an intentional, thoughtful break from the 'original', her focus is clearly on appropriation as product, the reimagined contours of genre or form in the appropriated work. When it comes to challenging Shakespearean performance as white property, however, the aim may not be to recraft the 'original' product like *Antony and Cleopatra*, *Richard III* or *Othello* through a wholesale transformation of form, genre or mode (i.e. the tragedy *Titus Andronicus* reimagined as the tragi-farce Broadway play *Gary*).[13] Indeed, because the 'original' product has held the most cultural authority, and therefore capital, this very type of performance has been a product conceptualised as white property. As such, the aim of appropriation may instead be to maintain the basic structure of the 'original' play while challenging the white-held ownership of Shakespeare as property. This means staging supposedly 'authentic' Shakespeare but in a way that extracts performance processes and expectations from white control in order to create space for BIPOC (Black Indigenous People of Color) bodies, voices and viewpoints. In short, it necessitates shifting who gets to freely 'use' Shakespeare in performance by allocating autonomy to BIPOC performers. As Cantanese contends, after all, 'black actors performing the works of Shakespeare could violate norms about race, space, and art'.[14] In this way, *appropriation*, what Sanders calls 'a new cultural product',[15] extends beyond genre, mode and form to a transformation of ideas, namely, of what counts as an authentic racial performance in Shakespeare, and even more radically, a challenge to whether the 'authentic' in fact should continue holding any value.

Sanders's emphasis on an intentional moving away can thus be paired helpfully with Linda Hutcheon's suggestion that appropriation entails a new process, a reimagined 'creative' and 'interpretive act'.[16] Appropriation as process therefore effectively focuses on perspective, reminding one that, as Desmet observes, 'evoking the term "appropriation" forces us to consider "where we stand"'.[17] The question of 'where we stand' is not only related to theoretical view (Desmet's emphasis), but also power. As the three plays discussed below reveal, when BIPOC actors and creators consider where *they* stand in regard to Shakespearean performance, its reality as white property – its continual placement in the power of whiteness – is too strong to ignore. Creating an alternative thus involves appropriating Shakespeare, seizing the great Western signifier, and with him, power, from predominantly white hands so as to open up the potential for racial equity in Shakespearean performance.

Shakespearean Performance as White Property: The Absolute Right to Exclude

In order to understand the imperative of appropriation as a response to traditional Shakespearean performance, one must first grasp the ramifications of Shakespeare as white property. In her 1993 article 'Whiteness as Property', Cheryl I. Harris traces the different characteristics of whiteness as property, delineating how 'the law has accorded "holders" of whiteness the same privileges and benefits accorded holders of other types of property'.[18] Harris's incisive analysis illustrates the shifting nature of property outlined above, moving from a concrete product owned by some and not others to ideological framings to sociological dynamics both formally codified and extra-juridical. Given the legal context in which she writes, it is unsurprising that not each privilege maps neatly onto a discussion of Shakespeare as white property. 'Laws' about Shakespearean performance and race are most often unstated yet culturally reiterated rather than formally mandated, for example. Yet homologies remain, as does *property*'s protean nature, parallels that reveal why Shakespeare has been and continues to be white property, including on the stage. *The Branch of the Blue Nile*, *The African Company Presents Richard III* and *Red Velvet* each grapple with these similarities, namely, the right to exclude and the right to use and enjoyment.[19] While the plays offer up differing, ambivalent responses to the ways Shakespearean performance mirrors facets of whiteness as property, they nevertheless posit appropriation, both product and process, as a vital way of prizing Shakespeare away from whiteness's powerful grasp.

Perhaps most significant for Shakespearean performance is 'The Absolute Right to Exclude'.[20] Just as with property, for which the right to exclude ensures 'use, disposition, and possession', whiteness likewise embraces exclusion, for it 'has been characterized, not by an inherent unifying characteristic, but by the exclusion of others deemed to be "not white"'. This exclusion of those 'not white' through the gatekeeping of the Shakespearean stage shapes *The Branch of the Blue Nile*, *The African Company Presents Richard III* and *Red Velvet*. In *Red Velvet*, a play that depicts the behind-the-scenes drama of Ira Aldridge's brief run as Othello at Covent Garden, actor Charles Kean expresses the idea that Shakespeare needs gatekeeping when he declares, 'I mean, if we don't maintain the standard of our business it will become accessible to every . . .' (44).[21] That Charles invokes an undefined standard to shore up his argument against having Ira play Othello makes it clear that, even if unspoken, this standard is tied to whiteness's primacy in Shakespearean performance.

Like whiteness, which defines itself not through an ontological reality but through restrictive contradistinction, the performance standard's primacy is established by constraining who can perform Shakespeare and how. Walcott's *A Branch of the Blue Nile* follows West Indian actors Sheila, Gavin, Chris and Marilyn under the direction of the white West Indian Harvey St. Just as they work to stage *Antony and Cleopatra*. In ways that Harvey is not, the actors are painfully aware that they tread on unwelcoming ground. As Joyce Green MacDonald argues, 'They can only approach and enact the Shakespearean text through the agency of their specifically colored and gendered Caribbean bodies, but these subaltern bodies' capacity to perform the cultural authority embodied by the Shakespearean text can barely be conceived, much less accepted.'[22] The struggle to conceive and accept their performance of Shakespeare appears in moments such as when Chris half-jokingly says to Sheila, 'Can't talk Shakespeare, though' (229), to which she responds, 'Lips too big.' 'No. No brains', he replies.[23] Even if mildly playful in tone, profound contentions reside in this back-and-forth. Sheila's comment about their supposed big lips illustrates precisely how 'racialized physical appearance functions as a powerful signifier of cultural integrity and authority' on the Shakespearean stage.[24] Their lips serve as the synecdoche for their 'dark bodies' and the fact that they 'are regarded as suitable for some kinds of performances and completely incapable of others'.[25] It is no wonder, then, that Sheila later castigates Harvey, reminding him, 'The theatre is okay for you, Harvey. You're white' (284). *The African Company Presents Richard III* exposes this dualism between Black and white when the Black actor, James Hewlett, responds to a review of his recent performance of Richard III that calls it 'a plausible imitation' (14).[26] He exclaims, 'Some fat, powder-face English man can be an African Moor, but let the Royal Plantagenet be "as black as the ace a spades" and it's "a plausible imitation"' (15). Whiteness may not be held to a standard of racial realism but Blackness is. Thanks to the exclusionary logic of whiteness as property, the Black actor never can be nor should play white, and therefore never can be nor really should embody Shakespeare's white characters. Hence the emphasis on 'imitation', mimicry by another name. Taken together, these examples highlight the history of Shakespeare as white property in performance, signalling that across places, stages and time, for Shakespeare to remain white property, Black bodies must be kept from inhabiting his characters.[27]

At stake is not only *who* can perform Shakespeare, but also *how* they do so. Notably, two of the plays especially emphasise how what Jennifer Lynn Stoever calls the 'sonic colour line', the 'process of racializing sound – how and why certain bodies are expected to produce, desire, and live amongst particular sounds – and its product, the hierarchal division between "whiteness" and "blackness"',[28] further maintains the exclusivity of Shakespeare as white property. To return to Sheila and Chris's discussion, not only are their 'big lips' aesthetically unacceptable, but so are the sounds that they make. Indeed, later in Walcott's play, Marylin angrily denounces the fact that 'We talking Shakespeare like "rangatang people"' (244), her simian reference signalling long-standing concerns about which racialised voices and accents may speak Shakespeare. A reviewer of *Antony and Cleopatra* suggests that Marilyn's concerns were well founded, criticising Harvey for 'desecrating the Bard' after 'rewriting the clown's speech' as well as other parts of the play 'in local dialect' (267). Harvey responds that 'since our dialect is so Jacobean, I felt quite justified' (268). By invoking Jacobean history, Harvey still authorises his artistic decision through the power of whiteness, appealing to a past only part of Trinidad's present due to England's imperial domination. In other words, the standard Harvey holds for determining acceptable Shakespearean speech is not all that different from the reviewer's that he so derides, for both determine value through whiteness.

Brown's play likewise explores the pressure placed upon how persons of colour speak Shakespeare. Brown puts the supposed standard in the mouth of Stephen Price, the white owner of The Park Theater attempting to dissuade Hewlett from having the African Company stage *Richard III* on the very night he is showcasing the same play with Julius Booth performing the titular role.[29] In a discussion with Hewlett, Price observes, 'I read your reviews. You've become a fine actor. Remarkably good diction and your pronunciations are quite good really' (46). In other words, Hewlett speaks Shakespeare correctly and therefore can be afforded a modicum of respect. Interestingly, the play's dialogue nowhere suggests that Price has watched Hewlett onstage. Instead, his impressions entirely derive from and are thereby authorised by reviews.[30] The criteria established for appropriate Shakespearean speech is thus not an idiosyncratic opinion but rather a nebulous yet racialised and reiterated cultural and social standard. In fact, just as speaking Shakespeare properly can be used for approbation for those who 'pass', the same expectation also becomes a measuring stick that justifies derision for those who cannot, as the character Papa Shakespeare reminds the audience. When he explains his name's history, he shares, 'My master 'dere he call me Shakespeare to mock me, 'cause I don't speak the way he do' (32). This is an express invocation of the history of enslavement that Harvey ignores in *The Branch of the Blue Nile*. Thus, what is or is not deemed appropriate oral performance on the Shakespearean stage, i.e. Shakespeare as white spoken property, cannot be divorced from whiteness's history of empire, domination and subjugation of Black and brown bodies and subjectivities.

Indeed, this suppression of Black subjectivity is the thematic beating heart of *Red Velvet*. Chakrabarti's play repeatedly meditates on the fact that, if actors of colour are allowed to perform Shakespeare at all, Shakespearean performance as white property profoundly circumscribes the dynamics of their performance. *Red Velvet*, however, shifts attention from matters of speech to the ways race informs performance traditions.[31] If white actors have overwhelmingly directed and embodied Shakespeare's characters, then one should remember that these performance traditions deserve the qualifying adjective, 'white'. This whiteness often remains obscured but nonetheless functions as a tool for delimiting how actors of colour may or may not interpret and embody a particular role. Once again, Charles becomes the mouthpiece for white elitism when he observes that 'Everyone will be expecting my father [Edmund Keene]. You cannot possibly think of replacing him with . . . him [Ira Aldridge]' (33). Charles's objection carries heavy signifying weight, for Ira not only introduces a different acting style and a reduced level of acting fame, but his status as a Black man also intensifies the racial difference explored in *Othello*. Ira therefore performs not simply against a previously established performance tradition, but specifically a *white* performance tradition that circumscribes how he can embody the titular character.

As the play unfolds, one sees that expectations imposed upon the people that society racialises collide with expectations for Shakespearean performance. In scene 2, Ira challenges actress Ellen Tree to play Desdemona and Othello's reunion on Cyprus differently, suggesting, 'the perfume of the moment must, how can I say it, envelop us. I'm seeing how beautiful you are, how you've trapped me entirely. I'm imagining our marital bed . . .' (37). The ellipses or performed pause carries the weight of the erotic unspoken, the sexual desire between the Black Othello and white Desdemona that now becomes mimetic 'reality' when Ira and Ellen embody them on stage. Put plainly, Ira asks for a heightened sexual charge between the lovers, and he also suggests that he must act more aggressively, for audiences 'have to feel the pain of his breakdown' (57). Yet Ira's, and eventually Ellen's, individual interpretations cannot withstand the onslaught from outside systemic forces, reminding both readers and viewers about the various stakeholders that work in concert to curtail Black subjectivity: theatremakers and actors, like Charles, but also reviewers, producers and audiences. While both *A Branch of the Blue Nile* and *The African Company Presents Richard III* mention reviewers and audiences, *Red Velvet* most powerfully draws back the metaphorical curtain on how theatre functions by exposing the clear interconnections between these parties. Reviews call Ira's performance 'monstrous' and 'upon the whole a failure' (71, 72), which leads to Ira's dismissal by the theatre's board. Significantly, when Pierre confronts Ira with his dismissal, the blame falls upon Ira's interpretations of the role. Pierre explains, 'I told you to play it gently [. . .] It was too strong . . . too intimate' (81). Pierre thus employs language drawing a direct corollary between Ira's performance choices and the audience's/reviewers'/board's rejection of him. Ira's vision does not conform to how the role has been performed previously, thus threatening Shakespearean performance as white property.[32] Because he cannot be controlled, he must be exiled, ensuring the exclusion he has resisted. The concept of exclusivity is vital to whiteness as property, meaning that whiteness is 'closely and grudgingly guarded'.[33] Exclusivity increases whiteness's value, Harris explains.[34] *A Branch of the Blue Nile, The African Company Presents Richard III*, and *Red Velvet* illustrate the parallels within Shakespearean performance, which is also closely guarded in order to affirm its status as a particularly valuable and therefore elevated form of performance. And just as reifying whiteness's exclusivity depends on 'the exclusion and subordination of Blacks',[35] so too, the plays lay bare, does maintaining Shakespearean performance as white property.

Shakespearean Performance as White Property: The Right to Enjoyment

Exercising the absolute right to exclude is one of many ways to maintain another right of whiteness as property, namely, the 'Right to Use and Enjoyment'.[36] When people use and enjoy whiteness, it 'can move from being a passive characteristic as an aspect of identity to an active entity that – like other types of property – is used to fulfill the will and to exercise power'.[37] Harris further explicates that a white person uses and enjoys whiteness whenever 'she [takes] advantage of the privileges accorded white people simply by virtue of their whiteness . . .'[38] Attending to the ways the right of 'enjoyment' gets stripped from BIPOC actors directs focus to the emotional and psychic ramifications of this exclusionary right to use that I have been tracing. Though Harris treats use and enjoyment together, I separate them here because the plays' explorations of exclusion already make clear who gets to use Shakespeare unabashedly: white people. Just as crucial to recognise, however, is the affective, psychological and material cost of this regulation, the way it sullies enjoyment of Shakespeare and/in performance for those restricted from uncontested use. To be clear, what I mean by 'enjoyment' is not enjoying a play as an audience member but rather the ability to 'enjoy', to get lost in, the embodied performance of Shakespeare. Enjoyment, then, becomes another forceful vehicle through which whiteness can flex its power. To be clear about the connections between the different rights I am discussing, for BIPOC actors, exclusive, racialised limitations upon how they use the white property that is Shakespeare circumscribes enjoyment of performance's embodiment and can exact an even more profound cost. As Cantanese explains, 'In the theater and in everyday life, knowing how and agreeing to perform your racial role correctly is often a guarantor of personal safety, financial reward, interpersonal respect, and even affection . . .'[39] Conversely, as *A Branch of the Blue Nile*, *The African Company Presents Richard III* and *Red Velvet* expose, disrupting this racial role and upsetting the whiteness of Shakespearean performance leads to adverse emotional, material and mental consequences that further solidify Shakespearean performance as white property.

In *A Branch of the Blue Nile*, Sheila serves as the character in which questions of enjoyment most crystalise. At the start of the play, she relishes playing Cleopatra, even screaming with joy, 'Sheila! Fuck Sheila! *My name is Cleopatra!*' (220). Yet even as she experiences this moment of transcendence, it soon diminishes, a fleeting possibility snuffed out when the reality of racial and gendered expectations intrudes. Speaking to Chris, with whom she is having an affair, Sheila rebuts her first exclamation: 'Fuck Cleopatra! My name is Sheila Harris and I came here like a shy little mamapoule because you said that I had it, and now I've found it . . . What am I going back to? Sheila Harris is a typist' (236). Sheila cannot reconcile what she experiences in rehearsal with the gendered, racialised roles society affords her. After all, she explains, 'I'm black. I'm a West Indian. Who needs a broke, black, West Indian actress over thirty' (238). While Sheila vacillates, declaring that she will 'shine again', she eventually leaves the company and joins a church, where she performs her societally expected role – a pious Black woman. But in the end, she does not find this role fulfilling either, for the draw of the stage intrudes upon her religious identity. She ultimately leaves the church and returns to the theatre, the only one from the company remaining. *A Branch of the Blue Nile* ends with Sheila weeping, left not with a speech that shines but rather on stage, alone, performing breathing exercises. Sheila's arc thereby exposes the social pressures that plague the gendered, racialised Shakespearean actor. Sheila has unfettered support from her Black, Trinidadian co-actors as well as from white director Harvey. But Sheila cannot reconcile the powerful, sexual, transcendent Cleopatra with the compliant, chaste, circumscribed Trinidadian woman expected of her, represented by her attempt to cloister herself through her church role. In other words, as a poor, 'over thirty' Black woman, Sheila does not believe she has the social capital nor the psychological wherewithal to give herself over to, to enjoy, performing Cleopatra. Through her trajectory, the play thus stages the divided self that Gavin speaks of in Act 1, scene 2. He recalls that when he was acting in New York, he would try to dazzle, but 'the mirror changed on me, the way you hate your passport picture . . . I began to believe what I saw in the mirror because that's how they [white people] wanted me to look' (225). Through meditations like Gavin's, but most poignantly, through Sheila's character arc, Walcott's play indicates that for some, enjoyment of Shakespeare remains out of reach, for their circumscribed social privileges based on race, and in Sheila's case also gender, create a psychic *frisson* that cannot be easily overcome.

In *The African Company Presents Richard III*, Ann's reticence to play Lady Ann even more explicitly uncovers the ways that all identities cannot immersively escape into their Shakespearean roles, with gender and race overlapping to create particular social and therefore emotional burdens. In short, Ann makes it clear that her identity as a Black woman challenges her embodiment of Lady Ann. Hewlett chides her, 'Is that what you're worried about? About people thinkin' you the same person as a part you're actin' in a play? Annie that's ridiculous' (21). Instead of being so worried, Hewlett advises, she needs to 'steam it down, 'til it gets to be a taste you can swallow. Lady Ann, she's in the king's kingdom, just like you in that man's house' (24). Hewlett's words betray him. The image of steaming something down to make it an acquired taste does not signal joy nor pleasure. In fact, what Hewlett does not understand is that the very conflation he suggests is precisely the problem. Ann counters:

Pretend? I don't know how to pretend . . . Every colored child come into this world in a little basket on somebody's door step [*sic*]. And if she's a little girl, when she gets old where she starts lookin' like a woman, there is always some King Richard who wants to lie with her . . . Pretend? There ain't no pretendin' to that. (24)

Ann's language signals the way that, as with Sheila, race and gender affect the enjoyment of performing Shakespeare as 'Every colored child' slips into the specificity of 'a little [colored] girl'. What for Hewlett is a challenging but doable exercise in suspension of concern is not possible for Ann because of the weight of both past and present. Her imagery invokes not only the King Richard figures who haunted enslaved Black women with the ever-present threat of physical, emotional and sexual violence, but also the King Richards in whose homes free Black women worked but remained unprotected. Ann's comments do not disregard the possibility that if a white woman were to play Lady Ann, she too would be disturbed by embodying a character so patriarchally subservient. But the specific racial history Ann invokes reminds audiences that the particular vulnerability experienced by Black women only increases this distress. Certainly, immersive enjoyment is not guaranteed for white Shakespearean actors. But given that BIPOC actors start from a systemically constructed position of deficit – they do not have access to and use of the property of whiteness – enjoyment is an even more vexed possibility for them as a result of converging and intensified social oppression, an oppression that robs them of the very self-assurance and emotional well-being that most effectively facilitates embodied enjoyment in Shakespearean performance.

Even if actors want to immerse themselves in and therefore relish a role less cautiously than do Sheila and Ann, because Shakespeare is white property, such a possibility of transcendent enjoyment often does not exist. *Red Velvet*'s Ira Aldridge quickly learns this lesson. As discussed above, Ira's full commitment to Othello, his absorption in the performance, becomes what supposedly costs him the role. When he debates this fact with Pierre, their dialogue makes the relationship between use and enjoyment clear. Because Shakespeare is white property and therefore should be used by white actors, the enjoyment of Shakespeare by a non-white actor cannot be withstood, for it is too threatening. Ira makes this double standard evident, declaring, 'So when Kean plays the Moor, we're amazed at how skillfully he descends into this base African tragedy but with me it seems I'm revealin' my true nature' (85). Ira thus puts more plainly the fears that plague both Sheila and Ann – that the potential slippage between person and character will result in social sanction on raced (and gendered) terms. The very immersion in performance that makes a white actor great thus serves as a liability for a Black actor. Pierre even admits, 'I told them in the heat of the moment you lost yourself in the play, your true nature surfaced and you descended into . . .' (88), the ellipses signalling the racial denigration Pierre has already enacted but is too cowardly to repeat. Thus, if enjoyment, truly losing oneself in a role, or shining as Sheila articulates it, is the goal for great performances, the fear of the cost imposed on actors of colour forecloses the very possibility. *If* they may perform Shakespeare, they must not only do so in ways that meet established white standards, but also keeping in mind that too much enjoyment may entail exclusion anyway. As these examples demonstrate, the cost is higher than simply being disallowed to perform Shakespeare. The price paid for threatening white property may entail a lost sense of selfhood, for as whiteness flexes its authority in an attempt to rectify the power imbalance created by the enjoyment of non-white identities, actors of colour risk coming to see themselves the way white eyes all too often see them.

Appropriation and the Shakespeare System

What is an appropriate personal, artistic and systemic response to the personal, artistic and material pain Shakespeare as white property imposes upon BIPOC actors? None of the plays provide an easy or clear answer. Nevertheless, undoubtedly, for each (though in distinct ways), appropriation serves as a tool that opens up the possibility of destabilising Shakespeare as white property. While overlaps exist between the way all three engage with appropriation, I want to focus on the distinct vision of appropriation each offers. *A Branch of the Blue Nile*, for instance, presents art itself as the appropriative tool. In Walcott's play, Chris has been writing a 'dialect piece' that Harvey says they can consider staging alongside *Antony and Cleopatra* (223). This piece turns into a play also called *A Branch of the Blue Nile*, which stages the very plot audiences have been following, from rehearsals for *Antony and Cleopatra* to Sheila leaving the company to Marilyn's ascendency. Audiences never get to experience Chris's play, but they can surmise that if it reflects what has happened thus far, then it not only focuses on West Indian experiences through its attention to the Trinidadian actors, but it also exposes the problems faced by Black identities staging the white property that is Shakespeare. What Chris crafts, then, is not a straightforward Shakespearean appropriation. But his play nonetheless functions as many appropriations do, casting a critical eye towards the original, here not a specific play, but rather on what Madeline Sayet calls the 'Shakespeare system', the 'complex and oppressive role his work, legacy, and positionality hold in our contemporary society'.[40] Indeed, Chris's play critiques that very system by exposing how performing Shakespeare entails negotiating Shakespeare as white property, namely, navigating the structures that create the 'naturalistic' or 'mimetic' white performance so valued on the Shakespearean stage. *A Branch of the Blue Nile* thus appropriates the concept of Shakespeare itself, not to reify whiteness and its historical authority, as Harvey does, but rather using yet sidelining Shakespeare to instead centre the overlooked West Indian identities and their striving for personal and artistic fulfilment.

In Brown's work, appropriation comes through championing a decidedly non-white style of performance. William Henry Brown, co-founder of the African Company, pushes Hewlett to stage the company's *Richard III*, but in a transgressive way. Brown declares:

> We tellin' everybody, that our ways, our ideas, our beliefs be just as good as theirs. These ain't no imitations. It's us [. . .] What you wear, the way you speak, what you do, how you feel. This is what we want to see and hear [. . .] say your Shakespeare like ya want. 'Now is de winter of our discontentment made de glorious summer by dis son a New York.' They gonna love it Jimmy. (43)

Even though the audience likewise never gets to see the African Company's *Richard III*, Brown's speech gives them a taste of it as he delivers Richard's most famous line in his West Indian accent. The dialogue is thus both Shakespeare's and not Shakespeare's, the revered text appropriated and transformed by a performance style that rejects the idea of Shakespeare as white property. Notably, the specific words Brown uses are not the entire point, for he makes it clear that this 'way' symbolises the 'ideas' and 'beliefs' of Black Americans so often rejected and devalued. In other words, Brown instantiates the 'translat[ion of] alienation into self-actualizing performance'.[41] His version of *Richard III* thereby signals that Shakespeare does not *have* to be white property. It can be seized from white ownership and offered up to audiences that are part of Brown's 'we', i.e. non-white audiences like him, in ways developed from unique value systems that afford the possibility for enjoyment, for 'what we want to see and hear'.

Red Velvet offers audiences the opportunity to see the type of performance suggested in both *A Branch of the River Nile* and *The African Company Presents Richard III*. It is itself a play in the hands of a creator of colour, centring the perspective of a character of colour, and championing the ability for actors of colour to perform Shakespeare as they desire, what

Lauren Eriks Cline calls a 'revisionist narrative' that offers up 'a method for reverse-engineering the protracted, contested, and partial processes of racialization'.[42] What allows a work like *Red Velvet* to exist is a point of view willing to appropriate Shakespearean performance history to find and make manifest the untold. Chakrabarti details how at university, 'part of my A-Level Theatre Studies syllabus was British Victorian theatre history. As a class we looked at Garrick, Kemble, Kean, Tree, Bancroft and Irving to name but a few. I was not taught about Ira Aldridge.'[43] Similarly, in her three years at the Royal Academy of Dramatic Art, where 'great Victorian practitioners were ever present' in the paintings and names inscribed on the walls, she 'still never once heard the name of Ira Aldridge'.[44] When she went looking for him, 'Finding any information about him proved very difficult', leading her to only 'one' accessible book.[45] Chakrabarti's journey to fill in her educational gaps, and subsequently create art that does so for others, thus '[reminds] us exactly who is folded into the history of Shakespearean performance'.[46] Her references to Garrick, Kemble, Kean, Tree, Bancroft and Irving – no first names needed – never mention race. Yet many readers will be able to fill in the missing information because as part of the grand signifier Shakespeare, Shakespearean performance history is also white property, a space of exclusion where those who long to transform it similarly confront racial inequity, as Chakrabarti's journey indicates. What Chakrabarti makes evident is that appropriation must therefore occur not just at the level of the performance, but also at the level of the entire Shakespeare system, challenging and changing white-oriented institutional emphases and points of view that maintain Shakespearean performance as white property. Vitally, metatheatrical appropriative works like *A Branch of the Blue Nile*, *The African Company Presents Richard III* and *Red Velvet* expose the Shakespeare system, laying it bare for discussion and systemic appropriation via transformative performance narratives, practices and structures.

This is not to be naïve about appropriation. To borrow Cantanese's framework, not all appropriations eschew the traditional view of performance as racially 'transcendent' – where people are encouraged to 'transcend racial consciousness' – in favour of racially 'transgressive' practices, which 'push at these very finite demarcations of the acceptable and the unacceptable, the just and the unjust, [to] enable and then create alternatives . . .'[47] In other words, creators of colour may still craft performances that advance ideologies propping up Shakespeare as white property.

Even so, the mere act of appropriating Shakespeare from white artistic control is itself a form of transgression, perhaps one not always taken far enough, but nonetheless an important first step. As the three plays indicate, with Shakespearean performance as white property whose value is maintained through circumscribed access, appropriation as theft is vital to retrieving that valuable property and offering it up to more diverse ownership and use. Yet the next step, creating an ideologically transgressive work of art that challenges the racial capitalist mindset reified by Shakespeare as white property, takes more work. As mentioned, audiences never see Chris's nor Brown's respective productions staged. They are only held out as a possibility, not a reality. But possibility is key. Read together through an understanding of Shakespearean performance as white property, *A Branch of the Blue Nile*, *The African Company Presents Richard III* and *Red Velvet* all signal appropriation undertaken as attitude or process as equally important to both 'authentic' performance and to works or products designated adaptions and even appropriations. Appropriation – wresting Shakespeare from white ownership and therefore power – is the tool that allows for what I elsewhere call the 'adaptive re-vision', the change in theatrical perspective necessary for disrupting Shakespeare as white property.[48] Appropriating Shakespeare is therefore the beginning of a multifaceted process that opens up the possibility for the unseen re-imaginings of Shakespeare – whether ones re-envisioning the racially 'authentic', more ethically adapting 'traditional' Shakespeare, or taking appropriation further to re-envision the Shakespeare system as a whole – waiting to be staged.

Notes

1. I am very thankful for the feedback provided by my colleague and friend L. Monique Pittman, as well as the incisive input of editors Louise Geddes, Kathryn Vomero Santos and Geoffrey Way. I also appreciate the editorial assistance of Alyssa Henriquez and Alex Hess. Unless otherwise noted, all citations are from William Shakespeare, 'The Merry Wives of Windsor', *The Norton Shakespeare*, ed. Stephen Greenblatt et al. (New York: Norton, 2008), 1255–320.

2. 'property, n.6', *Oxford English Dictionary Online*, Oxford University Press, December 2022, www.oed.com/view/Entry/152674. Accessed 25 February 2023.

3. 'property, n.3b', *Oxford English Dictionary Online*, www.oed.com/view/Entry/152674. Accessed February 25, 2023.

4. 'appropriation, n.1', *Oxford English Dictionary Online*, www.oed.com/view/Entry/9877. Accessed February 26, 2023.

5. Christy Desmet, 'Introduction', in *Shakespeare and Appropriation*, ed. Christy Desmet and Robert Sawyer, (London: Routledge, 1999), 4.

6. See Arthur L. Little Jr, 'Re-Historicizing Race, White Melancholia, and the Shakespearean Property', *Shakespeare Quarterly* 67, no. 1 (2016): 84–103; Ian Smith, 'We are Othello: Speaking of Race in Early Modern Studies', *Shakespeare Quarterly* 67, no. 1 (2016): 104–24; Kim F. Hall, 'Can you be White and Hear This?: The Racial Art of Listening in *American Moor* and *Desdemona*', in *White People in Shakespeare: Essays on Race, Culture, and the Elite*, ed. Arthur L. Little Jr (London: Bloomsbury, 2023), 219–34; and Ayanna Thompson, 'On Protean Acting in Shakespeare: Race & Virtuosity', The Center for Renaissance and Reformation Studies at the University of Toronto, 9 March 2021, Zoom.

7. Margaret Jane Kidnie, *Shakespeare and the Problem of Adaptation* (London: Routledge, 2009), 5.

8. Brandi Wilkins Cantanese, *The Problem of the Color[blind]: Racial Transgression and the Politics of Black Performance* (Ann Arbor: University of Michigan Press, 2011), 19.

9. Ibid. 19.

10. Margo Hendricks, 'Visions of Color: Spectacle, Spectators, and the Performance of Race', in *A Companion to Shakespeare and Performance*, ed. Barbara Hodgdon and W. B. Worthen (Hoboken, NJ: Wiley & Sons, 2007), 522.

11. Julie Sanders, *Adaptation and Appropriation*, 2nd ed. (New York: Routledge, 2016), 35.

12. Ibid. 37–8.

13. For more on *Gary*, see Louise Geddes, 'Taylor Mac's *Gary* and Queer Failure in *Titus Andronicus*', *Shakespeare Survey* 76 (2023): 137–49.

14. Cantanese, *The Problem of the Color[blind]*, 22.

15. Sanders, *Adaptation and Appropriation*, 35.

16. Linda Hutcheon, *A Theory of Adaptation*, 2nd ed. (London: Routledge, 2012), 8.

17. Desmet, 'Introduction', 4.

18. Cheryl I. Harris, 'Whiteness as Property', *Harvard Law Review* 106, no. 9 (1993): 1731. For further consideration of whiteness as property, see George Lipsitz, *The Possessive Investment in Whiteness: How White People Profit from Identity Politics* (Philadelphia: Temple University Press, 2006).

19. *A Branch of the Blue Nile* premiered in 1986 in Barbados and was subsequently performed in Trinidad. *The African Company* opened in February 1988 at the Penumbra Theatre in Minnesota, its only Black theatre company at the time. *Red Velvet* premiered on 11 October 2012 at the Tricycle Theatre in London with Adrian Lester as Aldridge and has subsequently been performed in both the UK and the United States.

20. Harris, 'Whiteness as Property', 1736.

21. All citations of *Red Velvet* are from Lolita Chakrabarti, *Red Velvet*, 2nd ed. (London: Bloomsbury, 2014).

22. Joyce Green MacDonald, *Shakespearean Adaptation, Race, and Memory in the New World* (London: Palgrave Macmillan, 2020), 86.

23. All citations of *A Branch of the Blue Nile* are from Derek Walcott, *Three Plays* (New York: Farrar, Straus and Giroux, 1986).

24. Angela C. Pao, *No Safe Spaces: Re-Casting Race, Ethnicity, and Nationality in American Theater* (Ann Arbor: The University of Michigan Press, 2010), 54.

25. MacDonald, *Shakespearean Adaptation*, 86.

26. All citations of *The African Company Presents Richard III* are from Carlyle Brown, *The African Company Presents Richard III* (New York: Dramatists Play Service, 1994).

27. Thompson addresses how even in contemporary performances, reviewers continue to single out the way multicultural actors speak, and how that speech disrupts expectations about appropriate Shakespearean performance. For instance, she notes that reviews of Peter Sellars's 2009 *Othello* frequently focused 'on the actors' mastery (or lack thereof) of Shakespearean verse as a type of code that reveals the racial makeup of the acting company' so that this attention to how the actors speaks offers readers 'a clear racial picture' of 'the actors' lack of fluency in "stage English"'. Ayanna Thompson, *Passing Strange: Shakespeare, Race, and Contemporary America* (Oxford: Oxford University Press, 2011), 174.

28. Jennifer Lynn Stoever, *The Sonic Color Line: Race and the Cultural Politics of Listening* (New York: NYU Press, 2016)

29. For a foundational history of The African Company, see Errol Hill, *Shakespeare in Sable: A History of Black Shakespearean Actors* (Manchester: University of Manchester Press, 1984). For a discussion of the company geared towards a general audience, see Vanessa I. Corredera, 'Pleasure and pain in Black Shakespearean performance history', *Shakespearesglobe.com*, 22 October 2020, https://www.shakespearesglobe.com/discover/blogs-and-features/2020/10/22/pleasure-and-pain-in-black-shakespearean-performance-history/. Accessed 2 August 2023.

30. Thompson illuminates the challenges posed by race, particularly non-traditional casting, in her article, 'To Notice or Not to Notice: Shakespeare, Black Actors, and Performance Reviews', *Borrowers and Lenders* 4, no. 1 (2008), https://borrowers-ojs-azsu.tdl.org/borrowers/article/view/145/287. Accessed 26 February 2023.

31. Speech is still racialised in many performances of *Othello*, however. Director Dawn Monique Williams contends that 'black actors get rewarded for what I have dubbed "the Paul Robeson effect." So that if it's in the voice, they're really left alone.' In dialogue with Williams, Thompson elaborates, 'And if you can get the timbre of your voice deep enough, then you're *really* ready for Othello.' 'Ayanna Thompson in Conversation with Dawn Monique Williams, 2 July, 2015', in *Shakespeare, Race, and Performance: The*

Diverse Bard, ed. Delia Jarrett-Macauley, (London: Routledge, 2017), 61–2, emphasis original.

32. Adrian Lester, who played Aldridge in *Red Velvet*'s initial run, comments on the fact that as an actor, he knows that others attempt to place these impositions on him, but in order for 'Shakespeare's works to live', and for him to live as a human being, it entails the same strategy: 'I will do what I will do with a complete disregard for what anyone wishes to think of me with regard to my colour. I will do what I do . . . I can't walk into the bounds of your limited conversation and then sit down and discuss with you what ignorances you have and how valid you feel they may or may not be.' Adrian Lester, 'In Dialogue with Ayanna Thompson', *Shakespeare Survey* 70 (2014): 14.

33. Harris, 'Whiteness as Property', 1736.

34. Ibid. 1737.

35. Ibid.

36. Ibid. 1734.

37. Ibid.

38. Ibid.

39. Cantanese, *The Problem of the Color[blind]*, 19.

40. Madeline Sayet, 'Interrogating the Shakespeare System', *HowlRound.com*, 31 August 2020, https://howlround.com/interrogating-shakespeare-system. Accessed 24 August 2023.

41. Daphne A. Brooks, *Bodies in Dissent: Spectacular Performances of Race and Freedom, 1850–1910* (Durham, NC: Duke University Press, 2006), 3.

42. Lauren Eriks Cline, 'Reviewing Ira Aldridge: *Red Velvet* and Revisionist Narrative', *Borrowers and Lenders* 13, no. 1 (2020), https://borrowers-ojs-azsu.tdl.org/borrowers/article/view/218. Accessed 26 February 2023.

43. Lolita Chakrabarti, 'Finding Ira Aldridge', in *Red Velvet*. 2nd ed. (London: Bloomsbury, 2014), v.

44. Ibid.

45. Ibid. The play *Keene*, by playwright Anchuli Felicia King, likewise meditates on the interconnections between school, training and their influence on race and performance. Ira Aldridge and his performance history is likewise a throughline of her play.

46. Ayanna Thompson, Introduction to *Red Velvet* by Lolita Chakrabarti, 2nd ed. (London: Bloomsbury, 2014), ix.

47. Cantanese, *The Problem of the Color[blind]*, 20–1

48. See Chapter 4 of Vanessa I. Corredera, *Reanimating Shakespeare's Othello in Post-Racial America* (Edinburgh: Edinburgh University Press, 2022), 156–205.

2

Hamlet as Resisting Subject: Intersecting Artistic Tactics in the *Mousetrap*s of Doran and Godwin

Kristin N. Denslow and L. Monique Pittman

Hamlet troubles the boundaries of knowing and not knowing, of seeing and not seeing, and, by means of its play-within-a-play, locates the problem of truth and its perception in the act of theatrical mimesis. Over the course of *Hamlet*'s performance history, the play-within-a-play has functioned as a metatheatrical tableau manifesting changing assumptions about the truth-telling potential of staged Shakespeare and the human subject's agency within networks of knowledge. By mirroring the representational act and multiplying the theatrical and fictive frames, Hamlet's playlet thus invites both creatives and audiences to examine epistemic assumptions, representational power and the human subject's capacity to act freely. Furthermore, *The Mousetrap*'s epistemic excavation operates as a crucial tool to resist an overbearing institutional power originally embodied in Claudius and reinterpreted over time and through performance history as various forms of harm curtailing human freedom. Two Royal Shakespeare Company filmed stage productions – directed by Gregory Doran (2008–9) and Simon Godwin (2016–17) – stage *The Mousetrap* to spotlight threats to human subjective freedom in the forms of surveillance capitalism and residual colonialism/neocolonialism. These parallel threats – both of which thingify, occupy and constrain the human – demand artistic resistance, which, in these filmed stagings of *The Mousetrap* rely on the intermedial techniques of theatre, film and artisanal craft. The range of artistic modalities in these two performances requires a critical praxis attuned to the 'productive tension' located at the intersection of performance, adaptation and appropriation, a tension which can be framed through Michel de Certeau's understanding of power and resistance.[1] These productions question and appropriate sites of epistemological authority – the (surveillance) camera and the institutional theatre – in acts of creative rebellion, relying upon the cunning and evasive tactics that might allow the digitally imbricated human subject, in de Certeau's terms, to 'poach' the 'property of others' and talk back to systems of power.[2] Yet, a closer study of these *Mousetraps* reveals ambivalence regarding the viability of such resistance, especially when institutional privileges, unconscious bias and racial prejudices stubbornly adhere to digital subjectivities as well as the in-person creative act.

Confronting the human subject's shrinking agency within the surveillance state, Michel de Certeau's *The Practice of Everyday Life* examines the individual 'tactics' designed to thwart the 'strategies' of institutional authority. According to de Certeau, institutional strategies rely on will and power to establish a realm of control, doing so by separating from and marginalising an exteriority – an Other. In contrast, the tactic is diffuse, non-totalising and heterogeneous: 'The place of a tactic belongs to the other. A tactic insinuates itself into the other's place, fragmentarily, without taking it over in its entirety.'[3] In de Certeau's well-known essay, 'Walking in the City', he aligns tactics with the infinite possibilities of the pedestrian who, though operating within the strategies of power figured in the city's grid of streets and buildings, may choose to walk an unanticipated alternate route through the scripted intersections of urban linearity. De Certeau describes the tactic as inherently creative, a '*bricolage*' with 'artisan-like inventiveness', a variety of 'clandestine forms taken by the dispersed, tactical, and makeshift creativity of groups or individuals already caught in the nets of "discipline"'.[4] Tactics are 'an art of the weak', a creative act of the powerless who 'must vigilantly make use of the cracks that particular conjunctions open in the surveillance of the proprietary powers. [The tactic] poaches in them. It creates surprises in them. It can be where it is least expected. It is a guileful ruse.'[5] When de Certeau describes the act of the reader-consumer 'poaching' the work of the producer-author, he suggests that such 'mutation makes the text habitable, like a rented apartment. It transforms another person's property into a space borrowed for a moment by a transient.'[6] Like de Certeau's renter, when Hamlet introduces changes and modifications into *The Murder of Gonzago* to create *The Mousetrap*, he does so as a transient, making the extant play he appropriates more habitable to his own ends and functioning provocatively as both producer and consumer of an artefact remade and transformed for his own resistant and tactical purposes.

Much as Hamlet poaches *The Murder of Gonzago* in his pursuit of truth within Claudius's regime, so directors occupy Shakespeare's oeuvre, making his work habitable and crafting new modes of tactical resistance. As artistic poachers, Doran and Godwin respectively appropriate *The Mouse-trap* to expose the surveillance strategies and the residual colonialisms constraining the digitally imbricated human subject. Whereas Doran represents efforts to elude the surveillance state nightmare, Godwin pursues through his predominantly non-white cast a fantasy of bodily representational autonomy targeting the racist-colonialist ideology long infecting both the state and Shakespearean performance history. In doing so, the productions endeavour to underscore key Certeauvian intuitions regarding the way that the disempowered and marginalised – by class, gender or race – vie for standing and a subjective self-determination in the face of overwhelming institutional authority. However, these two *Mousetrap*s ultimately illustrate the frailty of their resistant artistic modalities always-already imbricated within institutional strategies that defang opposition precisely because the human subject's own embeddedness in the biases and privileges of hegemony persist unacknowledged. In sum, Doran and Godwin present two sophisticated and highly 'knowing' *Mousetrap*s that thwart their own resistant artistic acts through a failure to account for the ways institutional productions silently benefit from status quo distributions of power and authority to white men.

A Networked Trap: Doran's *Hamlet*

In Doran's *Hamlet*, an ongoing and intensifying surveillance culture positions the individual as both the observer and the observed, demonstrating how overlapping technologies of communication and surveillance require and create a knowing and knowable human subject. Doran's *Hamlet* brings to light the paradox of the digital subject whose identity is being commodified and exploited by a surveillance capitalist regime which, in a form of data colonialism, turns human experiences, actions and emotions into behavioural data, transforming humans into 'natural resources', a twenty-first-century highly diffuse and yet targeted colonisation of the human subject on a massive scale.[7] The surveilled and enmeshed individual daily relies upon and places trust in various technologies of communication even while becoming increasingly aware of how these technologies turn the user's activity into data. While users may be active participants in these networked technologies, capable of sharing and withholding information that defines and describes the self, in reality that self-presentation may be irrelevant as the user becomes subjected to a constant and unrelenting gaze exerting total control, making the uses and misuses of the human-as-data unclear and all-pervasive.

Doran grapples with this contemporary anxiety, reinforcing and amplifying the play's interest in surveillance as knowledge currency. In the transition from the theatrical performance to a filmed version of the stage production, Doran heightens the audience's experience of a suffocating and all-encompassing epistemic access by means of inserted CCTV film footage. Sébastien Lefait explains that Doran 'adapts the play to a contemporary scopic regime that derives part of its essence from the spread of surveillance practices in everyday life'.[8] Unlike the prisoner in Michel Foucault's Panopticon who is subject to a centralised gaze that exerts total control, Hamlet (David Tennant) is subject to a multi-directional, decentralised panoptic surveillance system filled with technologies new and old: two-way mirrors, surveillance cameras and handheld video cameras.[9] In the filmed iteration, the CCTV camera appears frequently, signalled by sound effects, clicking and whirring noises that accompany the tracking of the cameras and are discernible by both the characters within the diegesis and the viewer, whose screen is made to look like a CCTV live feed. These technologies reflect de Certeau's strategies of power and motivate the ethical imperative of his interest in 'the *status of the individual* in technical systems', precisely because 'the involvement of the subject diminishes in proportion to the technocratic expansion of these systems'.[10] Tennant's Hamlet is immersed in what de Certeau calls the 'atopia–utopia of optical knowledge', in which the CCTV camera functions voyeuristically, creating a readable text out of what it captures in its viewfinder.[11]

Aware of his vulnerability within this surveillance culture, Tennant's Hamlet tactically resists the power of court through the practices of both performative and participatory surveillance, 'vigilantly [making] use of the cracks that particular conjunctions open in the surveillance of the proprietary powers'.[12] He achieves this trickery through performances meant for the surveillance cameras and by use of his own device, a handheld video camera, to film Claudius's reaction to *The Mousetrap*. By doing this, however, Hamlet deliberately entangles himself further in the technological realm. As such, Hamlet lives in a state of heightened performative surveillance, a term coined by E. J. Westlake to describe the voluntary engagement with the panoptic on social media as a means of bridging the chasm between defining one's own subjectivity and policing it within a community's norms.[13] The all-encompassing surveillance culture of Doran's *Hamlet* denies Hamlet privacy and opportunity for self-reflection, thus forcing self-expression into newly medial versions. This reinforces the possibility of an exclusively performative subjectivity constantly watched by electronic eyes, not unlike the experience of watching a play within a play. So, when Hamlet rips a CCTV camera from the wall before saying 'Now I am alone' and launching into his 'rogue and peasant slave' soliloquy (2.2.485), the viewer has reason to believe that Hamlet cannot actually think himself alone; as he learns in the nunnery scene when Claudius and Polonius spy not through the CCTV feed but rather a two-way mirror, there is always potential for 'low tech' forms of watching. Thus, anything Tennant's Hamlet may do or say must always be viewed through the lens of performative surveil-lance; he is always '[playing] on and with a terrain imposed on [him] and organised by the law of a foreign power'.[14]

Hamlet's knowing relationship with surveillance culture is also partici-patory, particularly when he chooses to deploy technology in the *Mousetrap* scene. Even with the awareness of the lethal capacity of technology to elude control and rebound on the human agent, Hamlet explores the capability of technology for resistance by 'directing' the performance of *The Mousetrap* and employing his own handheld, Super-8 video camera. Thus, Tennant's Hamlet appropriates the gaze that has previously been specifically trained upon him, turning his eye instead upon Claudius (Patrick Stewart) in order to ascertain the king's guilt (and the Ghost's truthfulness) – practising a de Certeauvian troubling of the agential assumptions embedded in the pro-ducer/consumer binary. Yet, hints that Hamlet's effort to command the gaze will not be conclusive abound throughout the playlet. Though his filmmaking contributes part of the scene's visual material, the televisual camera still makes Hamlet an object of the observing eye, implying the ultimate failure of Hamlet's oppositional tactics.

By means of a watcher/watched oscillation throughout the scene, the Doran *Mousetrap* dramatises the confused epistemology and agential strug-gle endemic to surveillance and digital subjectivities. Hamlet plays the role of sleuth-like filmmaker, documenting the truth by observation through a mediatic device. The television film intercuts between footage from the production cameras and material ostensibly taken on Hamlet's handheld device (though Director of Photography Chris Seager explains that the footage was shot on a standard television camera and the effects were added post-production).[15] Throughout the sequence, Hamlet's camera zooms around as rapidly and haphazardly as his eye, alternating between filming the action of the playlet and recording the reactions of Gertrude (Penny Downie) and Claudius. As the prince collects data, the hurried and necessarily fragmented nature of that process suggests that evidence always exceeds both the eye's capacity to observe and even the camera's ability to record. Though surrounded by digital surveillance technology,

Hamlet's device is, after all, still handheld and analogue, limited by human physical capacities and guided by distinctly singular intentions. The perspectively skewed and affectively heightened nature of that data is underscored by the look of Hamlet's footage; his intercut material in vibrant colour (contrasted with the desaturated tones of the televisual film itself) is taken at canted angles, flecked by film imperfections, and occasionally run off-kilter so that the frame edges are briefly visible. The noticeable distortions and disorientations of Hamlet's footage should throw into doubt the 'objectivity' of material gathered through other medial means – e.g. CCTV footage or even the sweep of the data mine or calculations of the digital algorithm, extensions of the surveillance camera's colonising gaze. Doran's film omits Hamlet's lines to Horatio (Peter de Jersey) to 'Give him [Claudius] heedful note, / For I mine eyes will rivet to his face / And after we will both our judgments join / In censure of his seeming' (3.2.80–3) because Hamlet believes he does not need Horatio's noting. He does not need to compare eyewitness evidence with another character because he stores his evidence in a more archivable and reproducible form through the camcorder. Yet, as the audience recognises, this is but another version of the truth, one Hamlet gathers precisely because he acts with considerable privilege, appropriating the tools of the oppressor. Hamlet may believe his data-capture to be the truest version of the event, but given the visual qualities of his footage, the context of the play-within-a-play, and his general condition as a medial subject, his collection of data can only be yet another unreliable record, another iteration of surveillance's distorting oppression.

Thus, the creative act in Doran's film is one of ambivalence. On the one hand, Hamlet appropriates technology with a Certeauvian 'dispersed, tactical, and makeshift creativity'.[16] Yet, on the other hand, his use of the camera replicates and extends the means of oppression restraining Hamlet and the inhabitants of Elsinore. Within the film, the CCTV camera embodies de Certeau's concern that 'our society is characterised by a cancerous growth of vision, measuring everything by its ability to show or to be shown and transmuting communication into a visual journey'.[17] The CCTV camera becomes a symbol of all that is wrong with this 'scopic drive' that makes the viewer a 'voyeur-god'.[18] By appropriating this gaze, Hamlet runs the risk of complicity as a participant in a pernicious system rather than as a creator who consumes in order to undermine institutional strategy – a sadly inevitable risk when forms of resistance poach within the productions of the powerful. The false ontology of Hamlet's film footage offers a clue: his 'handheld' and collected artistic material is really only made to look so by the creative team of the televisual film. Thus, what appeared to be a tactic is revealed to be a strategic and institutional mechanism masquerading as a resistant product. Similarly, the insidious need of de Certeau's strategy for an Other to enforce the boundaries and scope of power returns in the Doran production's racial representation.

A final detail from *The Mousetrap*'s dumbshow offers a further warning about the subjective constraints of the digital world and the vexed effort to deploy theatrical representation as resistant tactic. Indeed, twenty-first-century humans bring to their digital subjectivities all the racisms of their analogue selves.[19] In what could be described as yet another example of inattentive colour-blind casting, Doran's *Hamlet* features few persons of colour in major roles, Horatio being the only exception. As a result, the production expects its viewers to 'separate the fictional world of the stage from the world of lived experience,' regarding the actor's body as '"unmarked" in terms of race or ethnicity'.[20] This particular theatrical convention translates poorly to Doran's televisual film and breaks down profoundly during *The Mousetrap*, which features a glaringly racist trope in the dumbshow. The director explains in his commentary, 'We wanted to make it [the dumbshow] as burlesque as possible.' This burlesque approach includes a cross-dressed queen (Jim Hooper), a 'dwarf' king with oversized prosthetic ears (Samuel Dutton), and a stereotypical Black villain and sexual opportunist (David Ajala) as the poisoner Lucianus. In Doran's dumbshow, Lucianus, the lone Black actor in an otherwise white troupe, arrives on stage half-dressed, wearing only black spandex boxer shorts embellished with a large sequined red heart over the crotch. Casting and costuming trigger a reference to the 'Black buck' stereotype, which Vanessa I. Corredera describes as a 'sexual rapacity' imagined as targeting white women.[21] As he makes his advances on the widow player queen, Ajala's villain 'opens' the heart to reveal a comedically long metal slinky that drops between his legs. Here, as Ayanna Thompson points out concerning colour-blind casting, the depiction reinforces 'racist stereotypes' aligning Blackness with evil (a tradition that reaches deep into the Judeo-Christian canon) and with a threatening sexual virility endangering white womanhood.[22] This particular choice demonstrates the persistent blinders that prevent a skilful director like Doran from recognising the stereotype of Black male predatory sexuality operational within and mobilised by costuming and props selection.[23] Though inadvertent, this *Mousetrap* detail alerts viewers to the way in which racisms and privileges infiltrate the so-called objective gaze of digital networks and continue to compromise well-intentioned artistic efforts to oppose such strategies of power. Thus, both by means of the poacher's imbrication within the tools of oppression – Tennant's Hamlet wielding the scopic intrusion of the camera – and through the casual racism of the dumbshow, Doran's *Mousetrap* underscores the fragility of representational tactics of opposition, particularly when unacknowledged privileges underprop the theatrical institution.

The Artisanal Trap: Godwin's *Hamlet*

The surveillance culture of Doran's adaptation makes the body a readable, manipulatable text; Claudius can spy on Hamlet via the omnipresent CCTV camera, and Hamlet can both perform for the surveillor and participate in the surveillance by using the camera to document Claudius's guilt. Yet, even while the production pushes back against these systems of power and coercion, it participates in *another* system of power: white supremacy. In contrast to the digitally surveilled and overwhelmingly white Doran *Hamlet*, Godwin's RSC *Hamlet* (2016–17) resituates performed Shakespeare outside the landscape of whiteness, in what he describes on the DVD commentary as 'a state comparable to what you might find in West Africa today'.[24] In so doing, Godwin's production offers to redress the centuries-long demarcation of Shakespeare as exclusively 'white property'.[25] With a predominantly Black, Asian, Minority Ethnic (BAME) cast and a generalised West African *mise en scène*, *The Mousetrap*'s intersection of performance and surveillance necessarily invokes in Godwin's production the epistemic apparatus of Western colonial incursion that operates to name, codify and contain the people and commercial treasure of the region. The commodification of human preferences and decision-making parsed by Shoshana Zuboff as endemic to twenty-first-century surveillance capitalism finds an analogue in Godwin's postcolonial West African setting, gesturing to another phase of history in which humans were ideologically thingified and transformed into capital. Locating in surveillance capitalism a pernicious reboot of the commodifying strategies of colonialism should prompt an ethical response alert not only to the transformation of such strategies into a new form of data colonialism but also to the remainders of white supremacism and imperialism still threatening human thriving. The Doran production, highly attuned to the encroachments of digital surveillance, fails to connect that practice to older and persistent forms of dehumanisation as evidenced by the racist tropes of *The Mousetrap* that reside unapologetically and casually within the truth-telling playlet. In contrast, by transplanting the play to a visibly non-European world,

Godwin's *Hamlet* endeavours to reference that colonial framework and to resist the coloniser's all-knowing eye, proposing small-scale artisanal practices – both through Hamlet's own graffiti art and the itinerant creativity of the players – as a means to battle the panoptic control of networked and colonised human subjectivity.

By decentring whiteness, the production's representation of diasporic Blackness confronts both colonial and postcolonial epistemologies of the human subject and networked technologies that undermine human freedom and knowability.[26] Act 1 locates this West African Elsinore by combining traditional and modern images of West Africa, juxtaposing kente cloth, talking drums and carved thrones with camouflage-wearing, machine gun-wielding soldiers. Sujata Iyengar and Lesley Feracho characterise the production's diverse Black identities: 'Through a combination of cultural cues such as accent, dress, music and stage settings, the audience could identify characters from sites such as 1970s West Africa, East Africa, the Anglophone Caribbean (specifically Jamaica) and the United States.'[27] The production also highlights multiple modes of artisanal craft of African origin – including hand-carved wooden masks, kente cloth and other West African textiles, and the recycled/upcycled costumes worn by the members of the West African travelling actors – that function as multiple forms of resistance to Claudius's dictatorship and the unseen shadow of colonial and neocolonial capitalism.

This setting leads the production to adapt African forms of artistic expression and suture them to the look and politics of Jean-Michel Basquiat (the American artist of Haitian and Puerto Rican descent) whose work spotlights the enmeshment of white supremacism, colonialism and capitalism. Hamlet's engagement in handmade representation through an art form of his own – graffiti – continues the theme of art as postcolonial resistance. In the director's DVD notes, Godwin explains that Paapa Essiedu's graffiti art and jacket were inspired by Basquiat, and Iyengar and Feracho identify Basquiat motifs in Hamlet's work – particularly the crown and initial 'H' that operate as the prince's artistic signature.[28] Hamlet's costume in the *Mousetrap* scene extends this reference to Basquiat; Hamlet dons a cardboard *Tyrannosaurus rex* cap with scales that trail down his back. Atop the *T. rex* head sits a golden crown. This costuming, a visual reference to Basquiat's painting 'Pez Dispenser' (1984), reinforces Hamlet's challenge to Claudius's kin(g)ship while simultaneously underscoring a critique of commodified culture. The costume here, made from scrap materials, references via Basquiat's painting a vendable, ubiquitous product and links that product with kingship, artistic signatures and art as a form of resistance. In her searching assessment, bell hooks writes of Basquiat: 'Prophetically called, he engaged in an extended artistic elaboration of a politics of dehumanization. In his work, colonization of the Black body and mind is marked by the anguish of abandonment, estrangement, dismemberment and death.'[29] The Basquiat works infuse Hamlet's art of resistance with a critical commentary on Western culture's voracious transformation of animate beings into commercial commodities – a critique equally apt for both the digital economy and thriving neocolonial global enterprises. Even so, Basquiat's own uneasy enmeshment within the market for high-end goods should prompt questions concerning the Godwin production's appropriation of Basquiat as tactical resistance.

Whereas Doran's *Mousetrap* entangles the human through the omnipresent surveillance camera, Godwin's *Mousetrap* privileges live theatre characterised by an inventive poaching of costumes and props in an anticapitalist resourcefulness akin to aspects of Basquiat's work. Godwin describes the travelling actors as suited to the production's chosen context: 'In a West African setting, there's still a very strong presence of travelling theatre companies who use music, who move around with a kind of minimal story-telling props and yet are filled with dance and a kind of exuberance.'[30] During the impromptu performance Hamlet requests upon their arrival at court, the actors deploy carved wooden masks, handheld rather than worn, and rely upon ritualistic movement and gesture to convey the affective meaning of the recited lines (Movement Director, Mbulelo Ndabeni). This handcrafted and embodied display of truth typifies *The Mousetrap* performance that follows, exemplifying de Certeau's tactical and 'dispersed . . . *ways of using* the products imposed by a dominant economic order'.[31] The makeshift-as-creative materialises in the number of 'found' items that constitute props and costuming for the player king (Kevin N. Golding) and queen (Maureen Hibbert). For example, bottle caps replace jewels on the king's crown, and bright yellow galoshes substitute for the military boots that should complete the king's look. Similarly, the player queen sports long-sleeved, red gloves that look suspiciously like dish-washing gloves. The graphic and colourful prints associated with African textiles complete their sartorial arrangements. In an extension of Hamlet's artistic ethos, influenced by Basquiat, the acting troupe's approach to props and costuming relies upon a rich colour palette and the reuse of objects that resist commodity culture through recycling and upcycling. Furthermore, this ostensible resistance to commodity culture has specifically African connections, particularly in rubber gloves and galoshes, which may telegraph the horrific history of rubber harvesting in the Congo during the reign of King Leopold II of Belgium. In contrast to the traditional African clothing of the Ghost and the modern designer garb of the court, the players' costumes are pastiche – they include influences of popular culture, monarchical portraits (the player king's epaulettes resemble King Leopold's portraits), and commodity culture, rooted in the resources and history of the African continent. Like de Certeau's city-walkers, these players strive to elude institutional power structures and revel in the fragmentary, the multifarious, the 'contradictory movements that counterbalance and combine themselves outside the reach of panoptic power'.[32] Thus, Godwin's production constructs The Mousetrap not to elevate institutional theatre as epistemological authority but to highlight the informality and craft of itinerant artists reliant upon minimal props and traditional masks to truth-tell. By means of costuming, set design, music and mise en scène, Godwin's staging of The Mousetrap enacts a wishful return to the authentic modes of expression rooted in handcrafts and the body's capacities to communicate.

In her magisterial critique of surveillance capitalism's commodifications of human behaviour and foreclosure of human futures through predictive algorithms, Zuboff offers the home-granting space of 'sanctuary' as vital antidote. She explains: 'The sanctuary privilege has stood as an antidote to power since the beginning of the human story' and as a crucial 'exit from totalizing power'.[33] Paul Wills's stage design for Godwin's Hamlet reinforces this needed escape by means of Hamlet's artistic refuge, a space linked visually to the practices of the itinerant acting troupe and thus to the creative resistances of The Mousetrap. The colour scheme and mise en scène of The Mousetrap echo the aesthetics of Hamlet's graffiti art, the neon-infused 'punk style' Godwin describes. Since the production opts to stage The Mousetrap in Hamlet's artistic 'den', a subterranean space accessed by a steep set of metal stairs on stage right, this is a performance literally 'from below'.[34] This physical space offers Hamlet the right to sanctuary, which in turn grants him the capacity to create anew. As Zuboff contends, surveillance capitalism's invasive appropriation of human life and transformation of human decisions and preferences into future-predicting data points require 'the life-sustaining inwardness, born in sanctuary, that finally distinguishes us from the machines'; indeed, 'This is the well from which we draw the capacities to promise and to love, without which both the private bonds of intimacy and the public bonds of society wither and die.'[35] In the logic of Godwin's production, Hamlet's sanctuary and the dramaturgy of the itinerant players constitute crucial tactics of resistance that simultaneously endeavour to home-build spaces of safety for the human subject.

Godwin's *Mousetrap* incorporates the alienated Hamlet into in-person community and offers up artistic craft as epistemic tool and, more importantly, as refuge. This art binds humans together in face-to-face encounter rather than through disembodied digital networks; Godwin's playlet audience members – both courtiers and players not currently 'on stage' – are blocked as a circle around the square platform. In addition to colour palette sympathies, Hamlet signals his artistic affinity with the travelling actors by drumming throughout *The Mousetrap*, accompanied by other onstage musicians, including the production's composer, Sola Akingbola. Playbill materials for the 2016 run in Stratford-upon-Avon stress the craving for tangible belonging manifested in *The Mousetrap*. In his playbill essay, Augustus Casely-Hayford describes Hamlet's dislocation as representative of the viewing audience's alienation:

> He is traumatised by grief and injustice, but that is compounded by his broader disorientation after losing his epistemology . . . His psychological state is a poignant analogue for an ambient sense of disorientation and loss that stretches over the world, as an inexorable quickening pace of change impacts us all.[36]

Ekow Eshun's playbill contribution, 'A Place to call Home', explores the particular in-betweenness of diasporic Africans as akin to the out-of-jointness experienced by Hamlet, citing Basquiat as a creative who crafts art out of liminal dislocation.[37] Eshun concludes:

> What else is there to do when you have no home after all, but to create a place of your own? A home defined less by geography than by will and imagination. The fictional spaces of art are no less powerful than cities or nations for their power to inspire and connect and create communities based on shared affinities.[38]

And it is that faith in the capacity of art to combat the residue of colonialism and the alienations of the virtual world that the Godwin production affirms, returning to de Certeau's image of appropriative art as a poaching in and rendering habitable or 'home-like' the productions of another. Through an emphasis on the handmade and embodied, Godwin's *Mousetrap* imagines the human subject unencumbered by the punishing and ghostly control of digital forces. Indeed, Essiedu's Hamlet evades digital enmeshments through *techne* – the concrete, artistic work of the hand – rather than digital technology's invisible world of binary code.

However, by flattening the African context and appropriating Basquiat's oeuvre without adequate paratextual complexity, the Godwin production's embodied artistic resistance falters. Though Godwin's *Hamlet* promotes a more affirming approach to art and to the representation of Blackness than Doran's does, the choice of a generalised African context for this return to the 'primitive' traditions of in-person, hand-wrought artistry too easily seems yet another example of exoticising and Orientalising escape into the mysteries of the non-white world.[39] In her review essay, Grace Godwin identifies this danger in 'an abiding RSC tendency to elide distinct nations in its rare Afrocentric production'.[40] Furthermore, lurking in the production's Basquiat referencing is the tragic history of that artist's striving for fame in the white art world and his exploitation by dealers like Annina Nosei whose 'gift' of the basement art studio transformed into a 'sweatshop' pushing the young creator into inhumanly rapid production to meet a newly voracious art-as-commodity-market in the 1980s.[41] The visual appropriation of Basquiat is particularly problematic in light of the relatively scant attention he is given in the playbill and other production materials.[42] In addition, while the production ostensibly celebrates the handmade and the small-scale, these affirmations of art's home-building capacity and the agential resistance of de Certeau's Other ironically depend upon digitisation by a white institution for broader circulation via streaming and DVD sales. Though the repetition and recirculation of just such a *Hamlet* significantly pressures the received whiteness of the Shakespeare canon and performance history, troubling questions remain about the production's status as poacher's tactic. Indeed, might it be institutional strategy dressed up as tactic? In fact, the production's decentring of whiteness comes with a white man, a student of St Catharine's College, Cambridge and the London International School of Performing Arts, still at the helm. Though the RSC's paratextual elements insist that this is not a case of cultural appropriation whereby a dominant institution strategically appropriates the cultural register of the marginal for its own ends, that remains an uncomfortable possibility – especially in the context of the film production's 'unconscious biases' in the lighting of white and Black skin tones.[43] Thus, Godwin's production invites the audience to acts of artistic resistance and in-person community formation while not yet eluding the enmeshments of the institutional strategies that define the playing space and broadcast archive of the RSC.

Traps in Lockdown

Predating the COVID-19 pandemic, these two instantiations of Hamlet's *Mousetrap* anticipate both the inexorable spread of digital surveillance capitalism and the concomitant craving for in-person acts of agential resistance provoked by the health and justice crises of 2020–1. These *Mousetraps* ostensibly urge vigilance regarding the crisis of human subjectivity within networks of knowledge that appropriate digital data for a range of anti-human enterprises, ones that indeed replicate colonialism's thingification of humans for commercial gain. Following de Certeau, the depersonalised digital surveillances of the CCTV camera, the data mine and the algorithms of social networking (staged by Doran) can seemingly best be combatted from below in micro-gestures of resistance rooted in the creative and the face-to-face exchange (as seen in Godwin). But certain aspects of these productions trouble any tidy conclusions we may be tempted to draw, especially in the context of the pre-COVID-19 grappling with surveillance culture that characterises much of the 2010s. In *The Age of Surveillance Capitalism*, Zuboff concludes that 'The greatest danger [for the individual] is that we come to feel at home in glass life [of a total surveillance society] or in the prospect of hiding from it.'[44] Though the surveillance context is much more obvious in Doran's *Hamlet*, both *Hamlet*s studied here demonstrate the danger of the complacency/escape dichotomy outlined by Zuboff. In Doran's *Hamlet*, Tennant performs for and employs the camera himself, a knowing and known participant of the all-encompassing surveillance network. Thus, the work of the film camera, the surveillance camera and Hamlet's handheld camera converge into a space of constant scopic surveillance meant theoretically to reveal, to draw back the curtain on the crisis of human subjectivity within a surveillance state. Ironically, then, the production overlooks its own blind spots in the caricature of Black male sexuality. In other words, by highlighting the struggle of Hamlet to be granted personhood, the production ignores other forms of persistent dehumanisation. In Godwin, Essiedu's Hamlet does, seemingly, escape the world of the court in his literal refuge – both physical space and artistic sanctuary – yet the production itself follows the logic of Zuboff's surveillance capitalism in its mining of other cultures in order to accumulate depersonalised, disaggregated 'data' about a region, flattened and homogenised as 'West Africa'.

Thus, these two *Mousetraps* also prompt the very real questions of who is granted or denied personhood, as well as whether or not institutional theatre can defy the strategies of power that constitute its functionality. As both examples demonstrate, Hamlet's efforts to appropriate representational power by means of tactical practices do not operate independently from the structures that define and constrain. Like Shakespeare's Hamlet, Doran and Godwin remain deeply embedded in an institution directly benefiting from the unseen power network of hegemony. This does not, however, mean that all oppositional appropriation is futile; rather, that resistance dwells in the realm of de Certeau's tactic: at the intersections where everyday agents poach in the grounds of power to voice dissent. And with this in mind, we turn to the crises of 2020 and 2021 asking: Have the digital encumbrances of surveillance culture (so acutely understood in Doran's *Hamlet*) only further and dangerously enfolded humans as entire livelihoods, educations, businesses have moved into the online spatio-temporal field? Will the theatre's shift to home-streaming as an alternative income generator further trouble in-person performance's affordability, accessibility and viability? Or, will the COVID-19 pandemic's devastating impact on the performing arts renew the local, discrete and artisanal practices gestured towards in the communal homemaking of Godwin's *Mousetrap*? Indeed, what thoroughgoing reform of the theatre's imbrication within power hierarchies might now be possible to facilitate the everyday resistance of individual agents?

When Doran and Godwin appropriate Shakespeare through the lenses of surveillance culture and postcolonial artisanal practices, respectively, they make *Hamlet* newly habitable, liveable for a time. As this chapter has evolved over the course of the last seven years, we (Kristin and Monique) have experienced the habitability of these filmed stage productions wax and wane, drawing us closer to and distancing us from their world orientations, pulling us in surprising, new trajectories. Over its long performance history, Hamlet's *Mousetrap* has staged artistic mimesis as revealer of truth *and* effective oppositional tactic. But our convictions about art's capacities have, of late, been tested. We have witnessed democracy's fragility in the exponentially reverberating echo chambers of [anti-]social networks, the brutal suppression of peaceful protests against racism, and the ethical indifference of so many unwilling to curb individual freedom for the health of others. What, then, can creativity accomplish? The practices of these films, of Shakespeare appropriation, of the lives of two teacher-scholars during a pandemic – these paths intersect at new and unexpected points, perhaps recalling de Certeau's insight that 'The networks of these moving, intersecting writings compose a manifold story that has neither author nor spectator, shaped out of fragments of trajectories and alterations of spaces.'[45] Put into dialogue, the Doran and Godwin *Mousetraps* highlight Hamlet's paradoxical representational and political task – charting routes, perhaps in the unpredictable steps of the city-walker, by which to appropriate the strategies of power while simultaneously questioning and resisting those strategies (and our own reliance upon them) through dispersed and fragmentary tactics.

Notes

Kristin thanks the members of the SAA 2019 seminar, 'Refuge in Shakespeare's Europe', organised by Stephen O'Neill, as well as others who have given feedback: Richard Burt, R. Allen Shoaf, Terry Harpold, Brian Sutton, Vanessa I. Corredera and her student assistant, Jaclyn Myers. Monique thanks the members of the SAA 2015 seminar, 'Appropriation, Adaptation, or What You Will', organised by Sujata Iyengar; her colleagues, Karl Bailey and Vanessa I. Corredera, and her student assistants, Shanelle Kim, Ingrid Radulescu, Elianna Srikureja and Isabella Koh. Both thank Louise Geddes, Kathryn Vomero Santos and Geoffrey Way for their collegiality.

1. See Louise Geddes, Kathryn Vomero Santos and Geoffrey Way, in the Introduction to this volume, 4.
2. Michel de Certeau, *The Practice of Everyday Life*, trans. Steven Rendell (Berkeley: University of California Press, 1984), xii.
3. Ibid. xix.
4. Ibid. xviii, xiv–xv.
5. Ibid. 37.
6. Ibid. xxi.
7. Shoshana Zuboff *The Age of Surveillance Capitalism: The Fight for a Human Future at the New Frontier of Power* (New York: PublicAffairs, 2019), 100. Abeba Birhane, in 'Algorithmic Colonisation of Africa', writes that 'Algorithmic colonialism, driven by profit maximisation at any cost, assumes that the human soul, behaviour, and action is raw material free for the taking. Knowledge, authority, and power to sort, categorise, and order human activity rests with the technologist, for which we are merely data producing "human natural resources."' See Birhane, 'Algorithmic Colonisation of Africa', *SCRIPTed* 17, no. 2 (August 2020): 391.
8. Sébastien Lefait, 'This same strict and most observant watch' (1.1.71): Gregory Doran's *Hamlet* as Surveillance Adaptation', *Borrowers and Lenders* 8, no. 2 (Fall 2013/Winter 2014): 3.
9. Though outside the scope of this chapter and as noted by scholars such as Lefait, Doran adapts and extends Michael Almereyda's tech-heavy Elsinore in *Hamlet* (2000), relying less on the detritus of obsolescent technology and instead delving into the ethical dilemmas of a scopic surveillance culture.
10. De Certeau, *The Practice of Everyday Life*, xxiii.

11. Ibid. 92.
12. Ibid. 37.
13. E. J. Westlake, 'Friend Me If You Facebook: Generation Y and Performative Surveillance', *Drama Review* 52, no. 4 (Winter 2008).
14. De Certeau, *The Practice of Everyday Life*, 37.
15. All DVD commentary materials are transcribed by the authors from Gregory Doran, Chris Seager and Sebastian Grant, 'Commentaries', *Hamlet*. DVD. Directed by Gregory Doran (BBC Home Entertainment, 2010).
16. De Certeau, *The Practice of Everyday Life*, xiv–xv.
17. Ibid. xxi.
18. Ibid., 93.
19. See Mike Ananny, 'Toward an Ethics of Algorithms: Convening, Observation, Probability, and Timeliness', and Tarleton Gillespie, 'The Relevance of Algorithm', *Science, Technology, & Human Values* 41, no. 1 (2016): 93–117. Safiya Umoja Noble delivers an extended critique of 'digital sense-making' and 'the commercial co-optation of Black identities, experiences, and communities' by the largest technology companies, particularly Google. See Noble, *Algorithms of Oppression: How Search Engines Reinforce Racism* (New York: NYU Press, 2018), 2.
20. Angela C. Pao, *No Safe Spaces: Re-Casting Race, Ethnicity, and Nationality in American Theater* (Ann Arbor: University of Michigan Press, 2013), 29.
21. Vanessa I. Corredera, 'Far More Black than Black: Stereotypes, Black Masculinity, and Americanization in Tim Blake Nelson's *O*', *Literature/ Film Quarterly* 45, no. 3 (2017).
22. Ayanna Thompson, *Passing Strange: Shakespeare, Race, and Contemporary America* (Oxford: Oxford University Press, 2011), 77.
23. bell hooks urges a vital reckoning with the representation of race: 'Commodification of blackness has created a social context where appropriation by non-black people of the black image knows no boundaries. If the many non-black people who produce images or critical narratives about blackness and black people do not interrogate their perspective, then they may simply recreate the imperial gaze – the look that seeks to dominate, subjugate, and colonize.' bell hooks, *Black Looks: Race and Representation* (Boston: South End Press, 1992), 7.
24. All DVD commentary materials are transcribed by the authors from Simon Godwin and Anna Girvan, 'Commentaries', *Hamlet*. DVD. Directed by Simon Godwin (Opus Arte, 2017).
25. Arthur L. Little, Jr, 'Re-Historicizing Race, White Melancholia, and the Shakespearean Property', *Shakespeare Quarterly* 67, no. 1 (2016): 88.
26. Sujata Iyengar and Lesley Feracho, '*Hamlet* (RSC, 2016) and representations of diasporic blackness', *Cahiers Élisabéthains* XX (2019): 3.
27. Ibid. 3.
28. bell hooks explains: 'The image of the crown, a recurring symbol in his work, calls to and mocks the Western obsession with being on top, the ruler.'

She continues: 'In Basquiat's work the crown is not an unambiguous image. While it may positively speak the longing for glory and power, it connects that desire to dehumanisation, to the general willingness on the part of males globally to commit any unjust act that will lead them to the top.' bell hooks, 'Altars of Sacrifice, Remembering Basquiat', *Art in America* (1 June 1993).

29. hooks, 'Altars of Sacrifice'.
30. Godwin, 'Commentaries'.
31. De Certeau, *The Practice of Everyday Life*, xii–xiii.
32. Ibid. 95.
33. Zuboff, *The Age of Surveillance Capitalism*, 478.
34. This element of stage design also nods to Basquiat who famously created works in the basement of art dealer Annina Nosei's gallery. Stephen Metcalf, 'Searching for Jean-Michel Basquiat', *The Atlantic* (July/August 2018): 114.
35. Zuboff, *The Age of Surveillance Capitalism*, 492.
36. Augustus Casely-Hayford, 'The Limbo Between Worlds', Programme for *Hamlet*. Royal Shakespeare Company (2016).
37. Ekow Eshun, 'A Place to Call Home', Programme for *Hamlet*. Royal Shakespeare Company (2016). Grace Godwin's review points out that this passing reference in Eshun's playbill essay constitutes the only formal reference by the RSC to Basquiat, whose work clearly influenced the production. See Grace Godwin, 'Basquiat Cases: *Hamlet, Doctor Faustus*, and *The Alchemist* at the Royal Shakespeare Company', *Shakespeare Bulletin* 35, no. 4 (2017): 676.
38. Eshun, 'A Place to Call Home'.
39. Carol Magee describes this aggregating and homogenising practice in representations of Africa by Westerners: 'Africa is one cohesive entity – often referred to as a country not a continent, and cultural differences are subsumed under a general African identity' (5); 'Africa exists in the imaginary as a single entity' (9). Magee, *Africa in the American Imagination: Popular Culture, Racialized Identities, and African Visual Culture* (Jackson: University Press of Mississippi, 2012).
40. Grace Godwin, 'Basquiat Cases', 676.
41. Cora Marshall, 'Jean-Michel Basquiat, Outsider Superstar', *International Review of African American Art* 16, no. 4 (1999).
42. This visual reference of Basquiat's work with insufficient citation appeared again in the Fall 2021 Dallas Shakespeare 80s-inspired production of *Romeo and Juliet* (dir. Raphael Parry), in which the stage design included several paintings in the style of Basquiat, including the crown motif, without any clear citation or relevant reference points.
43. Pascale Aebischer, *Shakespeare, Spectatorship and the Technologies of Performance* (Cambridge: Cambridge University Press, 2020), 186.
44. Zuboff, *The Age of Surveillance Capitalism*, 492.
45. De Certeau, *The Practice of Everyday Life*, 93.

3

Jewishness between Performance and Appropriation: Music for *The Merchant of Venice* (2004)

Kendra Preston Leonard

The performance history of *The Merchant of Venice* is one entangled with what producers and directors hear as the sounds of Jewishness, be it traditional prayer, like the Shema or Kaddish, or contrived nonsense, like the 'old Hebraic song of sacrifice' sung by Anthony Sher in a 1987 stage production.[1] In this chapter, I interrogate composer Jocelyn Pook's score for Michael Radford's 2004 film adaptation of Shakespeare's *The Merchant of Venice*, using frameworks provided by Christy Desmet, Philip V. Bohlman and Barbara Mowat. In discussing both the film and Pook's score, which engages with specific cultural sounds both within and outside of the typical Western music purview, I rely on Desmet's theory of a 'dialogic concept of appropriation' in which appropriation represents a kind of response towards the source text, a gesture that is not to be understood as plagiaristic or theft, but something that stems from reception and contributes to the remaking of a text or an ornamentation of a text.[2] Desmet's theorisation of appropriation as reception and refashioning is particularly useful for framing the use of music, particularly unaccompanied vocal chant, that functions as part of the signification of Jewishness and Catholicism in the film and iterates the religious divide that serves as a fulcrum for the plot. While the appropriation of Catholic chant has become widely accepted and expected in films in which Catholicism plays a part, the use of Jewish-sounding music is more complex. The ways in which Pook appears to appropriate – or quote, or cite – Jewish music in order to convey Shylock's faith and world, can, as Desmet warns, be 'ethically fraught', verging on the edge of 'impersonation, speaking for someone else into satire, slander, or verbal hijacking'.[3] In sussing out how Pook uses or suggests Jewish music, I use Philip V. Bohlman's taxonomy of 'ontological moments of Jewish music', which serves as a guide for analysing music used to signify Jewishness and what it communicates. Bohlman defines these moments as follows:

1) Sacred ontologies/religious definitions: Revelation of sacred voice
2) Textual ontologies/linguistic definitions: Jewishness conveyed by Jewish language (Hebrew, Yiddish, Ladino, Judeo-Arabic, etc.)
3) Embodied ontologies/contextual definition: Genealogical descent and identity
4) Spatial ontologies/geographical definitions: Jewish music in the synagogue or ritual practices
5) Cultural ontologies/political definitions: Music and survival in a world of otherness.[4]

The score of a film is an integral part of the work. As film music scholar Anahid Kassabian writes, a film or show, 'as perceived by any kind of audience – public or scholarly – has words, sounds, images, and music. It is not merely *seen*'.[5] Music, she states, is 'at least as significant as the visual and narrative components that have dominated film studies'.[6] The music for a film can communicate a myriad of things: geographical and chronological setting; character thought, action, intent and emotion; atmosphere and mood; and more. Film composers rely on audiences – or perceivers, to use Kassabian's term that favours neither audio nor visual experience – to share with them an understanding of common musical tropes in order to communicate clearly through music. These shared references are what Barbara Mowat, borrowing from Claes Schaar, terms infracontexts, and Pook's score both assumes perceivers' shared infracontexts and seeks to create new ones through the film's historical contextualisation.[7]

Using these contexts, I examine Pook's score from the position that her score is a site of reception in regard to Catholic chant and early modern secular music and gestures towards that repertoire by appropriating its structures and styles; and that her use of music to signify Jewishness is likewise in conversation with the musical ontologies, limned by Bohlman, that serve to identify the Jew as separate from the Christian. Close listening, using Desmet's and Bohlman's work as guides, can give us a better understanding of how Pook's score functions in communicating Radford's adaptation. By 'close listening', I mean an aural analogue to close reading: the practice of actively paying attention to not just the melody, but to the various strata that make up the score, including the instruments or voices in use, their timbres, and how they are used; the texture of the music (is it sparse, with few instruments, or dense, or focused on specific instruments or ranges?); its rhythmical patterns; the regularity of the beat or lack thereof; its harmony; how it is structured over time; and the many infracontexts all of these elements have and how they can be interpreted. I argue that Pook uses the sounds of Catholic hegemony and tragic Jewishness as a method of supporting director Michael Radford's attempt to cast Shylock as a sympathetic character. In doing so, the score constructs a problematic environment in which the soundscape for the Christian world is one of power and pleasure, while the Jewish sonic world is focused exclusively on piety, lack of empowerment, and suffering, much – but not all of it – caused by the antisemitism of Venice's Catholics. Pook builds upon previous film scores like John Williams's score for *Schindler's List* that use the sounds of tragic Jewishness and the Jewish diaspora to create these identifications and their relationships, but ultimately, these tropes lead to an unsettling reading of the film.

Radford's *Merchant* incorporates an approach to the film that is, as L. Monique Pittman has written, one that relies on a 'William Shakespeare [who is a] liberal humanist, a non-racist, non-anti-Semite'.[8] In order to do this, Radford makes significant cuts to the text, the most telling of which is his removal of Shylock's aside in 1.3:

> How like a fawning publican he looks!
> I hate him for he is a Christian,
> But more for that in low simplicity
> He lends out money gratis and brings down
> The rate of usance here with us in Venice.
> If I can catch him once upon the hip,
> I will feed fat the ancient grudge I bear him.
> He hates our sacred nation, and he rails,
> Even there where merchants most do congregate,
> On me, my bargains and my well-won thrift,
> Which he calls interest. Cursed be my tribe,
> If I forgive him! (1.3.37–48)[9]

In removing Shylock's hostility towards Antonio and Christians in general, it is much easier to make him a victim, rather than the Christian-hating antisemitic figure of the playtext. This allows Radford to fully attribute Shylock's anger, hatred and bitterness to what Radford calls 'religious fanatics' in the film's introductory scrolling text. This introduction, using modern language that is usually used to describe Muslims and is suggestive of the conflict between Islamic and non-Islamic cultures, is particularly important in communicating Radford's interpretation of the play, in which he tries to express both the splendour of Catholicism and Judaism and the failings of their practitioners equally. This adaptive response to the playtext is an attempt to circumvent *Merchant*'s antisemitism by creating instead a reading that promotes the play as one pleading for tolerance and social justice. This is a common tactic for directors working with the play in a post-Shoah age who seek to make *Merchant* acceptable. While this may seem like a reparative adaptation that focuses on Shylock as a tragic figure, it also, as Alexa Alice Joubin writes, 'compartmentalize[s] social inequality by aestheticizing suffering in figures that are presented as larger than life'.[10] Shylock's suffering – which comes to stand in for universal Jewish suffering, interpreted as pleading for universality in his well-known and oft-cited 3.1 'Hath not a Jew eyes?' speech – is exploited, tragedising the lived experiences of every Jew. At the same time, this approach reifies what Judith E. Doneson identifies as the common image of the 'weak, feminised Jew', who must be saved by Christians because he cannot save himself. Shylock is made weak *and* his forced conversion to Christianity is the alternative to death. Jessica's story within *Merchant* also follows this trope, as she is 'saved' by Lorenzo from both her religion and her father; her line from 5.1, 'I am never happy when I hear sweet music', is accompanied by unseen performers singing and playing secular music, and Lorenzo insists that she must appreciate his culture's music in order to be trusted.[11] Additional sounds of the film, including Al Pacino performing a 'Jewish' accent as Shylock (chosen deliberately to be in contrast the British accents of the rest of the cast, creating what Jennifer Lynn Stoever theorises as a 'sonic colour line' in terms of race and religious otherness); the laughter and noise of the secular spaces and open to Catholics, such as in the feast and brothel scenes, as opposed to the quiet and solemnity of the ghetto; and Pook's score are all integral in presenting this interpretation.[12]

Pook's score supports Radford's reimagining of the play as one in which the Jew is the victim through the canny use of established musical tropes. Radford sets the film in Venice in 1596, the year of the play's creation; Pook states that in order to score the film for the place and period, she 'immersed [her]self in Renaissance music'. Her score, she says, was based on 'existing medieval or renaissance themes, others, including all the vocal pieces (except 'Song in Brothel') I wrote myself, setting them to various texts from the period, with the exception of 'Bridal Ballad' where I have used a text by Edgar Allan Poe'.[13]

Pook cites various kinds of music in her score, developing a dialogue between genres that engages with multitudes of infracontexts. While film music scholar Andrew Granade characterises the score as a pastiche, containing 'elements from Elizabethan popular music, Gregorian chant, Middle Eastern chant, lute songs sung by a countertenor, and modern strings', Pook is very deliberate in not using pre-existing music, which might carry with it specific infracontexts she does not wish to attach to the film or individual scenes.[14] Granade is correct in arguing that Pook tries to evoke, rather than recreate, a historical time period, but Pook herself acknowledges this, confirming her appropriative scoring practices and accepting responsibility for doing so. Her interactions with established sounds, such as her evocation of Gregorian chant and early modern lute song, are essential in establishing the Catholic world and its secular pleasures, just as her simulacrum of Hebrew cantillation is central to creating Shylock as a figure of Jewish tragedy. To this end, Pook employs newly composed chant and both new and traditional kinds of vocal cantillation in the score; and also interprets cantillation instrumentally, assigning cantillation-like melodies to the kanun, a Middle Eastern plucked string instrument similar to a zither.

Pook's Gregorian-influenced chant is performed by a mixed choir and an orchestra. That the work is entirely original to Pook and would be unfamiliar to those who are knowledgeable about chant is less important here than the sound itself; Pook draws on the sound of Gregorian chant in order to evoke its infracontexts of Catholicism, religious power and exclusion. Gregorian chant is often used in film and has become so closely associated with the use and abuse of power that it has its own page at TVTropes.org, called Ominous Latin Chanting.[15] As TVTropes. org notes, 'the actual meaning of the words is unimportant. [. . .] It's the sound that matters.' Pook is well aware of this – she has created chant before for film scoring, most notably for *Eyes Wide Shut* (1999), a film in which chant is sung by an ominous priestly figure presiding over an orgy held by social elites, a situation involving power imbalances not unlike those of Catholic and Jew in *Merchant*. Because of the ubiquity of chant in historical film, Pook is able to appropriate the sound of it in the score and to rely on perceivers to understand her intention in using it. Similarly, for both the vocal and instrumental forms of Hebrew cantillation Pook uses, she assumes perceivers will recognise this sound, music that is explicitly coded as 'Jewish'. By employing a representation of chant and by placing it in dialogue with cantillation and with secular music, Pook creates a score with highly specific musical references to the powers and

plots of the play: the performance of her new chant equals Catholic hegemony and freedom; the performance of authentic cantillation and new
cantillation-like music represents Jewish suffering and enclosure; and the
performance of secular music – which is more often shown in the film's
diegesis – signifies romance, or at least pleasure. Pook's score engages
in particular with what Bohlman terms the textual, spatial and cultural
ontologies of Jewish music and cultural performance, the infracontexts
associated with language differences, the geography of Venice's public
spaces and the ghetto. Her score is thus connected with previous uses of
these ontologies in developing the film as one focused on Jewish tragedy
and trauma. Appropriately for a film set in early modern Venice, a hub
of cultural exchange and home to five synagogues, Pook's Jewish music
also engages with Jewish diaspora through the use of the kanun, an instrument that originated in Assyria and is popular in North and West Africa,
the Middle East, Central Asia, and south-eastern Europe. Edwin Seroussi
writes that 'Jews certainly participated in their co-territorial landscape',
and Pook is either demonstrating her awareness of this in selecting multicultural sonic representations of Jews in Venice in 1596, or she is applying
the early modern Christian conceit that 'the music of any Jew, regardless
of ethnic origins [represents] the sound of the entire Jewish nation'.[16] By
appropriating the kanun, Pook is both citing Jewish culture per Desmet's
theory and referencing the textual and spatial ontologies of Jewishness:
the vocal performance of cantillation, diaspora, Otherness and segrega-
tion; the kanun, appropriated, performs Jewishness.

The film opens with an introduction establishing the power balance
between Catholics and Jews in early modern Venice and the treatment
of Jews in the city. Scrolling text provides contextualisation of the introduction's scenes, which begin with priests ferrying a cross across Venice's Grand Canal, accompanied by Pook's score. The music begins with
dense, slow-moving strings in a minor key (starting at 1:03), establishing
that the soundscape of the film's Venice is that of the familiar cinematic
Western art tradition. The film then cuts to an image of a torch setting
a Torah on fire (1:15). Pook provides three distinct sonic layers all in
dialogue for this scene: 1) an orchestra playing music in the Western art
tradition as the Catholic priests are in focus; 2) a kanun playing a line
that is very similar to the cantillation of Hebrew prayer as the Torah is
burning (starting at 1:17); and 3) the voice of Israeli singer Uri Yehuda
(starting at 1:23), who sings a Yemenite paraliturgical prayer, 'The Lord
of all revives every soul', to Pook's original melody using cantillation.[17] As
Yehuda sings, scrolling text informs perceivers of the oppression of Jews

in sixteenth-century Venice. The film then shows Catholic Venetians assaulting Jews on the Rialto Bridge while the priests in the boat preach against usury. One Jewish man is thrown into the canal (3:03), and Antonio, working his way through the mob, is stopped by Shylock, who calls his name; Antonio turns to Shylock and spits on him (3:15).

Following this pogrom on the Rialto, the sound of the kanun is transformed into the sound of a bolt being shot on a gate leading to the ghetto. The film's introduction ends with the sound of organ and Catholic chant that connects the assault of Jews – through Antonio, who leaves the bridge and enters a building where boats are being blessed – with Catholic privilege. Here the man who just spat on Shylock is blessed by a priest (4:15) to the sound of recognisably holy music. Although this sequence is the only one in which Pook uses pseudo-Catholic chant, it is crucial in understanding the film's structure, built on Radford's depiction of early modern Venice's Christianity, social and financial capital, and whiteness, all of which provide entrees to personal and institutional power. Gregorian chant, an art form almost exclusively associated with male composers and singers, represents here the advantages that Antonio, Bassanio and their friends and partners have.[18] By following the kanun and its associated scenes of oppression and bias with chant, Pook reiterates the religious conflict of the narrative. The visual aspects of the film and its score make it clear perceivers should understand the Venetians, Frank P. Riga writes, 'as intolerant and persecutorial'.[19] These musical strata of the introduction, which is perhaps the most musically significant part of the film, move in and out of primacy in the score in synchronisation with the visuals, making their significations as clear as possible. In just the first few minutes of the film, perceivers experience multiple ontologies of Jewish music: linguistic difference (between British-accented Catholics and the 'Jewish'-accented Shylock), musical conflict between the sonic environment of Catholic hegemony and the survival of the Jews (the orchestra, the orchestra plus chanting voices, and the kanun), and sounds redolent of the synagogue (Yehuda's vocal line).

Like her appropriation of Gregorian chant, Pook's use of the kanun is complex. First, it represents the linguistic ontology of Jewish music by mimicking the sound of cantillation. Second, it represents two geographical ontologies: that of the synagogue, one space in which cantillation takes place; and that of the Middle East, a place that is decidedly not Venice, but with which Venetians had contact, and the place from which the Jewish diaspora originates. Philippa Sheppard calls the music of the kanun's first appearance 'full of Eastern beats'; it is appropriated from Mizrahi

Jewish culture, and plausibly in dialogue with Venice and Venetian Jews, despite the fact that Pacino's unreliable accent seems to suggest Shylock is of Ashkenazi descent.[20] Throughout the film, the kanun calls on perceivers to identify these meanings, and Pook frequently puts the kanun in dialogue with the other major musical signifiers of the film, particularly those of the play's marriage plots. The kanun represents the Jewishness that Jessica renounces for Christian marriage, which is characterised by the use of Western instruments: the lute, bowed strings, high winds and secular song. Pook makes the low status of Venice's Jews obvious. The moment Lorenzo and his compatriots' boat enters the ghetto (5:04), the kanun takes over from the chant, making the difference between the outside world and this segregated space apparent. So as to leave no doubt in perceivers' minds as to where Lorenzo is, the kanun is briefly replaced by the sound of men chanting Hebrew prayers. This performance of Jewishness to establish a location is further emphasised when, a moment later, Radford shows the perceiver what Lorenzo sees: a Jewish congregation, the men davening (rocking back and forth) in a richly appointed synagogue (5:30) where the women are confined to the *matroneo*, or gender-segregated balcony. As Lorenzo's party watches Shylock and Jessica leave the synagogue, Pook layers the kanun, the orchestra and the lute. The kanun and its 'exotic' sound is subsumed by that of the normalised orchestra, creating a musical narrative for the film's Jews in which they are exoticised, segregated and exist beneath the control and tolerance of the Catholic government. Shylock is scored with the kanun taking a more prominent role than the orchestra, but Jessica's scoring is the reverse, making the sound of the Western orchestra more conspicuous than the kanun, a musical foreshadowing of the events to come. When Lorenzo picks up Jessica's handkerchief, the lute is joined by bowed strings and a recorder, which are later also associated with the romantic plots. Pook layers the kanun again over the orchestra as Antonio seals his bond with Shylock, pressing his ring into red wax (24:09), an identification of Shylock's suffering in his struggle for survival as well as his anger and bitterness.

The kanun's attachment to Jewish suffering intensifies as the film continues. In Shylock's dark and plain house, Jessica approaches Lancelet with a message for Lorenzo (30:53), and the kanun is layered over the music of the marriage plots' bowed strings and the lute. The mixture of musical elements here signifies Lancelet's immediate departure from Shylock's service as well as Jessica's later flight. When Jessica leaves Lancelet alone, the bowed strings and lute emerge as the kanun drops out, mirroring Jessica's presence; Pook very carefully accords music to character and place. When the camera cuts

back to Jessica as she promises to become Christian, the kanun is now notably absent, suggesting that the misery she experiences as Shylock's daughter
will end as soon as she is out of his home, his religion and his reach. As
Shylock leaves his home to dine with Antonio and Bassanio (35:53), Pook
brings back the kanun, signifying Shylock's continuing difference and, in the
context of Jessica's decision to leave her father and Judaism, re-emphasising
the concept that Jewishness itself is about suffering, that tragic Jewishness is
preordained. As Jessica watches Shylock leave, the kanun and the sounds
of his suffering are replaced with bowed strings, representing the marriage
plots, and her decision to choose happiness, which, according to the play,
can occur only by converting and marrying outside of her faith.

As before when partygoers entered the ghetto, the kanun accompanies the opening of the gate to the ghetto as Lorenzo and his party
make their way to Shylock's home (40:30), but by the time they reach
the house, the music has shifted into the bowed strings and lute associated with the marriage plots, and the kanun accompanies only Shylock's
chests of money as Jessica and Lorenzo remove them from the house.
The kanun returns to prominence as Shylock returns to his house,
searches for Jessica, finds her missing and goes out into the street to
call for her. Both here and as Shylock hears the story of Jessica trading
his ring for a monkey, Pook layers orchestral strings playing in a minor
key underneath the kanun, providing reinforcement for Shylock's tragic
Jewishness. The last time Pook uses the kanun is after Shylock's sen-
tence has been pronounced at the end of the trial scene and he makes
his way out of the courtroom (1:49:30). The kanun is present at this
point for a short time before Bassanio becomes the focus of the camera
and the music, but is nonetheless clear in signifying Shylock's tragic
Jewishness, a characteristic he will now lose, being forced to convert to
Christianity. The last time Shylock appears in the film, it is in the context of his new otherness in relation to the Jewish community. Radford
shows Jewish worshippers entering the synagogue, but Pook's score at
first seems entirely wrong, using a Catholic liturgical text. As the camera angle shifts, however, it focuses on Shylock, standing alone in the
courtyard, no longer a Jew, a man who must now hear the sacred music
of his oppressors. The synagogue door is shut against him, and the scene
cuts to Belmont, where Jessica, alone, watches men shooting fish as she
twists the ring that was her father's, not sold for a monkey after all.

Pook's soundscape of the Venetian ghetto in this *Merchant* repeatedly
connects the suffering of Shylock and Jessica with the exoticist and othering infracontexts created by her choice of the kanun and her use of it to

mimic Hebrew cantillation. While actual cantillation represents Jews as a whole in the film, such as the vocal performance by Yehuda over the burning of Torahs and the scene inside of the synagogue at the beginning of the film, the kanun specifically represents the pain, anger and bitterness Shylock feels and expresses in his dealings with the Catholic majority, and the psychological suffering Jessica endures as his daughter. By closely associating the suffering of Shylock and Jessica with the kanun, Pook has created a soundtrack for them that engages with the trope of tragic Jewishness. In using the kanun she exploits two technologies frequently used in film: the use of a solo, privileged instrument playing music that is appropriated from a specific Jewish culture but is broadly linked ontologically with a character's Jewishness; and the use of an instrument that is outside of the Western art tradition that is also, to at least inexperienced perceivers, connected with a character's Jewishness. Her techniques in doing this are not unique but appear in numerous scores for films centred on tragic Jewishness, and Pook builds on these existing cultural infracontexts that assign these sounds to Jewishness and, especially during the 1980s, 1990s and early 2000s, to tragic Jewishness in film.

This *Merchant of Venice* relies on perceiver familiarity with earlier films whose scores have created an aural ethos of tragic Jewishness, including *Playing for Time* (1980), *Au Revoir, les Enfants* (1987), *Europa Europa* (1990) and Steven Spielberg's epic about the Shoah, *Schindler's List* (1993), scored by John Williams. *Schindler's List* is perhaps the best known, and numerous films and scores made since it was released bear indelible marks of its influence. One of these later scores includes others by Williams, who, among other things, transforms the well-known Main Theme from *Schindler's List* into Hedwig's Theme for the Harry Potter movies, linking Harry's outsider status and tragic early life caused by genocidal forces with the genocide of the Shoah. The 2004 *Merchant* does not escape from this sphere of influence, and while Pook does not appropriate or adapt Williams's music, the visuals and score bear close parallels with *Schindler's List*, the first of which is the use of an introductory scene in which cantillation is used to set the stage for events in which Jewish voices are silenced. Instrument use is a second parallel. Although Williams's score for *Schindler's List* uses almost exclusively Western instruments and Western art music forms, the use of a solo instrument – Williams uses a violin; Pook uses the kanun – becomes indicative of the otherness of the Jews shown in the film, who are of course targeted for their religious difference, just as we see in *Merchant*. Thirdly, the scores for both films articulate a clear power structure in which Christian control results in the death of Jews, and in both films this Christian dominance is expressed through the visuals and the use of faux-Gregorian chant in the score. And finally, Radford shows Jessica, apparently accepted, at (Christian) Belmont at the end of *Merchant*, mirroring Spielberg's epilogue at the end of *Schindler's List*, which shows Schindler's grave in Jerusalem, carved with a cross and in the shadow of an even larger cross on a Catholic monastery, where the Jews he saved and their descendants place visitation stones on his grave as a mark of respect and remembrance.[21] Tragic Jewishness is thus commodified and framed in both films in such a way as to suggest that Christian figures of salvation – salvation from persecution and abuse in the ghetto, salvation from the camps – are inevitable, and that Jews, whether in early modern Venice or twentieth-century Poland, are powerless to save themselves. In *Merchant*, Jews must conduct transactions with the Catholic Church in order to survive; in *Schindler's List*, conversion is unnecessary, but Spielberg requires the surviving 'Schindler Jews' and their descendants to engage in a performance of Jewishness as part of revering a Christian saviour by gathering together to place stones on Schindler's grave.

The parallels between *Schindler's List*'s and *Merchant*'s scores are indicative of the zeitgeist surrounding narratives of tragic Jewishness. I do not suggest here that Pook plagiarises from Williams's score or any other score from this genre; I suggest that the cultural moment found meaning in specific musical elements, including cantillation and the use of a solo instrument playing in such a way as to express sadness. Spielberg's film opens with the lighting of Shabbos candles and Emil Katz chanting the Kiddush as the candles burn lower and lower and eventually burn out. This is the only example of cantillation in the film, but Williams's writing for solo violin is inspired to some extent by cantillation and traditional Hebrew and Yiddish songs along with nineteenth-century Romanticism and salon music. Where Williams uses the violin, the official state instrument of Israel and one closely associated with Eastern European Jewry, Pook uses the kanun as the sound of a more exotic Jewishness. While the soundtrack for *Schindler's List* includes situations in which the violin plays music that is neither Jewish nor composed by Williams, this is primarily in the context of the pre-existing music from the period included in the film, such as the music that plays on the radio as Oskar Schindler dresses in the beginning of the film. This use of the violin is generally diegetic, coming from a clear source within the film. Williams's own music for violin is acousmatic throughout the film, without a visual source, mirrored by Pook in her use of the unseen but repeatedly heard kanun. Williams's use of the violin and the themes he composed for it are used sparingly and in very specific situations, another technique paralleled by Pook in her employment of the kanun. Just as Williams introduces the violin to score the initial round-up of Krakow's Jews and dispersal of their belongings, Pook employs the kanun for the pogrom that takes place on the Rialto and the destruction of Torahs. The Main Theme for *Schindler's List* is in a minor key; the kanun plays in a non-Western mode that is similar to the Western concept of the minor: both are used to evoke sorrow. Williams does not use music that signifies Catholic chant for *Schindler's List*, but he does invoke the sacred in his cue 'Immolation', which accompanies the scene of camp prisoners being forced to burn the bodies of the dead. Here Williams uses the Hebrew text 'Im Hayeinu Anu Notim Hayim (With our lives, we give life)' as the lyrics for what critic Craig Lysy calls a 'requiem chorale'. The requiem is a specifically Catholic rite; by using Hebrew text in a traditionally Christian choral setting, Williams's score inhabits a decidedly problematic space in which Christian privilege appears to run roughshod over the performance of Jewishness. For the end of the film, Williams sets Naomi Shemer's 1967 Israeli song 'Jerusalem of Gold', which includes passages similar to cantillation, for chorus, recorder and guitar.[22]

It's clear that Pook's score engages with the sounds of tragic Jewishness made iconic by Williams's and similar scores, and that her score cites and reifies the matrices of referents and knowledge that have helped create shared infracontexts for the portrayal of Jewishness on the screen. Pook's music tells much of the story for Radford's *Merchant*: Venetian Jews, living in a Catholic world and reviled and miserable in the ghetto, make radically different choices in dealing with their situations. Both Shylock and Jessica leave the world of the ghetto, with its soundscape of the exotic, mournful kanun: Shylock, in his forced conversion, must now attend to the sound of Gregorian chant rather than Hebrew cantillation, and Jessica escapes to a world with both Christian and secular soundscapes, where the recorder and lute play for entertainment.

With the kind of attentive listening to the score's various layers and the ways in which Pook scores characters and locations, we hear how the score helps depict Shylock as a victim. At the same time, however, as we hear in the light and airy music of secular activities, of the privileged Christians, the score also implies that if only all of Venice's Jews would convert, their lives would become ones of greater beauty and pleasure. In doing so, the aesthetics of tragic Jewishness – amplified by the sadness of the lonely kanun playing its prayer-like phrases – become another facet of the play's antisemitism. While Radford and Pook are well-meaning in trying to rehabilitate *Merchant*, its 'cultural smear', to borrow from Charles Marowitz, is a strong one, and no amount of sympathetically intended cantillation can remove that.[23] In Season 2 of the Canadian television show *Slings and Arrows*, Nahum, a former theatre director from Nigeria, working as a custodian at a theatre, and Geoffrey Tennant, the theatre's director, discuss *Macbeth*. Nahum says, of the play, 'I do not like that play. It teaches us nothing.' Tennant replies, 'It teaches us about evil', to which Nahum offers a rejoinder: 'No! It *shows* us evil; it's a portrait of a psychopath.'[24] Despite Radford's and Pook's desires to make *The Merchant of Venice* a play that teaches us about antisemitism, careful listening demonstrates that, at least in this case, it shows us antisemitism and remains antisemitic.

Notes

1. Charles Edelman and William Shakespeare, *The Merchant of Venice*, ed. Charles Edelman (Cambridge, Cambridge University Press, 2002), 241.

2. Christy Desmet, 'Recognizing Shakespeare, Rethinking Fidelity: A Rhetoric and Ethics of Appropriation', in *Shakespeare and the Ethics of Appropriation*, ed. Alexa Alice Joubin and Elizabeth Rivlin (New York: Palgrave Macmillan, 2014), 41, https://doi.org/10.1057/9781137375773_3. Accessed 7 August 2023.

3. Ibid. 47.

4. Philip V. Bohlman, 'Ontologies of Jewish Music', in *The Cambridge Companion to Jewish Music*, ed. Joshua Walden, (Cambridge: Cambridge University Press, 2015), 14.

5. Anahid Kassabian, *Hearing Film: Tracking Identifications in Contemporary Hollywood Film Music* (New York: Routledge, 2001), 5.

6. Ibid. 1.

7. Barbara Mowat, '"Knowing I Loved My Books": Reading *The Tempest* Intertextually', in *'The Tempest' and Its Travels*, ed. Peter Hulme and William H. Sherman (London: Reaktion, 2000), 28.

8. L. Monique Pittman, 'Locating the Bard: Adaptation and Authority in Michael Radford's *The Merchant of Venice*', *Shakespeare Bulletin* 25, no. 2 (2007): 15, http://doi.org/10.1353/shb.2007.0038. Accessed 7 August 2023.

9. All subsequent play citations are from William Shakespeare, *The Merchant of Venice: Third Series*, ed. John Drakakis (London: Bloomsbury Arden Shakespeare, 2011).

10. Alexa Alice Joubin, 'Screening Social Justice: Performing Reparative Shakespeare Against Vocal Disability', *Adaptation* 14, no. 2 (August 2021): 190, https://doi.org/10.1093/adaptation/apaa031. Accessed 7 August 2023.

11. Judith E. Doneson, 'The Image Lingers: The Feminization of the Jew in *Schindler's List*', in *Spielberg's Holocaust: Critical Perspectives on* Schindler's List, ed. Yosefa Loshitzky (Bloomington: Indiana University Press, 1997), 145.

12. Jennifer Lynn Stoever, *The Sonic Color Line: Race and the Cultural Politics of Listening* (New York: NYU Press, 2016).

13. Jocelyn Pook, '*The Merchant of Venice* | Jocelyn Pook', https://www.wisemusicclassical.com/work/14731/The-Merchant-of-Venice--Jocelyn-Pook/. Accessed 7 May 2022.

14. Andrew Granade, 'The Merchant of Venice Soundtrack (2004)', *Soundtrack. Net*, https://www.soundtrack.net/album/the-merchant-of-venice/. Accessed 7 May 2022.

15. 'Ominous Latin Chanting', *TV Tropes*, https://tvtropes.org/pmwiki/pmwiki.php/Main/OminousLatinChanting. Accessed 7 May 2022.

16. Edwin Seroussi, 'Jewish Music and Diaspora', in *The Cambridge Companion to Jewish Music*, ed. Joshua Walden (Cambridge: Cambridge University Press), 31, 34.

17. My thanks to Jacqueline Feldman Smilack for helping me identify this text.

18. Alan Horrox's 1996 film of *The Merchant of Venice* also opens with the sound of Gregorian chant and a procession of a cross by altar boys and priests, establishing the Catholic dominance of the setting.

19. Frank P. Riga, 'Rethinking Shylock's Tragedy: Radford's Critique of Anti-Semitism in *The Merchant of Venice*', *Mythlore* 28, no. 3/4 (2010): 14.

20. Philippa Sheppard, *Devouring Time: Nostalgia in Contemporary Shakespearean Screen Adaptations* (Montreal: McGill-Queen's University Press, 2017), 91.

21. Doneson, 'The Image Lingers', 148.

22. 'Jerusalem of Gold' is closely associated with the Six-Day War, and in Israel objection to its use in *Schindler's List* was so strong that it was replaced with 'Halikha LeKesariya', a song written by a World War II resistance fighter and associated with the Shoah in Israel. See Haim Bresheeth, 'The Great Taboo Broken: Reflections on the Israeli Reception of *Schindler's List*', in *Spielberg's Holocaust: Critical Perspectives on* Schindler's List, 205.

23. Charles Marowitz, 'Shakespeare Recycled', *Shakespeare Quarterly* 38, no. 4 (1987): 469, https://doi.org/10.2307/2870426. Accessed 7 August 2023.

24. *Slings and Arrows*, directed by Peter Wellington, (2005) television series.

4

Rita Dove, Blues Aesthetics and Shakespearean Improvisation

John S. Garrison and Saiham Sharif

There is a quotation attributed to Miles Davis, phrased variously as 'It takes a long time to sound like yourself' or 'It takes a long time to play like yourself.' It is widely quoted or misquoted (if we can use such terms with a possibly fictitious attribution) across the Internet. Crucially, both the sentiment and the status of the quotation speak to the dynamics that we explore in this chapter. On the one hand, our individual subject-formation relies on integrating previous voices and then separating ourselves from them. On the other hand, these previous voices have their own curious relationship to authenticity as they are often filtered through the unreliable lens of cultural memory. Defining one's own voice in relation to Shakespeare's voice represents a particularly charged challenge, given that its centrality and pervasiveness within the canon grants it a gravity that is near inescapable. James Baldwin once counterposed himself to other readers by declaring that 'the most illiterate among them is related, in a way I am not, to [. . .] Shakespeare'.[1] However, several years later, he would reconsider this claim and suggest, 'My relationship, then, to the language of Shakespeare revealed itself as nothing less than my relationship to myself and my past.'[2] We hear in this declaration how reconciliation with the language and legacy of Shakespeare can contribute to an author's self-fashioning yet also how it might have added dimensions of complexity for Baldwin and other Black authors.

This chapter examines a cluster of case studies – two poems and two songs – in order to explore the complex dynamics of Shakespearean appropriation in relation to subject-formation. Rita Dove's 'Blues in Half-Tones, 3/4 Time' modifies lines from *King Lear* and *Hamlet* in order to contemplate the role of misquotation in the resuscitation of previous voices. Dove's

'Shakespeare Say' goes even further as it showcases the voice of blues singer Champion Jack Dupree, who misattributes quotations to Shakespeare and goes on to even fictionalise Shakespearean language during an improvised song. As discussed below, Dupree's own creative processes link to Dove's as they both test the limits of appropriation. In different ways, poet Rita Dove and musician Champion Jack Dupree contemplate the implications of improvisation as a means of both connecting to and counterposing one-self to Shakespeare. Taken together, the poet and the musician then offer an intriguing case study for exploring the unique operations of improvisation in contemporary works, specifically depicting or occurring within African American musical contexts, that seize upon elements of Shakespeare.

Both Dove and Dupree incorporate elements from Shakespeare within the context of off-the-cuff musical performance, employing a form of improvisation that disrupts the notion of a stable originary script. Though they both showcase Shakespearean elements in their creative work, their methods seem to stray far from adaptation, when we consider Sujata Iyengar's alignment of that mode with 'fidelity' or 'truthfulness to an inherent textual, historical, or writerly authority'.[3] Instead, the elements – quotation without citation, misquoting of the original, and blurring of original blues lyric with Shakespearean dialogue – generate what Iyengar aligns with *appropriation*: 'a variable meaning- and subject-making position' tied to a mode that 'involves a wholesale remaking or transformation of the Shakespearean intertext in the context of the linguistic, social, media, and cultural landscape of the appropriating artwork'.[4] However, we will see both the poet and the musician call into question how concretely one can identify appropriation at work, especially as these creators dramatise the interplay between the pervasiveness of Shakespeare's influence and the performative act of improvisation.

The Appropriation of Nothing

Dove interpolates Shakespeare's language into her poem 'Blues in Half-Tones, 3/4 Time' and makes clear how appropriation takes on the feel of improvisation within the space of blues poetics. The poem opens, 'From nothing comes nothing' (1).[5] Framed as a stand-alone line at the top of this visually narrow poem, this phrase functions as an aphorism and as an impetus to begin. It is, of course, a nod to *King Lear* where the king says to his daughter Cordelia, 'Nothing will come of nothing' before he adds 'speak again' (1.1.99).[6] In the play, the king's retort is a father's wisdom and a ploy to garner the speech he desires. However, the poem takes a different turn. Rather than framing its variation on 'nothing will come of nothing' to be fresh and as vital wisdom, it asks, 'Don't you know that by now?' as it reveals itself and its readers to be consciously aware of the pervasiveness of Shakespearean aphorisms (2). The poem starts in a curious place, then, telling us that we already know what it has told us. It appropriates the line from Shakespeare not to adapt the story of the play but to place the language in the new context of blues performance. Then it does more than that: it tells us that even in a new context the language and notion are not novel.

Instead, the poem seems fixated on its own propensity for misquoting. A few lines later, we are told parenthetically '(There's a typo somewhere.)' (8). However, there is no visible 'typo' in the poem. There are misquotations from Shakespeare rather than typos, as in the first line. Even though the meaning between the original line in *King Lear* and the misquotation in Dove's poem remain essentially the same, the poet makes it her own through slight variation. Peter Erickson characterises Dove's relationship to the Shakespearean tradition as one in which the poet is 'ranging across its spectrum, playing with her own combinations, and freely creating new variations'.[7] Such a description of method – with its emphasis on 'playing', 'combinations' and 'variations' – speaks very much to the performative dynamics of blues and jazz music. We recognise that this is not Shakespeare's line, all the while that we know it is from Shakespeare. It feels as if it is improvised, quoted from memory in the moment. Not only do the poem's opening two lines showcase the productive role of appropriation in poetic creation but they also elevate the status of the contemporary poet above that of the medieval king. Lear speaks the line with all the power of a monarch and a father who can command a kingdom and a daughter. This poet speaks the line to evince command of the canon only to undermine the power of the line by characterising it as common knowledge.

The poem's speaker will continue to connect the quotation and dismissal of Shakespeare with creative authority, all the while complicating that authority. The speaker says:

> I'm not for sale because I'm free.
> (So they say. They say
> the play's the thing, too,
> but we *know* that don't play.) (15–18)

Here, the poem correctly quotes *Hamlet* as it draws from the famous line that attests to the power of literature to move people to self-identification and self-knowledge: 'The play's the thing / Wherein I'll catch the con-science of the King' (2.2.633–4).[8] Yet, mirroring the discursive move we saw in its first two lines, the poem rejects the wisdom of the play. 'Blues in Half-Tones, 3/4 Time' thus offers a useful object with which to begin to answer Peter Erickson and Kim F. Hall's call for 'more studies of race and performance that themselves theorise/critique race rather than sim-ply document the activities of people of colour in the service of proving Shakespeare's universality'.[9] The Black poet and her poem in the African American blues tradition draw upon Shakespeare in such a way that acknowledges his recognisability but rejects his universality. By stating 'we *know* that don't play', the poem frames common knowledge as seeing no truth in Hamlet's claim. The playwright's persona and language do contribute to the authority of this poem and of its poetic speaker. How-ever, Shakespeare's words are deployed only to be dismissed rather than concretised as a shared experience of wisdom. Shakespeare's phrases have lost their power as universal wisdom, even if they do represent a canon against which a poetic voice must position itself.

'Language is never innocent', Roland Barthes once remarked.[10] That is, any language taken up by the writer will necessarily draw upon the extant words and figurations of previous writers. The poem states as much above when it immediately undermines the italicised phrase '*I'm not for sale because I'm free*' with the parenthetical 'So they say.' On the one hand, the voice here differentiates itself by separating from the previous voice of Shakespeare as it dismisses its blanket applicability. At the same time, misquoting that originary source renders the previous voice unstable. His words resemble the 'nothing' of the poem's first line and the play's famous line. Just as Cordelia's claim in *King Lear* is not enough because it simply states the common knowledge of what a daughter owes a father, so too does Shakespeare's aphoristic wisdom become a commodity to be appro-priated even if it holds little value in its discrete state.

The poem ends by underscoring Shakespeare's place in the past but also nodding to his resonance in the present:

Well, you know what they say.
What's gone's gone.
No use crying.
(There's a moral *some*where.) (25–8)

The line 'what's gone's gone' brackets the previous voices of the past from the present and perhaps, too, brackets their power. W. E. B. Dubois famously remarked, 'I sit with Shakespeare and he winces not.'[11] We find a similar sentiment here when we detect that this poem is ultimately a poem about reading and about the power of the reader over the author. Here, parallel construction maps the hidden 'moral' to the 'typo' noted early in the poem, suggesting that misspeaking and misquoting have a place in the creation of art. Yet it is left up to the reader or hearer to find both the moral and the typo.

The instabilities in the poem can be explained partially by the 'blues' named in the poem's title. This places the text in a musical tradition characterised where creative work is generated in the moment, appropriating elements from previous performances and improvising content on the fly. At the same time, this musical tradition itself has been a rich source for appropriation by broader, hegemonic performers and audiences. Dialectically, jazz and blues belong to those strains of music that constitute a 'chief source of distinctiveness as well as the main source of innovation for those Black musical sensibilities that diffuse into and are appropriated by the white-dominated wider culture'.[12] Dove's poem alters such dynamics. The Black poet and her poetic voice of the blues performer appropriate work from a figure often posed as paradigmatic of the white hegemony that often appropriates style and content from the musical genre. The poem then subsequently undermines the power of that figure by claiming his language as its own to misquote and to dismiss.

Appropriation and Improvisation

In 'Shakespeare Say', Dove plays even more imaginatively with the received language and reputation of the playwright. Despite the centrality of the figure in the poem's title, he is not mentioned until the middle of the poem and even then it is within a performance by Champion Jack Dupree. As the musician 'drums the piano wood, / crowing', readers find themselves guided in and out of his lyrics, his physical movement and the thoughts going through his head (1–2).[13] Intriguingly, the poem opens by introducing the blues performer not by elevating him but by humanising him:

Champion Jack in love
and in debt,
[. . .]
with a red eye
for women, with a

diamond-studded
ear, with sand
in a mouthful of mush − (3–11)[14]

The opening of the poem immediately blurs Dupree's public performance as he plays piano and sings in the first two lines, with his inner life
of desire and debt, before returning the public performance only to reveal
'a mouthful of mush'. This final phrase suggests that his singing is a mix or
a jumble while he is perhaps drunk or tired, as already implied by the 'red
eye'. Yet 'mush' need not have a negative connotation. It proves an apt
term for describing the mode of appropriation that we find in the poem,
where lived experience and language from varied traditions become so
intermixed as to become indiscernible from each other.

In lyrics rich with rhyme, lines from Dupree's performance are inter-
polated into the text and appear to reflect the romantic and other troubles
that characterise the depiction of his lived experience that opens the poem:

poor me
poor me
I keep on drifting
like a ship out
on the sea
[. . .]
I love you, baby,
but it don't mean
a goddam thing. (12–16, 31–3)

The lyrics seem to run counter to the poem's claim that 'tonight / every
song he sings / is written by Shakespeare' (28–9). These lines are clearly
not written by Shakespeare. Instead, they are written by Dove and made
up on stage by her version of Dupree. Erickson suggests that, in Dove's
poem, Dupree is 'using Shakespeare's name as an ironic, all-purpose
endorsement for whatever he improvises on the spot'.[15] The enjambed
ending that follows 'Shakespeare' is 'and his mother-in-law', suggesting
the way that one's authorial influences intermingle with one's personal
past (30). Dupree has remarked in an interview, 'if you've never had
no miserable life you cannot [play the blues.] It's always a life story, it's
not just playing.'[16] So lived experience contributes to the creation of art,
but art contributes to the experience of life too. The lyrics with which
Dupree describes his life may sound hauntingly like previous song lyrics

or love poetry one has heard. However, he misattributes his lyrics to the Renaissance writer as their original author.

While 'Blues in Half-Tones, 3/4 Time' misquoted Shakespeare and called his universality into question, 'Shakespeare Say' even further desta-bilises the playwright's voice as recognisable. While Dupree at first claims to be ventriloquising Shakespeare broadly, the performer claims to quote him specifically at the poem's midpoint when we encounter the singer

> Going down slow
> crooning *Shakespeare say*
> *man must be*
> *careful what he kiss*
> *when he drunk.* (40–4)

The line is presented as a quotation or a paraphrase of Shakespeare. But what could Dupree refer to when he says, 'Man must be / careful what he kiss / when he drunk'? One might track this line to a situation that a character such as Bottom, Falstaff, Stephano, or especially Titania might find themselves in. Yet Shakespeare never *says* this, even if he might show the lesson being learned on stage. Dupree seems to relish in the fiction of it all, as he claims to pull an axiom out of the canonically esteemed author's work and to seemingly reaffirm the author's legacy. And, as we know from the opening of the poem, he is actually the one who is intoxi-cated and has romantic problems. The advice rings true, at least for this performer, who stumbles through the bar with 'the bourbon in his hand / some bitch's cold / wet heart' (49–51). The intoxication and the bitter memories generate a performance where 'even the mistakes / sound like jazz' (55–6). In an interview, Dove zeroes in on this operation as the engine behind the performer's genius. The poet has commented that, while he may be 'drunk' and 'not at the height of his powers' and even 'at his worst', Dupree's audience finds that 'the mistakes still sound like jazz'.[17] By repeating the line verbatim from the poem in combination with the devaluation of his prowess, Dove showcases the role of on-the-spot creation in blues and jazz performance. The method of improvi-sation, especially one that appropriates language from other sources or misattributes quotations, thus represents a tool of artistic authority. To incorrectly quote Shakespeare or to erroneously assign him as an author is in fact the marker of a skilled performer in the blues or jazz traditions.

In the final lines of the poem, Dove adds yet another dimension to the interplay between improvisation and appropriation seen in the poem. Adding to the notion that Dupree's music intermingles personal biography, the poem ends with him moaning in such a way that 'no one hears', as he sings:

I'm broke and can't hold
my piss;
my mother told me
there'd be days like this. (59, 61–4)

Once more, the figure of the mother returns and she seems to possess the same type of common knowledge that Shakespeare does. Nita N. Kumar finds that the parallel structure here ends up 'pitting Shakespeare against the *mother*', yet a focus on the operations of appropriation allows us to complicate Kumar's characterisation of the tension between figures and discourses.[18] As we will see below, these lines constitute a vital crux in the poem where Dupree engages in a multivalent conflation of sources from which he appropriates content. Dove has remarked that it is in this moment – when Dupree can draw from 'stuff about Shakespeare' and from 'blues lyric' – when 'the art and the life come together'.[19] So, on some level, we see here a seemingly strict depiction of the mode of appropriation described by Iyengar above. That is, Shakespeare enters a new cultural context and subsequently becomes the artist's own language. However, there is much more than that here.

The phrase 'my mother told me / there'd be days like this' productively complicates our understanding of appropriation. It paraphrases the opening line and chorus from the Shirelles' song titled 'Mama Said'. The tune was a top-ten hit in 1961, reaching the number four spot on the *Billboard* Hot 100 chart and the number two spot on the R&B chart. The song's memorable refrain, 'Mama said there'll be days like this / There'll be days like this, mama said',[20] resonates in cultural memory. It also predates not only Dove's poem but also much of Dupree's career, especially the latter period depicted in the poem. So, it is not actually his mother but just a general saying of maternal wisdom and of common knowledge, yet the particular line is drawn from a rhythm and blues group who captured such wisdom. When Dupree appropriates the lyric and works it into his performance just as Dove does for her poetry, he finds a discourse to describe his own life in other people's art.

Improvisation on the Blues Stage: Champion Jack Dupree's *Shakespeare Says*

While the Shirelles' hit 'Mama Said' may be the most direct reference for this line in Dove's poem, a look at Dupree's own body of work finds another antecedent. In the 1976 song, 'Million People Live the Same Way', Dupree replaces 'Mama' in the Shirelles' lyrics with 'Shakespeare' in his own:

> Ah, that's what Shakespeare said: There would be days like this.
> Say you'll be in Paris, playing the blues. And I never believed it.
> Now I believe everything Shakespeare says.[21]

So, it turns out that Shakespeare said this, even before the Shirelles sang it and before Dove's poetic version of Dupree's own mother said it. The performer creates the illusion of appropriation as he names his source and conjures a familiar phrase. Simultaneously, he troubles the notion that even attributed quotation has any tie to appropriated content. The very name of the song, 'Million People Live the Same Way', stresses that lived experience generates shared knowledge. So, the song is at once a common-sense response to Shakespeare, undermining the notion of his universalism or his deep insight into human nature. The song's misattribution of the Shirelles' phrase to Shakespeare instantiates Ayanna Thompson's claim that 'to engage contemporary notions of Shakespeare, race, and universalism, one must be attuned to a wider variety of sources: one must be willing to engage in cultural studies in the broadest sense'.[22] Here, Shakespeare is not actually the author of the phrase, but its very place in the cultural aether gives it the same status as Shakespeare's oft-quoted phrases. In the imaginary of the song, this adage can also be understood to be composed by Shakespeare simply because it has achieved a pervasiveness where everyone already knows this wisdom.

The performer comes to 'believe everything Shakespeare says' because he finds himself playing the blues in Paris. The notion that the playwright offers universal wisdom and predicts our modern lives becomes an object of playful derision even if the singer affirms it with conviction. A few lines later in the song, Dupree even says 'Do what Shakespeare said!' What begins to emerge then is the idea that Dupree specifically or common sense more broadly can actually embody Shakespeare, and that retroactively all good advice must stem from Shakespeare. The merging of life and art here privileges the former in its superior wisdom of the latter. Dove has remarked that it is in her poem's line, 'Mama told me there would be days like this', that the performer has 'found his art again'.[23] In Dupree's own artistic process, he can replace 'mama' with 'Shakespeare' and still claim it as a valid quotation of a named source. His art, we can see, places the work of appropriation at a far distance from that of adaptation by suggesting that the new contexts and meanings of the appropriated element make it entirely anew.

While Dove uses the figure of Champion Jack Dupree specifically and the blues genre more generally for her poetic exploration of improvisation as art form, the performer himself used Shakespeare's work liberally towards similar ends. Consider, for example, Dupree's song 'Big Legged Sally'. It dramatises self-appropriation through its construction as a duet for one person. Dupree engages in a question-and-answer format with himself, which quickly leads to discussion of Shakespeare. One persona asks, '*What was – what was I used to sing?*'[24] And the other responds:

Ah . . . the one about . . . what Shakespeare wrote . . . you know: 'Mama move your false teeth papa wanna scratch your gums' or somethin' like that you know – you understand, yeah. All right, now look. You sing a verse and then I'll sing a verse.

Shakespeare, of course, did not say this. Yet the song sets up a dynamic where one persona knows the work of Shakespeare and must remind the other persona of that work in order to stimulate the creation of art. Yet the early modern figure who inspires him is, to borrow a useful term from Ruben Espinosa, one of a 'stranger Shakespeare'. That is, misquoting the playwright gives us access to the 'rich strangeness of Shakespeare' and 'allows for a stranger Shakespeare not yet filtered through a critical apparatus that often privileges and takes for granted his universality'.[25] Dupree can choose to create his own Shakespearean dialogue and thus *be* a blues-infused Shakespeare. As we come to recognise his efforts at self-fashioning involve framing himself as a previous voice from which he draws, we might recognise him as *a Shakespeare* even as we know he is not *the Shakespeare*.

The title of Dove's poem, 'Shakespeare Say', constitutes an appropriation of the title of Dupree's album upon which 'A Million People Live the Same Way' and 'Big Legged Sally' appear: *Shakespeare Says*. We are cautioned in the two poems to be on the lookout for a 'typo' and Shakespeare-sounding 'mistakes', and perhaps here is the only one we can find. It is a slight modification to the title of the album by the appropriated figure, but it is not simply a one-to-one relationship between the previous and later works. Both the album and the poem triangulate to point to Shakespeare and to what Shakespeare says, even if neither quotes Shakespeare correctly and both go as far as to attribute to the playwright phrases which he never said. And they work together to add a new dimension to Ayanna Thompson's claim that 'instability is the nature of the relationship between Shakespeare and race in American popular culture'.[26] Both the poet and the musician integrate the playwright into African American musical contexts, even as they trouble the verifiability of their quotations or even a sense of who the 'Shakespeare' of their lyrics might be.

Coda: The Appropriation Blues

Each of the works described in this chapter embrace the unexpected and unplanned performative elements at the heart of the jazz and blues genres. Dupree's appropriation of Shakespeare occurs in a medium that is never the same twice. The poems and the songs thereby reveal a pattern of thought that positions the logics of musical performance, especially those genres which have improvisation built into them, as an analogue for how Shakespeare's work can be continually repurposed. In turn, these case studies suggest at least some ways that African American creative artists have placed themselves in conversation with the canon, particularly seizing upon how context-based and spontaneous improvisation might allow writers to situate themselves in the shadow of Shakespeare's language. Christy Desmet has suggested that appropriation constitutes a 'dialogical phenomenon' that is 'not simply a conversation or collaboration between appropriating and source texts, but an exchange that involves both sharing and contested ownership'.[27] We find here that improvisation functions as an unauthorised appropriation that can never happen the same way twice, yet nevertheless constitutes a legitimate and legitimising use of Shakespeare, who seems now a baseless fabric in the shadow of these contemporary figures.

Notes

1. James Baldwin, *Notes of a Native Son* in *James Baldwin: Collected Essays* (Boone: Library of America, 1998), 121.
2. James Baldwin, *The Cross of Redemption: Uncollected Writings*, ed. Randall Kenan (New York: Vintage, 2011), 68.
3. Sujata Iyengar, 'Woman-Crafted Shakespeares: Appropriation, Intermediality, and Womanist Aesthetics', in *A Feminist Companion to Shakespeare*, 2nd ed., ed. Dympna Callaghan (Oxford: Wiley-Blackwell, 2016), 508.
4. Iyengar, 'Woman-Crafted Shakespeares', 508.
5. Rita Dove, 'Blues in Half-Tones, 3/4 Time', in *American Smooth: Poems* (New York: W. W. Norton, 2004), 97–8.
6. William Shakespeare, *King Lear*, ed. Barbara A. Mowat and Paul Werstine (New York: Simon and Schuster, 2004).
7. Peter Erickson, *Citing Shakespeare: The Reinterpretation of Race in Contemporary Literature and Art* (New York: Palgrave Macmillan, 2008), 22.
8. William Shakespeare, *Hamlet*, ed. Barbara A. Mowat and Paul Werstine (New York: Simon and Schuster, 2012).

9. Peter Erickson and Kim F. Hall, '"A New Scholarly Song": Rereading Early Modern Race', *Shakespeare Quarterly* 67, no. 1 (Spring 2016): 9.

10. Roland Barthes, *Writing Degree Zero*, trans. Annette Lavers and Colin Smith (New York: Hill and Wang, 2012), 16.

11. W. E. B. Dubois, *The Souls of Black Folk*, in *Writings: The Suppression of the African Slave-Trade / The Souls of Black Folk / Dusk of Dawn / Essays and Articles* (Boone: Library of America, 1987), 438.

12. Perry A. Hall, 'African-American Music: Dynamics of Appropriation and Innovation', in *Borrowed Power: Essays on Cultural Appropriation*, ed. Bruce Ziff and Pratima V. Rao (New Brunswick: Rutgers University Press, 1997), 48.

13. Dove based the poem on a live performance she had seen, where Champion Jack Dupree did actually use the phrase 'Shakespeare Say' as a running joke. She describes the performance during an interview included in Erickson, *Citing Shakespeare*, 24.

14. Rita Dove, 'Shakespeare Say', in *Museum: Poems* (Pittsburgh: Carnegie-Mellon University Press, 1983), 33–4.

15. Erickson, *Citing Shakespeare*, 31.

16. 'Champion Jack Dupree interviewed by James Hogg', recorded c. 1967/8 by James Hogg, British Library, shelfmark C122/312.

17. Malin Pereira, 'Rita Dove', in *Into a Light Both Brilliant and Unseen: Conversations with Contemporary Black Poets* (Athens: University of Georgia Press, 2010), 93.

18. Nita N. Kumar, '"Shakespeare Is a Black Woman": African American Women Writers and Shakespeare', in *"No other reason but a woman": Women on Shakespeare*, ed. Krystyna Kujawinska-Courtney, Izabella Penier, Katarzyna Kwapisz-Williams (Frankfurt: Peter Lang, 2013), 68.

19. Pereira, 'Rita Dove', 93.

20. The Shirelles, 'Mama Said', written by Luther Dixon and Willie Denson, Track 1 on *The Shirelles Sing to Trumpets and Strings* (Scepter Records, 1961).

21. Champion Jack Dupree, 'Million People Live the Same Way', Track A1 on *Shakespeare Says* (Saravah, 1976).

22. Ayanna Thompson, *Passing Strange: Shakespeare, Race, and Contemporary America* (Oxford: Oxford University Press, 2011), 43.

23. Pereira, 'Rita Dove', 93.

24. Dupree, *Shakespeare Says*, track B3.

25. Ruben Espinosa, 'Stranger Shakespeare', *Shakespeare Quarterly* 67, no.1 (Spring 2016): 61.

26. Thompson, *Passing Strange*, 5.

27. Christy Desmet, 'Recognizing Shakespeare, Rethinking Fidelity: A Rhetoric and Ethics or Appropriation', in *Shakespeare and the Ethics of Appropriation*, ed. Alexa Huang and Elizabeth Rivlin (New York: Palgrave Macmillan, 2014), 42.

5

'Ich leb', was ihr rappt': Confronting Racism through Consumption in OG Keemo's *Otello*

Kirsten N. Mendoza and Oliver Knabe

The cover of the extended play (EP) *Otello* (May 2019) by Black German rapper OG Keemo disturbingly depicts the artist's body at the fore of the image with the face of white German beat producer Funkvater Frank transposed onto his neck. With sunglasses resting just low enough on his nose to allow his left eye to be exposed, Funkvater Frank stares calmly and directly at the viewers. The sight of his right eye is obstructed by OG Keemo's clenched hand and arms that pull downward as though putting a mask on Funkvater Frank, which evokes the practices of blackface. However, the mask is actually a clear plastic bag stained with bright red paint dripping like blood onto the sunglasses. Beneath the bag, OG Keemo gasps for breath, suffocating from the plastic that he, himself, pulls. This visceral image of asphyxiation cannot be seen without remembering Eric Garner's final words: 'I can't breathe. I can't breathe.' before he was murdered by NYPD forces in 2014. The name 'otello', which hovers in the top-left corner of the cover in a slightly squiggled and transparent font outlined in white, haunts the violent image that dominates the frame.

The juxtaposition of 'otello' with the brutal image of a Black man dying as a white man coolly stares back evinces the relationship that exists between an early seventeenth-century English play and Black experiences in twenty-first-century Germany.[1] With the name 'otello' – barely noticeable but nonetheless there – OG Keemo prompts viewers to think about the long history of *Othello*, its reiterative accumulation over time, that has influenced race relations today and, specifically, the harm experienced by Black men in the twenty-first century. The cover exists as a powerful indictment against one of the most debilitating portrayals of Black masculinity made canonical by a white man for white audiences.[2]

Figure 5.1 Cover of OG Keemo's EP *Otello*, 2019. Image courtesy of Chimperator

OG Keemo's *Otello* is both a political as well as a personal act that speaks to Christy Desmet's argument about the ethical dimensions of appropriating Shakespeare. Appropriations, Desmet explains, are dialogic and responsive and 'every "response" of one text to another also renders that discourse "responsible"'.[3] OG Keemo's response to *Othello* – his 'talking back to Shakespeare' – makes canonical Shakespeare accountable for the violence and oppression against Black people not only in anglophone nations but across the globe.[4] As he levels this charge against *Othello*, his EP also encourages us to think critically about white allyship in two fundamental ways. OG Keemo's rap has the potential to make listeners think about the complicity of Desdemona and the Venetian senate in Othello's negative perception of himself. Additionally, he encourages reflection on the ways that (white) audiences and consumers of Shakespeare today are complicit in enabling the reproduction of the conceptual ties that have linked Black masculinity to Othello. Through *Otello*, OG Keemo critiques his white German listeners who consume his art and believe themselves to be his ally but who nonetheless support his performance based on a damaging and singular representation of Black culture tied to sex, violence, drugs and the pursuit of wealth. In doing so, OG Keemo can also help Shakespeare scholars, practitioners and students to reflect on their role as anti-racist allies who are complicit in the reproduction of negative stereotypes about Black men every time *Othello* is performed.

'Ich bin kein Nazi': Racism in Post-WWII Germany[5]

In the aftermath of World War II, discussions of race in Germany have been generally avoided in public discourses due to the centrality of the term 'Rasse' within the Nazi movement and the genocides committed during that regime. However, this vigilance against discussions of race have stifled necessary conversations on white privilege and the continued subtle as well as overt acts of racism experienced by many non-'white' Germans, immigrants and refugees. Despite the fact that the country has been shaped by people of colour, and although more than one million people of African descent currently live in the Federal Republic, the national self-perception appears to be built around the presumption of whiteness for the majority of German society.[6] This, in turn, hinders conversations about racial privilege in the first place. Particularly, Black Germans have been excluded from the nation's self-image, as Green Party politician Aminata Touré asserts when she talks about efforts to raise awareness of race-based discrimination in the country:[7]

> Beim anti-Schwarzen Rassismus merkt man, man fängt total bei null an. Weil es erstmal überhaupt kein Bewusstsein darüber gibt, dass es viele schwarze Menschen hier gibt. Was mich immer sehr wundert, weil, wenn ich in den Bus einsteige, treffe ich viele schwarze Menschen. Und trotzdem tun wir in Deutschland immer so ein Stück weit, als würde es hier keine schwarzen Menschen geben.

> *In terms of anti-Black racism, you quickly realise that you start at zero since there is no awareness that many Black people actually live here, which really surprises me because when I get on a bus, I meet a lot of Black people. And yet, in Germany we act to a certain extent as though there were no Black people here.*[8]

In practice, the Federal Republic of Germany does not acknowledge deviations from this self-image through ethnicity, as the data collection of the nation's Federal Statistical Office demonstrates. Information on race and ethnic descent of Germans is not gathered at all. Instead, the government records these demographics exclusively through the vague and broad category of 'migration background' ('Migrationshintergrund').[9] Much like the so-called practice of colour-blind casting, this decision not to collect racial or ethnic data and, thereby, not to categorise and differentiate Germany's population may be informed by anti-racist intentions.[10] However, as Ayanna Thompson, Lisa M. Anderson and Ania Loomba have argued, the refusal to acknowledge racial difference elides with a refusal to recognise and reckon with the entwinement of power and race that have impacted the lived experiences of people past and present. Furthermore, without a clear picture of the nation's diverse ethnic composition, conversations about ongoing racism in Germany will continue to prove difficult. Moreover, debates among white Germans about their race-based discriminatory practices are often evaluated through the narrow lens of the country's Nazi past. Racist acts are either measured against the atrocities committed by Hitler's Germany, which absolve everyday forms of racism since these quotidian acts seem incomparable to the crimes committed during the Third Reich, or all forms of prejudice result in the label of fascist or Nazi, which thereby end the possibility for communication and for more nuanced understandings of systemic racism.

The 2010s brought forward an increase in media attention to racist acts and terror, which pushed the public towards a crucial examination of the country's treatment of its non-white citizens and visitors. At the beginning of the decade, German media reported widely on the 'National Socialist Underground' terror group trial (NSU, 2013) and the anti-Islam movement PEGIDA (founded in 2014). Shortly thereafter, the nation saw a rise in antagonistic responses from Germans towards the influx of refugees and displaced persons from countries, such as Syria, Iraq, Afghanistan, Sudan, Senegal, Somalia, Libya, Eritrea and Nigeria (2015–16). The latter half of the decade then witnessed the rapid rise of the far-right party Alternative für Deutschland (AfD), neo-Nazi violence in Chemnitz (2018), the assassination of refugee-supporting politician Walter Lübcke, as well as the attempted mass murder at a Synagogue in Halle (both in 2019). As the 2010s came to an end, Germany faced a public reckoning that was advanced through social media. Specifically, the #MeTwo movement on Twitter manifested a collective narrative of everyday racism in Germany that was further amplified through the divisive debates that resulted from the resignation of German soccer star of Turkish descent Mesut Özil from the national team.

German Rap as Social Critique: OG Keemo's *Otello* in Five Tracks

Within the realm of popular culture, Germany's rap scene represents another significant stage that has allowed minorities to articulate their critical messages, including on issues of national belonging.[11] German rap began in the 1980s and produced a milestone in anti-racist music shortly after the fall of the Berlin Wall. After the homes of asylum seekers and guest workers were set on fire during the 1992 pogrom in Rostock-Lichtenhagen, rap-crew Advanced Chemistry released the groundbreaking track 'Fremd im eigenen Land' (*'Foreign in your own country'*), in which they called out the systemic nature of racism against non-white Germans as well as the ongoing neo-Nazi violence in the newly reunified nation. Almost thirty years later, with racial discrimination once again on the rise, German rapper OG Keemo has become a distinctive figure among German rappers and a mouthpiece for many members of the Black German community.[12] Born in Mainz as Karim Joel Martin, the son of a Sudanese immigrant father, OG Keemo has been releasing his work since 2017. Especially through his 2019 lead-single '216' from his debut album *Geist*, the artist positions himself as a critical political voice within the hip hop scene. In '216,' he confronts Germans with the unsettling picture of everyday racism in the country including racial profiling, police brutality and conflicts within the Afro-German community.

No less political is his five-track extended play *Otello*, which he released a few months prior together with Funkvater Frank in May 2019. Through naming his EP after one of the most infamous and harmful representations of Black men, OG Keemo places his work in dialogue with Shakespeare whose purported universality has contributed to making Othello one of the most well-known and recognisable of the playwright's characters. Although Shakespeare is often lauded as being 'good for you', Ayanna Thompson has stressed that *Othello* is far from edifying but is, in fact, one of Shakespeare's 'three toxic plays'.[13] Thompson states that the play – a drama 'written for a white man in blackface' – feels 'like it's damaging your soul', especially for Black actors.[14] While the racism of *Othello* can sometimes be obscured due to the projection of Shakespeare's universal 'goodness', adaptations like OG Keemo's EP make explicit the pervasive racism that forms the foundation of the Othello narrative. Vanessa I. Corredera has importantly argued that adaptations have the potential to 're-mediate' Shakespeare's tragedy by reorientating the focus of scholars, teachers, students, practitioners and audiences such that the central issue is no longer 'questions about a black man's humanity' but more so the 'racist inhumanity directed against him through the shifting, potent tools of white supremacy'.[15] OG Keemo's *Otello* points to an important mechanism of white supremacy – the means by which racist ideologies are reproduced and presented positively as inclusion, white allyship and a celebration of Black culture.

OG Keemo's critique of his white German listeners forces us to interrogate how even the Shakespearean characters who admired and loved Othello, namely Desdemona, esteemed a racist caricature of Black hypermasculinity that was bound to the inevitable endangerment of his body. *Otello* begins with a song titled after the namesake of the EP and a second track, 'Tanamo', that reiterate reductive racist assumptions about Black culture. Particularly, these initial songs reify images of Black criminality, antagonism with police, as well as a desire for sex and money. As Priscilla Layne has pointed out, German conscious rap and gangsta rap might both include exaggerated representations of an 'other' as well as social critique. However, gangsta rappers' willingness to perform these caricatures implies a degree of adoration for the circumstances that create the poverty and violence commonly associated with these identities'.[16] In 'Tanamo', the lyrics express the predetermined expectations for the lives of Black rappers like him – 'meiner Art (*my kind*)' – to revolve around the valorisation of violence, male sexual virility and the ambition for the accumulation of wealth.[17] Despite his regurgitation of gangster rap stereotypes, OG Keemo foreshadows the social critique he will eventually voice in the later three songs of the EP.

The final line of the first track 'Otello' raises the status of being both within and outside of German culture. 'Ach Gott, der anner von Mannem, mir nenne den den schwarze Deifel, kann der Deutsch? Ich weß gar net. (*Oh God, that guy from Mannheim. We call him the black devil. Can he speak German? I do not know.*)'[18] As is implied in the Shakespearean title *Othello, the Moor of Venice*, Othello is both incorporated within and yet separated from the general perception of a homogenous Christian Venetian society. However, the wealth of early modern Venice derived from hundreds of years of imperial enterprises, commerce and trade, which made the city a melting pot for various religions and ethnicities. *Othello*, Ambereen Dadabhoy poignantly argues, ultimately 'investigates and denies the possibility of incorporating alien others into a European imperial body politic'.[19] Similarly, despite global immigration into Germany, the national image is based on the assumption of whiteness. Through the appropriation of Shakespeare's play – a canonical work that begins with the fantasy of assimilation and ends with the tragic rejection of the possibility of inclusion – OG Keemo points to the pervasive narratives that produce expectations of failed assimilation. While these assumptions often put the onus on immigrant communities to assimilate, OG Keemo's turn to *Othello* makes plain how the national self-image of a European body politic has historically been constructed through the possibility of inclusion but ultimate exclusion of Black people.

With a nation that perceives itself as white, Black Germans find them-selves – like Othello – limited in their inclusion within the state and excluded from the national self-image.[20] Through his references to slurs like the 'black devil', OG Keemo points to daily forms of othering that Black Germans experience. Iago and Emilia similarly refer to Othello as a 'devil' (1.1.124; 5.2.161,163), which therefore marks Othello not only as an 'other' but as an enemy of Christian Venice.[21] References to Black Germans as devils, therefore, reifies the association of Blackness with vil-lainy. Afro-Germans are both physically marked as an 'other' and are therefore assumed not to be from Germany. This is suggested through the question of whether or not the man *can* speak the language, which is delivered in a menacing, synthetic deep voice that also is unidentifiable. The song, thus, exposes the kinds of racist microaggressions that Black Germans experience daily that undermine their belonging in Germany. OG Keemo – himself – is the 'schwarze Deifel'. However, his rap – an art that requires fluency in the German language – points to the flawed logic of such racist assumptions about belonging and ability.[22]

This fraught relation between a rap artist who produces German con-scious music and the genre's complicity in maintaining negative stereo-types that reduces Black culture to a single idea continues in the second song. 'Tanamo' feeds into the desire of white middle-class audiences to hear about OG Keemo's street credibility, a desire for money, drugs and sex, and Black hypermasculinity. The hook of the second song, how-ever, 'Ich wollte verdienen mit dem Set (*I wanted to make money with this set*)' begins to address the relation between audience expectations and their influence on a rapper's work. Specifically, if the purpose of the song is to sell and make money, then he is – to a certain extent – com-pelled to cater to the image that his white fans have of Black culture. The namesake of the song references Lord Tanamo, Joseph Abraham Gordon, most known for his work on ska that popularised the genre globally, a genre that promoted social justice and racial tolerance. The dissonance between the title and the content of 'Tanamo' expresses the tensions produced between OG Keemo's own vision for his art to bring forth equality and the appropriation of Black culture by middle-class white Germans.

Although 'Otello' and 'Tanamo' hint at the social criticism the EP will later provide, these opening songs to *Otello* nonetheless reinscribe negative stereotypes that fetishise Black hypermasculinity and tie Black cultures to lust, criminality, drugs and violence. Although in Shakespeare's play, Othello presents his union with Desdemona as lawful and not driven by lust, Iago arouses Brabantio's fears and anger through racist and demeaning rhetoric.[23] Desdemona has committed 'treason' (1.1.170) to be embraced in the 'gross clasps of a lascivious Moor' (1.1.127). The language used presents the marriage of Othello and Desdemona as unlawful, animalistic and carnal. Negative associations tied to Black masculinity were reinscribed and perpetuated by Shakespeare's canonical work and reverberate today in the kinds of contemporary representations of Black culture consumed by white audiences. In other words, OG Keemo gives his audience the white man's Othello, a caricature of Black German culture that (initially) fulfils the expectations of his listeners. This performance of street credibility that positions Blackness as outside of hegemonic German culture provides white fans with the ability to appropriate Black culture as a symbol of their anti-racism and anti-establishment politics. As Priscilla Layne compellingly reveals, the appropriation of Blackness in German culture has long been employed discursively as a means to signify white male rebellion.[24] This appropriation and utilisation of Black culture to serve the interests of white audiences, Layne critiques, 'read[s] blackness as always already rebellious' and 'strips black culture and black people of their complexity. Moreover, if blackness is always already coded as Other, then it is impossible for individuals to be both Black and German.'[25]

'Obi-Wan', the third song in *Otello*, features a marked shift in the EP. Similar to the structure of a Shakespearean play, this third song or act explicitly states a provocation that departs from the previous tracks when it contends that his rap challenges systemic racism, anti-Blackness and oppression rather than perpetuating the reduction of Black German culture to a homogenous and othered group. OG Keemo opens 'Obi-Wan' with an expression of an obsession with symbols:

Schon immer Eurozeichen in mei'm Fokus
24/7 kokaweißes Vintage-Polo . . .
Bitch, ich war ein Pimp, auch schon als Kind nur in Dior und Ralphy-Sweater, fuck it.
Ich war ein King, ich hatte Dornenkranz und Zepter, fuck it.

Always had Euro signs in my focus
24/7 coke-white vintage-polo . . .
Bitch, I was already a pimp as a kid only in Dior and Ralphy-Sweater, fuck it.
I was a king, I had a crown of thorns and scepter, fuck it.[26]

The first lines point to the fact that since bodies are read, OG Keemo attempts to shape how people interpret him through the usage of signs that can adorn his body, such as designer brands, logos and jewellery. However, the song almost immediately critiques the simple syllogism, 'one is what one symbolises', when it gestures towards the ways that signs are slippery and often signify beyond the intention of the bearer. For example, while sceptres represent monarchical dominion, the curious inclusion of the Christian symbol of a *crown of thorns* as a sign of sovereign power underscores the dangers of potential misinterpretation. Although Jesus of Nazareth's professed kingship referred to the heavenly realm, he was understood by those who persecuted him as a political threat who endeavoured to forge his kingdom on earth.[27] The tensions between one's desired identity and how one is interpreted by others also hearkens to the titular character of the EP. Like Othello's evocative 'Speak of me as I am' (*Othello* 5.2.351), OG Keemo emphasises the power of audiences who will interpret his rap and him, conferring identity and meaning to what he endeavours to represent and be. More importantly, just as Othello – circumscribed by early modern race discourses – evinced a crisis of self-identity when he stabs himself as he recalls killing the 'turbaned Turk', the political and religious enemy of the Venetian State, OG Keemo's rap conveys the difficulty for Black men to claim an identity when their representation is overdetermined by negative stereotypes within contemporary German popular culture.

OG Keemo challenges the quotidian forms of racism that label him as outside of German culture. In 'Obi-Wan', he proclaims himself to be 'der beste deutsche Rapper, Punkt (*the best German rapper, period*).'[28] The usage of the superlative, itself, is less important than the implications of the statement. First, it directly undermines the conclusion of the first song 'Otello', which voices the prejudiced assumption that the German language remains somehow inaccessible to Black Germans. Second, not only does his statement go beyond access to claim mastery of the German language; he asserts a German identity and belonging within the nation. OG Keemo does not just simply rap in the language nor does he cast himself as a Sudanese-German, an ethnic other despite having German nationality; he centres himself as German. OG Keemo goes further yet when he explicitly states the purpose of his music: 'ich mach' Rap für Gleichberechtigung (*I make rap for equality*)'.[29] In doing so, he confronts his listeners with the challenge to understand the music he creates as participating in the collective endeavour to dismantle systemic oppression and anti-Blackness. While he levels overt criticism towards structural and flagrant forms of racism, he also provides a subtler critique of his own audiences who are drawn to Black culture as a sign of their defiance of German hegemonic society. When audiences perceive him as outside of German culture and celebrate his critique of society as an 'other' from outside rather than within, this implies that they do not see him as German and, thus, belies their inability to accept his assertion that he is the best 'deutsche Rapper'.

The last two songs of *Otello* express the psychological toll and physical harm that result from quotidian as well as more flagrant forms of racism influencing the lived experiences of Black people in Germany. In particular, these final two tracks emphasise who pays the price for the white privilege enjoyed by OG Keemo's fans. For example, throughout the music video for 'Schnee (*Snow*)' – the fourth song of the EP – OG Keemo holds a bloodied knife with drops of red splattered on his white polo shirt and shorts. The song opens with 'Vergib mir meine Sünden, Gott (*Forgive me my sins, God*)', which matches the visual of OG Keemo's expressions of mental anguish in the video.[30] He describes himself as 'Der schwarze Vincent Vega, renne vor den Cops (*The Black Vincent Vega, running from the cops*) / Die Belohnung ist ein M auf meinem Kopf, so wie Majin Vegeta (*The reward is an M on my head, just like Majin Vegeta*).'[31] The negative stereotypes that link violence with Black culture enable hostilities between police and racialised groups within Germany. In a critical comparison, OG Keemo expresses similarities between Vega's profession in *Pulp Fiction* (1994) as a contract killer and Black rappers who make money and gain fame through violence – albeit imagined rather than real. His audiences expect him to rap about his anger and desire for harm targeted against racist German authorities who enforce systemic oppression. The 'M' that marks the forehead of the manga series *Dragon Ball* character Majin Vegeta symbolises his coerced and unwilling submission to the evil Babidi. Thus, the mark serves as a sign of Vegeta's identity and conversely as a symbol of compulsion. OG Keemo poignantly underscores how within Germany Blackness is read as a negative sign of belonging to an outside culture immersed in drugs, violence, sex and rebellion.

As a Black rapper whose fans expect an antagonistic persona from him, OG Keemo is compelled – like Vegeta – to perform a (self-)destructive

Black hypermasculinity in order to 'make money with [the] set'.[32] From giving audiences insight to the pressures that circumscribe his experiences as a Black German rap artist – especially one who endeavours to work against racism – OG Keemo then turns his attention more explicitly to those who consume and appropriate Black rap culture:

> Ihr seid keine Gangster, ihr seid Modeblogger
> Keine Rapper, ihr seid Drogenopfer . . .
> Niemand sieht mich liegen, bis die Ärzte meinen Körper autopsieren

> *You are no gangsters, you are fashion bloggers*
> *Not rappers, you are drug victims . . .*
> *No one sees me lying, until doctors autopsy my body.*[33]

White privilege allows the social-media-obsessed to perform street credibility through their affinity to OG Keemo. It is his experiences of anti-Blackness and his perceived position as outside of German culture that white German middle-class audiences consume and exploit to construct themselves as gangster rebels.[34] The experiences of violence romanticised and rapped about by middle-class white Germans are part of his quotidian existence: 'Guck, ich leb', was ihr rappt (*Look, I live what you all rap*).'[35] Like the Venetian state that uses Othello, audiences use OG Keemo to give themselves desired labels, which in turn makes money for him. However, as 'Schnee' poignantly depicts, the compulsion he experiences to perform racist stereotypes comes at the cost of psychological duress and potential physical harm. Even those who claim to be anti-racists, in fact, perpetuate the consumption of Black culture for white gain, and this is most strikingly underscored when OG Keemo states that his death will not be seen until his body is invaded for bureaucratic purposes by a medical examiner performing an autopsy.

'Whitney', the final song – Act 5 – of the EP explicitly tackles the associations of Black men with sexual virility, domestic violence and self-destruction. In Shakespeare's play, Desdemona prefers Othello over the privileged and protected 'wealthy curled darlings' of Venice (*Othello* 1.2.69). When asked to recount how he wooed Desdemona, Othello began with a description of Brabantio's incessant desire to hear Othello's stories about his life, '[F]rom year to year, the battles, sieges, fortunes / That [Othello had] passed' (1.3.129–30). Like her father, Desdemona was similarly drawn to Othello's stories and with her 'greedy ear / devour up [his] discourse' (1.3.148–9). Her eager consumption of the trials and tribulations he experienced – his exotic stories of pain, abuse and redemption – won her heart for 'She loved [him] for the dangers [he] had passed' (*Othello* 1.3.166). Like Desdemona – drawn to the hardships Othello faced in his life – a white female figure expresses her attraction towards OG Keemo for the narratives of discrimination, poverty and violence he tells, for the image he creates.

> Sie streichelt mein'n Kopf, als ob sie mich leiden kann
> Fängt zu weinen an, redet nicht zu Ende
> Für die Kids bist du 'ne lebende Legende!', sagt sie zitternd
> Ich sag', 'Ich bin nur'n Trap-Nigga, der gut schreiben kann!'

> *She caresses my head, as if she could stand me*
> *Starts crying, does not finish speaking*
> *'You are a living legend to the kids!' she says trembling*
> *I say, 'I am only a Trap N****, who can write well!'*[36]

Both Desdemona and the white woman are moved by the stories of these particular Black men because they fulfil certain stereotypes that white people have about being Black. Desdemona consumed Othello's exotic stories of hardship and gave him 'a world of kisses' (1.3.158) while the woman in 'Whitney', similarly moved by OG Keemo, caresses him. As previously stated, OG Keemo critiques the ways that white audiences consume and exploit representations of Black men that hinge upon negative associations with violence, drugs and poverty. In 'Whitney', the fetishisation of a homogenous and reductive idea of Black culture is not simply commodified as a symbol of white rebellion. Rather, the song points to the usage of Black bodies as signs of the progressiveness of white liberal Germans. Proximity and affinity to Black culture, therefore, could be less about anti-racist allyship than about the social benefits that such associations confer upon white middle-class persons. With the inclusion of 'als ob sie mich leiden kann (*as if she could stand me*)', OG Keemo sees through Whitney's hyperbolic performance of adoration.

On an affective level, Whitney's performed empathy and attraction to OG Keemo could be self-gratifying and pleasurable since these actions may give her a sense of righteousness.[37] After all, her tears – which (are designed to) show how deeply she has been moved and perhaps even the 'pain' she has felt – are shed for a 'legend to the kids', someone who is an inspiration to the youth, a hope for the future. Whether OG Keemo's image as a Black rapper is used by middle-class white audiences as a sign

of rebellion or as a sign of their progressiveness, they are nonetheless commodifying him and appropriating a certain simplified idea of Black culture. Through his incisive critiques, OG Keemo challenges his audiences
to develop a more nuanced understanding of racism that goes beyond the
extremes represented by the political views of the AfD, white supremacy
and the historic mass genocides committed by the Nazis. Our erotic lives,
Sharon Patricia Holland asserts, have been shaped by everyday racist practices.[38] Desire, itself, evinces the workings of racist ideologies even among
self-proclaimed anti-racists. Implicit within this song is a challenge for
OG Keemo's listeners to self-reflect and to confront the ways that racism
is pervasive and embedded within all lived experiences.

As in 'Schnee', OG Keemo again contests the romanticisation of Black
resistance to systemic oppression and racism when he responds to Whitney's
praise by downplaying his accomplishments and stating that he has simply
used his talent as a writer. With his artistic ability to construct narratives in
critique of society, OG Keemo fleetingly raises a hopeful potential for words
to bring forth social change. He, a *'hooligan sent by prophets'*, serves contemporary Germans as a Martin Luther-like figure.[39] But, when he asks, 'sag
mir, was ist mächtiger, ein Buch oder 'ne Waffe? (*tell me, what is more powerful, a book or a weapon?*)', he forces his audiences to recognise the pervasive
destruction that books can inflict on a par with actual weapons.[40] Shakespeare's *Othello*, a canonical work globally recognised, helped to perpetuate
and give credence to destructive images of Black masculinity. In *Othello*,
audiences are given a valiant and accomplished man who loathes his dark
complexion and comes to see himself through the racist ideologies espoused
by Iago as unworthy of Desdemona's love and affection.

Furthermore, *Othello* reified the perception of Black men as a threat
to white womanhood, a fear that has been used to justify slavery, seg-
regation and atrocious acts of violence. Hortense Spillers, in 'Mama's
Baby, Papa's Maybe', underscores the fatal consequences of the written
and the verbal: 'We must concede at the very least, that sticks and stones
might break our bones, but words will most certainly *kill* us.'[41] In Mississippi 1955, the words of a white woman took the life of a Black child.
Carolyn Bryant Donham lied that fourteen-year-old Emmett Till had
made menacing advances towards her. The perceived sexual threat to
the ideological protected status of white womanhood led to the brutal
abduction, torture and murder of Emmett Till. Although OG Keemo
momentarily voices the revolutionary potential for words to bring forth
social change, he more keenly exposes the psychological and physical
damage caused by written works that have the power to cultivate and

perpetuate racist ideologies. Through the title of this EP, OG Keemo explicitly names *Othello* (including its print and performance history) for its participation in reifying a destructive representation of Black masculinity for, as Peter Sellars explains, 'Shakespeare's *Othello* is a permanent provocation, for four centuries the most visible portrayal of a black man in Western Art.'[42]

Othello's evocative 'Speak of me as I am' (5.2.340) that precedes his suicide conveys care about what might be remembered of him and, perhaps, a hope that he can somewhat shape the narratives others will tell. The self-destruction of Shakespeare's Othello has a long history of being interpreted by scholars as Othello's self-identification as a protector of Venetian interests who must eradicate the outsider within himself.[43] According to this interpretation, when Othello kills himself while describing the time he 'took by th' throat the circumcised dog / And smote him – thus!' (5.2.53–4), it is his last act in service to the state. Othello's suicide at the end of the play is represented in 'Whitney's' hook when OG Keemo raps about driving a car into an oak tree at 130 kilometres per hour. However, the affective motivations in these representations vastly differ.[44] In OG Keemo's *Otello*, visions of 'Magenta, Weibern und Gold (*Magenta, Broads, and Gold*)' accompany death, and cars – the means of his demise – serve as symbols of acquired wealth, status and masculinity.[45] The first hook ends with the motto: '"Fick die Welt, ich hab' die Scheiße gewollt!" Ja (*'Fuck the world. I had wanted this shit!' Yes*).'[46] What has been glorified in stereotypes of German gangster rap – the acquisition of wealth and women – fails to bring him satisfaction. Furthermore, he possesses what he is expected to desire but only through his adherence to performing a fabricated, simplified and negative view of Black culture consumed and appropriated by his white middle-class fans.

The song ends with a slight difference in the final hook that seems to undo the hope that surfaces momentarily throughout the EP: 'Diese Welt wird eh zu Grunde gehen, also was soll's! Amen' (*This world will perish anyway, so why bother! Amen*).[47] The religious affirmative mirrors the secular 'ja' from the previous hook and poetically ties the conclusion of 'Whitney' with the opening of the song. Unlike Shakespeare's *Othello*, who is concerned with what the white Christian Venetians will remember of him, OG Keemo's *Otello* ends with an expression of frustration and hopelessness in the face of pervasive and systemic racism that can lead to a refusal to care. But, as the vision of suicide suggests, a disinterest in fighting against racial injustice – a lack of hope and acceptance of the status quo – leads to a figurative (and potentially real) death.

Für Gleichberechtigung (*For Equality*)

Remediating Shakespeare's play through OG Keemo's EP shifts attention to invite a more critical view of the play's representation of a 'liberal' and 'inclusive' Venetian state. It encourages scholars to consider that, even when the Venetians praised Othello, their celebration of him was always tied to Othello's willingness to render himself vulnerable and to endanger his body for Venice. Thus, the ability to exploit Othello for Venice's gain masqueraded as white magnanimity. Although Othello represents a Black man, OG Keemo's EP cover outlines that name in white. In doing so, he expresses how this character – which has dominated representations of Black masculinity for hundreds of years – is not a Black man at all but derived from the fantasy of white men.

OG Keemo's *Otello*, however, is not a white man's *Othello*. Unlike Shakespeare's work, his rap derives from a place of hope and is part of his ongoing effort for social change. OG Keemo challenges listeners to recognise not only the flagrant acts of race-based violence but also the everyday racism that they have enabled and have benefited from in their appropriation of Black culture. OG Keemo likens the tendency of white Germans to appropriate and reductively exploit Black German experiences to a form of blackface, which he makes apparent in the EP cover of *Otello*. The evocative visual of OG Keemo suffocating beneath a clear plastic bag that he pulls onto the face of his white friend and fellow artistic collaborator Funkvater Frank conveys the violence of appropriation that benefits middle-class white Germans while inflicting detrimental consequences on Black lives. Overtly racist Germans – who vilify racial minorities for presumed criminality – participate in the perpetuation of racist ideologies, but so do those who see themselves as allies and who support the hip hop scene by lauding violent caricatures of Black hypermasculinity as part of their anti-racist politics. Through their consumption and appropriation of a caricature of Black culture, even white progressive rap audiences reify the stereotypes of Black criminality and violence that have been used to justify the murder of Black men, women and children.

Less than four months after releasing *Otello*, OG Keemo confronted audiences with his powerful indictment of ongoing racism in Germany in his acclaimed single '216' (September 2019).[48] As stated previously, the 2010s have brought forth an alarming rise in racist political agendas and white supremacist visibility. OG Keemo's *Otello* prepares audiences to view '216' and to recognise that contemporary German racism is a continuation of the ingrained history of reducing and vilifying Black people.

He challenges his fans to continue their support of him despite his painful criticisms of the manifold kinds of discrimination and racist thinking from which no one is exempt. Anti-racism – as *Otello* makes clear – begins with self-reflection and a recognition of the privilege that one enjoys with disastrous consequences for Black lives. In doing so, OG Keemo helps audiences of his rap and of Shakespeare to recognise our ability to contribute to anti-racist efforts by demanding a change in the narratives we consume.

Notes

1. OG Keemo's twenty-first-century response to Shakespeare continues a long tradition of German engagement and fascination with the early modern playwright. Shakespeare captured the minds of countless German intellectuals over the centuries: from the Storm and Stress writers (Herder, Goethe, Lenz) and dramatists from the Romantic era (A. W. Schlegel, Tieck) to twentieth-century artists like Gerhart Hauptmann and Ludwig Fulda – the latter two claimed that Shakespeare was really German at heart. During the Third Reich, the Nazis appropriated and used Shakespeare's works in the context of their race politics and antisemitic propaganda, particularly through the figure of Shylock.

2. Dympna Callaghan reminds readers: 'Othello was a White man' (a phrase originally coined by Mary Preston during the Civil War Era of the 1860s). Dympna Callaghan, '"Othello was a white man": properties of race on Shakespeare's stage', *Alternative Shakespeares: Volume 2*, ed. Terence Hawkes (London: Routledge, 1996), 193–215. See also Ayanna Thompson's 'The Blackfaced Bard: Returning to Shakespeare or Leaving Him', *Shakespeare Bulletin* 27, no. 3 (2009): 437–56.

3. Christy Desmet, 'Introduction', *Shakespeare and Appropriation*, ed. Christy Desmet and Robert Sawyer (London: Routledge, 1999), 19.

4. Ibid. 11.

5. 'Ich bin kein Nazi'. (*I am not a Nazi.*)

6. See 'Afrozensus'. *Afrozensus*, https://afrozensus.de/?lang=en. Accessed 5 May 2022. African American GIs played a crucial role in reorganising post-war Germany, and it was people of colour who provided their labour through guest-worker programmes to the Federal Republic (starting in the 1950s) and the German Democratic Republic (starting in the 1960s but particularly in the 1980s).

7. Aminata Touré is the daughter of Malian refugees and was elected vice president of Schleswig-Holstein's state parliament in 2019.

8. Arte Tracks. *Afrozensus – Mit Megaloh, Aminata Belli Und Aminata Touré.* Video, https://www.youtube.com/watch?v=I57LePt0cgc&ab_channel= ArteTRACKS. Accessed 5 may 2022.

9. Philip Oltermann and Jon Henley, 'France And Germany Urged To Rethink Reluctance To Gather Ethnicity Data'. *The Guardian*, 16 June 2020, https://www.theguardian.com/world/2020/jun/16/france-and-germany-urged-to-rethink-reluctance-to-gather-ethnicity-data. Accessed 5 May 2022.

10. The term 'colour-blind', which refers to specific practices and ideologies, demonstrates the pervasiveness of ableist rhetoric in scholarly discourse. This problematic term 'equates blindness with ignorance' and with a refusal to acknowledge racial inequalities, as Subini Ancy Annamma, Darrell D. Jackson and Deb Morrison have argued (157). Subini Ancy Annamma, Darrell D. Jackson and Deb Morriso, 'Conceptualizing color-evasiveness: using dis/ability critical race theory to expand a color-blind racial ideology in education and society', *Race Ethnicity and Education* 20, no. 2 (2016): 147–62.

11. See David Chemeta, 'Deutsche Identität, Kultur Und Sprache Im Deutschen Rap', *Zeitschrift Für Ethnologie* 138, no. 1 (2–13): 37–54. https://www.jstor.org/stable/24364888. Accessed 5 May 2022.

12. Ralf Bosen, 'Racism On The Rise In Germany', *DW.COM*. 6 September 2020, https://www.dw.com/en/racism-on-the-rise-in-germany/a-53735536. Accessed 5 May 2022.

13. Ayanna Thompson, 'All That Glisters Is Not Gold'. Interview with Gene Demby and Shereen Marisol Meraji. NPR Code Switch. Podcast transcript, 21 August 2019. See also Vanessa I. Corredera, who states that 'Shakespeare's universality finds its limits in Othello's inauthentic experience' (29). Vanessa I. Corredera, '"How Dey Goin' to Kill Othello?!": Key & Peele and Shakespearean Universality', *Journal of American Studies* 54, no. 1 (2020): 27–35.

14. Thompson, 'All That Glisters Is Not Gold'. In the interview, Thompson shares that her help has been repeatedly sought after by major theatre companies to assist Black actors playing Othello as they experienced mental breakdowns. See also Keith Hamilton Cobb's *American Moor* that shows the deeply vexed relation *Othello* has with Black actors: 'I was ashamed that any reasonable person would look at me and see him . . . [but] I could not *not* care for Othello.' Keith Hamilton Cobb. *American Moor* (London: Methuen Drama, 2020).

15. Vanessa I. Corredera, '*Get Out* and the Remediation of *Othello's* Sunken Place: Beholding White Supremacy's Coagula', *Borrowers and Lenders* 13, no. 1 (2020), https://borrowers-ojs-azsu.tdl.org/borrowers/article/view/219. Accessed 5 May 2022.

16. Priscilla Layne, 'One Like No Other? Blaxploitation in the Performance of Afro-German Rapper Lisi', *Journal of Popular Music Studies* 25, no. 2 (2013): 200.

17. 'Tanamo', 4.

18. 'Otello', 44–5. OG Keemo delivers this line entirely in the local Electoral Palatinate dialect. The phrase 'der anner' conveys a derogatory tone.

19. Ambereen Dadabhoy, 'Two Faced: The Problem of Othello's Visage', *Othello: The State of Play*, ed. Lena Cowen Orlin (London: Bloomsbury, 2014), 142.

20. Derived from the German word 'Deutungshoheit', which describes who has the authority of interpretation, 'Deutschungshoheit' – coined by Afro-German artist Malonda – signifies the exclusionary practices of white Germans who claim the authority to determine what counts as German and what does not.

21. Christian iconography of the mediaeval period often depicted devils as black figures.

22. In this context, OG Keemo's spelling of 'Otello' that places him in a musical tradition with its references to Verdi's *Otello* (an Italian opera based on Shakespeare's *Othello*) can also be understood as an effort to further assert his 'Germanness' by adhering to the linguistic rules of the German language in which 'th' is found less frequently.

23. Othello admits that he had 'married her' (1.3.79) and emphasises the importance of Desdemona's consent when he has Desdemona speak for herself and compels the senate to listen to her will (1.3.116, 259). In doing so, Othello underscores their lawful union and the importance he places in her mind and consent, which deviates from the hypersexualised rhetoric used by Iago to demean their union.

24. Priscilla Layne, *White Rebels in Black: German Appropriation of Black Popular Culture* (Ann Arbor: University of Michigan Press, 2018), 189.

25. Ibid. 196.

26. 'Obi-Wan', 1–2, 5–6.

27. John 19: 13–16.

28. 'Obi-Wan', 11.

29. Ibid. 13.

30. 'Schnee', 2.

31. Ibid. 34.

32. 'Ich wollte verdienen mit dem Set' ('Tanamo', 19, 46).

33. 'Schnee', 35–6, 42.

34. See Priscilla Layne, *White Rebels*.

35. 'Schnee', 2.

36. 'Whitney', 21.

37. For more on how learning about systemic oppression can bring a sense of emotional catharsis rather than lead to activism, see Kimberly A. Nance, 'Reading Human Rights Literature in Undergraduate Literature Classes: Professorial Desire, Disciplinary Culture, and the Chances of Cultivating Compassion', *Journal of Human Rights* 9 (2010): 161–74.

38. Sharon Patricia Holland, *The Erotic Life of Racism* (Durham, NC: Duke University Press, 2012).

39. 'Whitney', 23.

40. Ibid. 8.
41. Hortense J. Spillers, 'Mama's Baby, Papa's Maybe: An American Grammar Book', *Diacritics* 17, no. 2 (1987): 68.
42. Peter Sellars, 'Foreword', in *Desdemona*, Toni Morrison (London: Oberon Books, 2012), 7.
43. See Dennis Austin Britton, 'Re-"turning" *Othello:* Transformative and Restorative Romance', *English Literary History* 78, no. 1 (2011): 44; Virginia Mason Vaughan, *Othello: A Contextual History* (Cambridge: Cambridge University Press, 1994), 34; Kim F. Hall, *Othello, The Moor of Venice: Texts and Context* (Boston and New York: Bedford/St. Martin's, 2007), 177–9.
44. 'Whitney', 16, 32.
45. Ibid. 15, 31. Magenta serves as a synecdoche for the 500-euro bill, which stands for money and wealth.
46. Ibid. 17.
47. Ibid. 33.
48. In '216', OG Keemo tackles self-loathing due to internalised racism and complicity in the oppression of other marginalised groups. Two versions of OG Keemo exist. A fairer-skinned, decorated Black military officer dressed in a white suit hangs the darker complexioned version of himself (donning blackface dressed in black).

6

Mythical Geographies: Race, Nationalism and Shakespeare's Pronunciation

Chris Klippenstein

There are no neutral accents, only naturalised ones. Whether in the early modern period or the twenty-first century, pronunciation is an inescapable aspect of any performance that includes spoken language – but the ubiquity of pronunciation does not make it value-neutral. This chapter will explore the implications of Shakespearean performance accents in constructing an image of people from certain social backgrounds as part of a privileged Shakespearean legacy. Situated at the intersection of performance and appropriation across the long twentieth century and into the present moment, my analysis revolves around two distinct movements – the myth of an Appalachian Shakespearean accent, and the original theatrical practice known as Original Pronunciation (OP) – that claim to preserve or reconstruct Shakespeare's own pronunciation. Each of these movements positions certain speakers in honoured proximity to Shakespeare, though with different political and cultural implications, and I will use this pairing to interrogate how hegemonies of so-called 'Anglo-Saxon' whiteness are upheld through the pursuit of Shakespeare's pronunciation on (and beyond) the contemporary stage. By linking these geographically and socially disparate traditions, this chapter frames pronunciation as the connecting thread of a profoundly unsettled, transnational and transregional reimagining of Shakespearean geography: an expanded map of aural identifications that nevertheless reproduces entrenched paradigms of racial and class privilege.

For more than a hundred years, there has been a surprisingly persistent belief that, somewhere in the isolated mountains of Appalachian America, people still speak English with the same pronunciation as Shakespeare. In its most romanticised form, the myth of Appalachian Shakespeare offers the fantasy of an intimate connection both to Shakespeare himself and to early modern England, glowingly described in 1929 by Charles Morrow Wilson as 'a nation of young life which had just found its prime, a nation of energy and daring, a nation leaping from childhood into manhood'.[1] But the borders of Appalachia itself are surprisingly difficult to define. To begin with, they emphatically resist being mapped onto state boundaries: Appalachia crosses into New York, Pennsylvania, Maryland, Ohio, West Virginia, Virginia, Kentucky, Tennessee, North Carolina, South Carolina, Georgia, Alabama and Mississippi alike.[2] Because Appalachia is a region rather than a state, its coherence relies on having characteristics that are distinct from surrounding areas. Topography surely offers the most straightforward basis for defining Appalachia, since this area is famously mountainous, but this, too, ultimately seems inadequate; the Appalachian Mountains continue north from the United States into Atlantic Canada, but references to Canada are vanishingly rare, if not non-existent, in discourse around Appalachia. Instead, the boundaries of Appalachia seem to be defined by social expectations as much as topography. As linguist Chi Luu has written, '[p]eople don't always agree on what counts as the Appalachian region, except, it seems, no matter where you are geographically on the mountain range, if you're poor, white and rural, you must be in Appalachia'.[3] While Luu points to the social expectations of class, whiteness and rurality as ways of locating Appalachia, Elizabeth Catte suggests that difference itself, rather than any particular difference, is at least partly responsible for distinguishing the region from its surroundings. Between the Civil War and World War II especially, Catte writes, '[i]t mattered little whether the characteristics ascribed to Appalachia were desirable or deplorable as long as they were different'.[4] As I will show, both these topographical and social boundaries contribute to the myth of an Appalachian Shakespearean accent.

The famed ruggedness of the Appalachian landscape has translated into the idea that this region is also rooted in a more distant time, laying the groundwork for the fantasy that Shakespeare's pronunciation has been immaculately preserved there. Writing in 1899, on the cusp of the twentieth century, William Goodell Frost makes the remarkable claim that '[i]t is a longer journey from northern Ohio to eastern Kentucky than from America to Europe; for one day's ride brings us into the eighteenth century'.[5] To venture into the mountains is to go back in time, both linguistically and culturally. Frost's writings set the tone for many subsequent descriptions of Appalachia; as linguist Michael Montgomery explains, Frost was one of the first and 'most influential' propagators of 'the view that mountain speech and culture were legitimate survivals from older times'.[6] Across the long twentieth century, proponents of American nationalism increasingly adopted the idea that Appalachian speech was intimately connected to a gilded white racial history in which Shakespeare played a starring role. As Charles Morrow Wilson boasts in 1929:

> We know a land of Shakespearean ways, a country of Spenserian speech, Shakespearean people, and of cavaliers and curtsies. It is a land of high hopes and mystic allegiances, where one may stroll through forests of Arden and find heaths and habits like those of olden England. We are speaking of the Southern highlands – Appalachia and Ozarkadia.[7]

Wilson positions himself as someone who is able to draw back the curtain on this hidden, extravagantly romantic world, using his access – 'We know a land of Shakespearean ways' – to centre the insider/outsider dichotomy that consistently reappears in discussions of Appalachia.

Although it might be reasonable to assume that twentieth-century Appalachia would be considerably removed in space and time from 'olden England', proponents of the Appalachian legend often brought the two into greater proximity by conflating a Shakespearean inheritance with a legacy of so-called 'Anglo-Saxon' pride. During what Kim Sturgess calls 'the main period of [American] appropriation of Shakespeare'[8] in the nineteenth century, the word 'Anglo-Saxon' dominated American media because it allowed for the separation of 'heritage and the political system of England', and thus permitted Americans 'to promote widespread acceptance of Shakespeare while England itself was seen as the enemy'.[9] By centring the idea of an Anglo-Saxon race that could transcend national borders, Americans could lay claim to Shakespearean proximity while distancing themselves from England. As medievalists Mary Rambaran-Olm and Erik Wade have shown, the term 'Anglo-Saxon' does not refer in any impartial way to a racial or historical group; rather, it has long been 'rebranded . . . to include false narratives around white racial superiority',[10] such that the term cannot be divorced from its racist and white supremacist contexts. Although Rambaran-Olm has persuasively argued for an end to 'Anglo-Saxon studies' as the name of a sub-field within mediaeval studies,[11] I have retained this term in my chapter in order to interrogate the white supremacist legacies with which Shakespearean pronunciation remains entwined, and which the term insistently evokes. Early twentieth-century interlocutors like Frost, for instance, saw the racial and cultural implications of Saxon heritage as a way of drawing closer to a privileged connection to Shakespeare:

> Spinning [wool] . . . has helped to form the character of our race, and it is pleasant to find that here in Appalachian America it is still a contribution to the health and grace and skill of womankind. Along with these Saxon arts we shall find startling survivals of Saxon speech. The rude dialect of the mountains is far less a degradation than a survival.[12]

'Mountain speech' escapes being a degradation precisely because it offers a connection to Saxon history and attendant 'arts' that contribute to 'the character of our race'. By framing the Appalachian accent in this way, Frost inscribes himself into an ongoing tradition of white nationalists who see themselves as stewards of a glorious past that must be protected from the perceived cultural degradations of their current moment. Alongside his racial emphasis, Frost also characterises Appalachia as a place of nationalist American purity because '[as] Appalachian America has received no foreign immigration, it now contains a larger proportion of "Sons" and "Daughters" of the Revolution than any other part of our country'.[13] By drawing on a shared heritage of Anglo-Saxon whiteness, American writers could claim special proximity to Shakespeare even as they rejected his ties to England.

These claims about privileged cultural connections to Shakespeare feel all the more significant because they centre on a region that has long been stereotyped for poverty, rurality, lack of education and low social capital. Although Wilson proudly characterises Appalachia as the living echo of a golden age, a self-contained 'country of magnificent isolation, one little touched by the ways of a modern world',[14] he also notes that '[a]s a race they place inestimably more confidence in elves than in elevators'.[15] As this comment suggests, Appalachia's place on the pedestal of Saxon heritage is complicated by the disdain that writers often mixed with their praise. Even as Frost lauds the Shakespearean characteristics of Appalachian speech, he also refers to Appalachians as 'primitive folk'[16] who live in a 'ward of the nation'[17] and lack education about such basic subjects as 'hygiene, United States history, and settling quarrels without bloodshed'.[18] In this telling of the myth, there is something insistently 'primitive' about the guardians of Shakespearean speech: Appalachians are portrayed not only as guardians of a sacred Shakespearean cultural resource, but also as too isolated and old-fashioned to develop a more modern version of language or society. A similar mixture of commendation and condescension persists throughout the century. In a double-edged compliment from 1976, literary agent William Aspenwall Bradley claimed that '[w]ords and turns of expression employed by Shakespeare and in the King James version of the Bible are of such common occurrence in the mountain speech that . . . the purest English on earth is that of the Kentucky mountain[s] – however unpolished and crude it may be grammatically'.[19] Proximity to Shakespearean pronunciation was laudable for upholding Anglo-Saxon pride, but the otherness of Appalachia also translated into complex condescension towards the people who lived there.

In spite of the persistence of the Appalachian Shakespearean myth, however, there is little truth to the idea that people in Appalachia speak in a perfectly preserved Elizabethan English accent. Across the twentieth century, as Montgomery demonstrates in some detail,[20] arguments in favour of Appalachian Shakespeare have been hampered by vague evidence, absolute claims, and the casual conflation of Englishes with substantial differences, such as the English of fourteenth-century Chaucer and sixteenth-century Shakespeare. However persistent the myth of Appalachian Shakespeare might be, there is simply no linguistic basis for the idea that an Appalachian accent is an immaculate reproduction of Shakespeare's English. As linguist Jennifer Cramer puts it, '[l]inguists know that all languages change, all the time, thus there can be no language that has been untouched by time'.[21] Certain characteristics of seventeenth-century English do linger in some American accents, as we will see in my discussion of OP, but Appalachia does not appear to have an especially significant share of these features. To insist on a privileged connection between Appalachia and Shakespearean pronunciation is to cling to the false narrative of a homogeneous racial and cultural past.

Myths, however, are not about facts; they are about faith. Although academics may agree that Appalachia has not preserved Shakespeare's accent to anywhere near the degree claimed by Frost and others, it is also true that scholars are not the target audience for this fantasy. As Cramer writes, 'a recent online news story glorified the Elizabethan status of Appalachian English, further indicating how little is thought of the expert status of linguists . . . It seems, then, that linguists are not the ones who have the right kind of knowledge about this myth.'[22] Indeed, the myth of Appalachian Shakespeare remains surprisingly persistent into the present moment, especially in the context of tourism, which I interpret as an attempt to translate Shakespearean proximity into an appealing vision of cultural exoticism (though still a white, and therefore reassuringly bounded, exoticism). In the mid-1960s, a document entitled *A Dictionary of the Queen's English* was printed for complimentary distribution at state welcome centres in North Carolina.[23] Drawing on the same idyllic images that have persisted for a century, this booklet promised that travellers would 'hear the Queen's English in the coves and hollows of the Blue Ridge and the Great Smoky Mountains and on the windswept Outer Banks where time moves more leisurely'.[24] In 2009, Georgia-born senator Zell Miller claimed that 'mountain dialect . . . largely, but not completely, stems from the same archaic English' of both Chaucer and Shakespeare.[25] And as recently as 2017, the website of Tennessee Mountain Tours characterised Appalachia as a place with a unique and regionally specific connection to Shakespeare:

> The predominate [sic] theory is that the existence of Appalachian-English is the result of the isolation the mountains beyond the Blue Ridge ensured – making our dialect one of the most ancient and protected dialects in the nation. While our high-browed relatives who moved to the big city and lost their accent may frown upon our words and pronunciations, it is believed that the Appalachian dialect is a remnant of Elizabethan English.[26]

Here, the long-standing dichotomy between Appalachian insiders and outsiders manifests as a division between urban and rural. Those 'high-browed' Appalachian relatives in 'the big city' have lost more than their Appalachian accents, they have lost their capacity to understand those accents as part of a privileged Shakespearean inheritance. According to the myth of Appalachian Shakespeare, Shakespeare's closest successors and legacy-keepers are not members of an academic or social elite, but the people whom Wilson calls 'counterparts of rural Elizabethans'.[27] Whether or not outsiders recognise the value of a supposed Appalachian connection to Shakespeare, the myth of that accent seems to be a source of continued pride to at least some Appalachians.

The myth of Appalachian Shakespeare has a complicated legacy. There is work to be done on how (and whether) Appalachia's localised claims to Shakespearean pronunciation translate into social, economic or other forms of capital for the region. Professor Rochelle Smith, writing about the Shakespeare festival she organised with university and high school students in an 'isolated and depressed rural community'[28] in Appalachia, suggests that 'Shakespeare's immense power as a marker of cultural capital, his privileged place in a contested canon, turns out to have great value for places like this that are distinctly lacking in privilege.'[29] Smith makes no mention of an Appalachian Shakespearean accent, but many of her claims nevertheless describe the atmosphere from which the myth of Appalachian Shakespeare arose. 'The nostalgia for a more glorified past is almost palpable around here,' writes Smith,

> and Shakespeare, who is as canonical an author as they come, somehow fits right in. In a community wary of change, a community proud of its working-class character and suspicious of intellectual elitism, a major exception is made for Shakespeare.[30]

Here is a further manifestation of the long-standing appropriation of Shakespeare for America, and not only for America, but particularly for a region where Shakespearean affiliation coexists (and contrasts) with rural and working-class identities. Smith acknowledges the white nationalist elements of Appalachia's Shakespearean entanglements – 'Shakespeare's firm position in the canon and his status as the ultimate "dead white male" author appeals in ways not necessarily admirable to the strongly conservative streak in regions like this one'[31] – but also maintains that engagement with Shakespeare holds meaningful benefits for 'parts of the country where poverty is all too prevalent and "privilege" something that often seems permanently out of reach'.[32] Because of the sheer force of Shakespeare's cultural capital, Appalachians may benefit from greater proximity to Shakespeare even though they do not share his accent. 'When high school students discover that they can read Shakespeare and even enjoy him', Smith writes, 'they start to wonder what else they might be up for.'[33]

At first blush, the highly regional and white supremacist implications of Appalachian Shakespeare seem to be a world away from the linguistic reconstruction and original theatrical practice known as Original Pronunciation (OP). Spearheaded in its current incarnation by British linguist David Crystal, whom Keith Johnson rightly calls 'the doyen of the most recent OP studies',[34] OP puts forth a significantly transnational reimagining of Shakespearean proximities through accent and across the lines of social class, especially in contrast with Received Pronunciation (RP), the hegemonic accent for Shakespearean performance in Britain. At the same time, even as OP allows a wider range of audience members to hear themselves in Shakespeare, it nevertheless speaks predominantly to an audience from the whitest corners of the British Empire. Both promising and problematic, the use of OP poses important questions about the racial and class implications encoded in the accents of Shakespearean performance.

For most of the twentieth century, OP was a relatively underex-plored performance possibility. Experiments with Elizabethan pronun-ciation date back to at least 1902,[35] but Crystal recounts that there had been no full-length OP productions since John Barton's 1952 *Julius Caesar* for the Cambridge Marlowe Society,[36] 'and there had never been one on a London stage'.[37] The contemporary wave of interest in OP began in 2004 with *Romeo and Juliet* at the Globe, a production with which Crystal was extensively involved. In part because the Globe was uncertain whether audiences would be alienated by an unfamil-iar accent, the 2004 *Romeo and Juliet* ran for only three performances in OP, with the rest of the run performed in modern English.[38] The anxiety around audience reception, as well as issues raised by actors and others involved in the production, usefully de-naturalises a vari-ety of social expectations regarding pronunciation in a Shakespearean production. In particular, Crystal notes that certain features of OP can sound rural to many modern audience members, leading him to won-der about the capacity of such accents to delegitimise Shakespeare's text: 'Can the older Capulets and Montagues, the Prince, and Romeo and Juliet themselves all sound rural without the effect becoming ludi-crous?'[39] Whether this attitude is attributed to audience members or theatremakers, it speaks not only to the notion that certain accents come with genre expectations, but specifically to the idea that people with rural accents are inherently difficult to take seriously as figures of authority ('the older Capulets and Montagues, the Prince') or as lead-ing protagonists in a tragedy ('Romeo and Juliet').

The discourse around OP particularly highlights the entrenched asso-ciations between comedy and classism in Shakespearean performance. Elaborating on how OP makes Shakespeare more accessible, Ben Crystal comments that in any Shakespeare production, '[t]he temptation is to add sex jokes and toilet jokes and bum jokes where there aren't any to make it funnier so you enjoy it more. But there *are* these sex jokes there, but they only work in OP' (emphasis original).[40] Hearing the same vowel pronunciation for 'hour' and 'whore' in Shakespeare's *As You Like It*, for example, allows audiences to enjoy newly apparent puns about venereal disease: 'from hour to hour, we ripe and ripe, / And then, from hour to hour, we rot and rot'.[41] By illuminating hidden wordplay, journal-ist Megan Garber suggests, OP brings out the kind of bawdy humour that is meant to be accessible to everyone – including, but not limited to, 'groundling[s] at the Globe [who] may have been illiterate'.[42] Of course, not every audience member agrees that OP makes Shakespeare's language more accessible. When the Orlando Shakespeare Theatre produced *Twelfth Night* in 2018, critic Matthew Palm wrote that its use of OP 'can be detrimental to getting the full value from Shakespeare's words, especially in big emotional moments . . . Luckily, [director] Howarth has stocked the play with physical comedy scenes, all of which work delightfully.'[43] By implying that OP is ill-suited for 'big emotional moments' but that the production compensates through 'physical comedy', Palm contributes to the cultural anxiety around the rural and classist implications of this accent and its implications for Shakespearean performance.

The way that OP shares certain features with contemporary rural accents also draws attention to the long-standing privileging of RP – famous as the accent of BBC announcers and the British royal family – as a Shakespearean performance accent that conveys posh education, high social class, urbanity, and often implicitly, whiteness. As Crystal explains, RP itself emerged as an 'attempt by upper-class speakers to distinguish themselves from those of the "lower orders"'[44] – it was, and remains, an accent designed to uphold class hierarchy. Delving into the history of RP to contextualise its ongoing hegemony in Shakespearean productions, Alec Paterson highlights a number of actors (including Andrew Scott, Christopher Eccleston, David Tennant, Patrick Stewart, Derek Jacobi and Ian McKellen) who have adopted RP in performance instead of their native accent.[45] Eccleston explicitly links his decision to RP's cultural dominance, stating that 'I don't get offered Shakespeare roles because I have a northern accent . . . I didn't go to the right university or the public schools'[46] and underscoring the tension between rural accents and widespread cultural notions of how Shakespearean text should sound. And although I echo Paterson's claim that '[n]on-standard accents can bring vitality to the performance as well as convey complexity of thought',[47] I want to propose that the stakes of pronunciation are also higher and more political than this statement suggests. Because of the powerful social implications inherent in accents, the choice to perform a classical text in OP or a rural, regional or other non-RP accent can actively push back against the idea that Shakespearean actors must sound a certain way in order to be legitimate. Choosing OP over RP can not only contribute to a shift away from what Don Weingust calls 'elitist conceptions of the plays of Shakespeare in modern performance',[48] it can also push audience members and theatremakers to confront their expectations about who is encouraged to hear themselves in the mouths of Shakespearean actors.

Since 2004, there have been approximately twenty-nine full-length OP Shakespeare productions around the world,[49] predominantly in university settings and in cities with resource-rich theatrical ecosystems. As Johnson reports, five OP productions have taken place in the UK, while seventeen occurred in the United States:

> A full-length run of OP *Troilus and Cressida* followed [the 2004 *Romeo and Juliet*]. Then America became interested. There was a 2010 *Midsummer Night's Dream* in Kansas, a 2011 *Hamlet* in Nevada, a 2012 *Cymbeline* in Oregon, followed by *Julius Caesar* in Texas, *Twelfth Night* in Minneapolis and *The Merchant of Venice* in Baltimore. OP returned to the London Globe in 2014 with a *Macbeth*, and a 2015 *Henry V*.[50]

To my knowledge, none of these OP productions have taken place in Appalachia. Indeed, Appalachia is largely absent from the discourse around OP; at best, it makes an appearance as merely one accent among many, as in artistic director Jim Helsinger's claim that OP resembles 'a blend of American Appalachian, Western England and a bit of Scottish'.[51] Given the ongoing vitality of the Appalachian Shakespeare myth in its home territory, the absence of this region from discussions of OP underscores both the lack of linguistic basis for Appalachian Shakespeare, and the wide cultural gap between the appropriative claims of Appalachian Shakespeare and OP.

One of the most prominent claims about OP is the idea that this accent is transnational, and therefore makes Shakespeare sound more accessible to a wider range of audience members. Theatre critics and journalists have described OP as 'a hodgepodge of several different modern accents, among them the English spoken in Cornwall, Somerset, Ireland, Black Country, Lancashire, and Australia. . . . In some ways, it's closer to American English than to British'[52] and as an accent that produces 'the odd sensation of having strayed into an Irish-American bar somewhere in Warwickshire'.[53] One of OP's diphthongs also appears in modern Canadian English.[54] Because of these many echoes, OP seems to encourage audience members from disparate parts of the world – though still only certain parts – to connect with Shakespearean performance in a way that is often described as fresh, exciting and accessible. Garber enthuses that 'OP helps to reclaim Shakespeare for modern audiences – to demystify his words, and to democratize them',[55] while Alexander Aciman claims that OP 'allows us to hear [Shakespeare] in the accent we ourselves speak. It not only feels more personal, but it's easier to understand.'[56] Speaking of the Globe's 2004 *Romeo and Juliet*, actor Jimmy Garnon recounts that '[t]imings within scenes went awry because the OP moves quicker. . . . The whole thing was more exciting somehow. Words felt like fireworks again.'[57] Many audience members and theatremakers seem to find that OP augments the familiarity, intelligibility and even the relevance of this classical playwright.

Accessibility through accent seems to increase theatrical immediacy in other ways, as well. Crystal reports that audience members from the OP *Romeo and Juliet* 'made the point that they felt closer to the characters . . . [OP] presented a more immediate opportunity to access the speaker's thought.'[58] Similar claims about immediacy and dynamism are often also made about other original theatrical practices, which can include historical costumes, single-gender (typically all-male) casts, relatively bare stages and universal lighting. As W. B. Worthen writes of immersive theatre, 'the low-tech approach to performance is designed to foster the pleasures of "interactivity" between stage and audience'.[59] As a representative example, Worthen cites the Portland Original Practice Shakespeare Festival's 2014 claim that their 'fast paced, energetic acting' generates 'lots of audience interaction. This lends a much more immediate, organic, and improvisational feel to the performances.'[60] Much of the discourse around OP emphasises a less elitist and faster-paced vision of Shakespeare that implicitly or explicitly offers more direct access – to the words, to the play, to a Shakespearean experience – even as this earthiness and immediacy stand in contrast with the specialised knowledge that is often required to put original practices into action.

Even as OP allows for a more expansive view of who can hear themselves in Shakespeare, however, its map of aural identifications nevertheless remains part of the legacy of British colonialism. I want to explicitly draw out the imperial inheritance that lies behind Crystal's comment that OP is 'the ancestor of the accents we hear in English today. And not just British English, but English all over the world.'[61] Although OP is indeed, arguably, less exclusionary than RP, racialisation still plays a role in discussions of countries in relation to OP. India, for instance, is rarely mentioned in such discussions, while the places whose pronunciation is said to echo OP – Ireland, Scotland, America, Australia, Canada – mirror the list of British colonies that clergyman Josiah Strong once called 'Anglo-Saxon dominated countries' destined to help Anglo-Americana 'give its civilization to mankind'.[62] By making such points, I am not trying to discourage theatremakers or scholars from taking an interest in OP; rather, I want to affirm that part of this interest must involve a deep and active reckoning with the ways that white imperial legacies remain bound up even in practices that offer productive alternatives to traditional theatrical practices.

What does it mean to reimagine Shakespearean pronunciation as the lodestone of a mythical geography, one that draws forth unexpected relationships between spatially disparate places? This chapter has called for critical engagement with pronunciation as a tool of social representation, highlighting the need to consider which people, regions and legacies are implicated in Shakespearean appropriations through accent. By focusing on this often-overlooked aspect of performance, I have taken up Richard Paul Knowles's warning that seemingly neutral theatrical devices are in fact 'vacuums to be filled by the unquestioned because naturalised assumptions of (dominant) ideology'.[63] Although OP and the Appalachian myth use Shakespeare's pronunciation to create proximity with very different audiences, both remain entwined with living hierarchies of white nationalism, class and empire. And while I echo Paterson's appeal to move away from standard performance accents such as RP, I am cautious about sharing in his desire 'that the transmission of Shakespeare's thought via his language becom[e] simply a matter for the actor to speak with clarity of thought, clarity of intention, and attention to the verse structures rather than any standardised or socially constructed accent'.[64] Pronunciation is so deeply entwined with class, education, race, rurality and other social factors, that I hesitate to believe those associations can ever simply disappear. Rather, movements like Appalachian Shakespeare and OP surely act as invitations to think more consciously about whose accent is heard, and with which implications. It is my hope that a deeper and more critical perspective on pronunciation can lead to more inclusive representation in performance, expanding the range of people who can hear themselves in Shakespeare.

Notes

1. Charles Morrow Wilson, 'Elizabethan America', *The Atlantic Monthly (1857–1932)* 144 (1929): 240.
2. Appalachian Regional Commission, 'Map of the Appalachian Region', *The Appalachian Region*, https://www.arc.gov/appalachian_region/mapofappalachia.asp. Accessed 8 January 2022.
3. Chi Luu, 'The Legendary Language of the Appalachian "Holler"', *JSTOR Daily*, 8 August 2018, https://daily.jstor.org/the-legendary-language-of-the-appalachian-holler. Accessed 8 January 2022.
4. Elizabeth Catte, 'There is no neutral there: Appalachia as a mythic "Trump Country"', *Elizabeth Catte*, 17 October 2016, https://medium.com/@elizabethcatte/there-is-no-neutral-there-appalachia-as-a-mythic-trump-country-ee6ed7f300dc. Accessed 8 January 2022.

5. William Goodell Frost, 'Our Contemporary Ancestors in the Southern Mountains', *The Atlantic Monthly* 83 (1 January 1899): 1.
6. Michael Montgomery, 'In the Appalachians They Speak Like Shakespeare', in *Language Myths*, ed. Laurie Bauer and Peter Trudgill (New York: Penguin Books, 1998), 69.
7. Wilson, 'Elizabethan America', 238.
8. Kim C. Sturgess, *Shakespeare and the American Nation* (New York: Cambridge University Press, 2004), 106.
9. Ibid. 108.
10. Mary Rambaran-Olm and Erik Wade, 'The Many Myths of the Term "Anglo-Saxon"', *Smithsonian Magazine*, 14 July 2021, https://www.smithsonianmag.com/history/many-myths-term-anglo-saxon-180978169. Accessed 11 April 2022.
11. Mary Rambaran-Olm, 'Anglo-Saxon Studies [Early English Studies], Academia and White Supremacy', *Medium*, 27 June 2018, https://mrambaranolm.medium.com/anglo-saxon-studies-academia-and-white-supremacy-17c87b360bf3. Accessed 12 April 2022.
12. Frost, 'Our Contemporary Ancestors', 3.
13. Sturgess, *Shakespeare and the American Nation*, 3.
14. Wilson, 'Elizabethan America', 240.
15. Ibid. 243.
16. Frost, 'Our Contemporary Ancestors', 2.
17. Ibid. 9.
18. Ibid. 9.
19. William Aspenwall Bradley, 'In Shakespeares [*sic*] America', *Appalachian Heritage* 4, no.4 (1976): 27–8.
20. Montgomery, 'In the Appalachians', 70–3.
21. Jennifer Cramer, 'Is Shakespeare Still in the Holler? The Death of a Language Myth', *Southern Journal of Linguistics* 38, no.1 (2014): 200.
22. Cramer, 'Is Shakespeare Still in the Holler?', 201.
23. Montgomery, 'In the Appalachians', 66.
24. Quoted in Montgomery, 'In the Appalachians', 66.
25. Quoted in Cramer, 'Is Shakespeare Still in the Holler?', 198.
26. Tennessee Mountain Tours, 'The History of Appalachian English: Why We Talk Differently', *Tennessee Mountain Tours*, 23 November 2017, https://www.tnmountaintours.com/single-post/2017/11/23/the-history-of-appalachian-english-why-we-talk-differently. Accessed 8 January 2022.
27. Wilson, 'Elizabethan America', 240.
28. Rochelle Smith, 'Poverty and Privilege: Shakespeare in the Mountains', in *Shakespeare and the 99%*, ed. Sharon O'Dair and Timothy Francisco (Cham: Palgrave Macmillian, 2019), 144.
29. Ibid. 144.
30. Ibid. 146.

31. Ibid. 154.

32. Ibid. 54.

33. Ibid. 154.

34. Keith Johnson, *Shakespeare's Language: Perspectives, Past and Present* (Abingdon: Routledge, 2019), 120.

35. Ibid. 119–20.

36. David Crystal, *Pronouncing Shakespeare: The Globe Experiment* (Cambridge: Cambridge University Press, 2005), 21.

37. Ibid. 21.

38. Ibid. 169.

39. Ibid. 22.

40. Hannah Furness, 'Shakespeare read in Elizabethan accent reveals "puns, jokes and rhymes"', *The Telegraph*, 11 October 2013, https://www.telegraph.co.uk/culture/theatre/william-shakespeare/10372964/Shakespeare-read-in-Elizabethan-accent-reveals-puns-jokes-and-rhymes.html. Accessed 27 February 2023.

41. Shakespeare, *As You Like It*, 2.2.26–7.

42. Megan Garber, 'Such Ado: The Fight for Shakespeare's Puns', *The Atlantic*, 1 March 2016, https://www.theatlantic.com/entertainment/archive/2016/03/loves-labours-found-saving-shakespeares-puns/471786/. Accessed 8 January 2022.

43. Matthew J. Palm, '"Twelfth Night" Finds the Funny, in Elizabethan Style', *Orlando Sentinel*, 8 March 2018, https://www.orlandosentinel.com/entertainment/arts-and-theater/os-et-mjp-twelfth-night-review-20180308-story.html. Accessed 27 February 2023.

44. David Crystal, 'Received Pronunciation Old and New', *World of Better Learning*, 15 June 2020, https://www.cambridge.org/elt/blog/2020/06/04/received-pronunciation-old-and-new/. Accessed 8 January 2022.

45. Alec Paterson, 'How Should Shakespeare Sound?: Actors and the Journey from OP to RP', in *Shakespeare and Accentism*, ed. Adele Lee (New York: Routledge, 2021), 82–99.

46. Anita Singh, 'Christopher Eccleston: I don't get offered Shakespeare roles because I have a northern accent', *The Daily Telegraph*, 22 February 2018, https://www.telegraph.co.uk/news/2018/02/22/christopher-eccleston-dont-get-offered-shakespeare-roles-have/ . Accessed 27 February 2023.

47. Paterson, 'How Should Shakespeare Sound?', 95.

48. Don Weingust, 'Early Modern Theatrical Practice in the Later Modern Playhouse: A Brief Overview', in *Thunder at a Playhouse: Essaying Shakespeare and the Early Modern Stage*, ed. Peter Kanelos and Matt Kozusko (Selinsgrove, PA: Susquehanna University Press, 2010), 256.

49. David Crystal, 'Events', http://originalpronunciation.com/GBR/Events?event=7. Accessed 27 February 2023.

50. Johnson, *Shakespeare's Language*, 129.

51. BWW News Desk, 'Photo Flash: Orlando Shakespeare Theater in Partnership with UCF presents *Twelfth Night*', *Broadway World*, 13 February 2018, https://www.broadwayworld.com/orlando/article/Photo-Flash-Orlando-Shakespeare-Theater-in-Partnership-with-UCF-presents-TWELFTH-NIGHT-20180213. Accessed 8 January 2022.
52. Garber, 'Such Ado'.
53. Robert McCrum, 'RP or OP? That is the question', *The Guardian*, 20 August 2005, https://www.theguardian.com/stage/2005/aug/21/theatre.classics. Accessed 8 January 2022.
54. Crystal, *Pronouncing Shakespeare*, 87.
55. Garber, 'Such Ado'.
56. Alexander Aciman, 'Shakespeare the Way It Was Meant to Be Spoken', *Time*, 20 September 2013, http://entertainment.time.com/2013/09/20/shakespeare-the-way-it-was-meant-to-be-spoken/. Accessed 27 February 2023.
57. Crystal, *Pronouncing Shakespeare*, 65.
58. Ibid. 142.
59. W. B. Worthen, 'Interactive, Immersive, Original Shakespeare', *Shakespeare Bulletin* 35, no. 3 (2017): 408.
60. Quoted in Worthen, 'Interactive, Immersive, Original Shakespeare', 408.
61. Crystal, *Pronouncing Shakespeare*, 92–3.
62. Quoted in Sturgess, *Shakespeare and the American Nation*, 116.
63. Richard Paul Knowles, 'Shakespeare, Voice, and Ideology: Interrogating the Natural Voice', in *Shakespeare, Theory and Performance*, ed. James C. Bulman (London: Routledge, 2005), 97.
64. Paterson, 'How Should Shakespeare Sound?', 95.

7

Shakespeare and Gentrification in Regional Theatre

Niamh J. O'Leary

This chapter asks questions to uncover methods for studying regional Shakespeare. Can Shakespeare reflect a community's identity, or is he always an instrument of gentrification and local erasure? What is the iterative potential for a theatre to make reparations to the local community through performative and adaptive engagements with Shakespeare, a symbol of upper-class, white cultural hegemony? How does a theatre company balance commitment to Shakespeare with engagement of its immediate surroundings? My exploration of these questions will be informed by my experience working with and studying the Cincinnati Shakespeare Company who, in 2017, moved their theatre to the gentrified neighbourhood of Over-the-Rhine in Cincinnati. I will examine the demographic and economic context of this regional Shakespeare theatre company, how performance is shaped when the actors are also citizens of the theatre's city, and what it means for those actors to plant Shakespeare as their flag to claim space locally.

Regional Shakespeares: Methods and Challenges

To approach a study of regional Shakespeare is to join a growing conversation at the intersection of community practice, amateur theatre, critical regionality and global Shakespeare. This conversation shares with appropriation theory questions about cultural appropriation: Who is empowered when speaking Shakespeare into their community? What makes the perspective of an artist from Idaho, Arkansas or Maine worthy of intervening with Shakespeare? In the introduction to our co-edited volume of *Shakespeare Bulletin*, 'Shakespeare on Regional American Stages', Jayme

M. Yeo and I formulate a theoretical framework for studying regional Shakespeare. We describe regional Shakespeare as (1) primarily embodied and immediate; (2) characterised by interpersonal and social commitments; (3) illuminating the internal diversity of a region; (4) tying regional concerns to national and global ones; and further note that (5) regions shape and are shaped by Shakespeare.[1] These characteristics form the fundamentals for the methodology of studying regional Shakespeare I outline here, centring reparations, critical regionality, local engagement and scholarly position. Studying regional Shakespeare with these principles allows us to craft a dialogic relationship between Shakespeare and the regions that produce his work. This relationship directly contributes to a democratising of both Shakespeare and performance scholarship.

A regional theatre can make reparations to the local community through performative and adaptive engagements with Shakespeare. Regional theatre is inherently an activist practice because of its emphasis on locality. Describing 'theatre of place', Todd London argues that it is 'an often-activist, community-based art that dreams globally and acts locally . . . [T]hese artists dig their heels into the soil of established communities, either for extended stays or for good. Professional artists work with, and not just *for*, audiences and amateurs.'[2] London's description underscores the defining feature of regional theatre: it is intrinsically connected to (complex and varied) regional identity and concerns. The reparations regional theatres can offer are both material and cultural. A theatre can bring resources into the region through job opportunities and patrons who spend money at local businesses. Additionally, theatres can interact with educational and charitable institutions to enhance services available not only to economically privileged subscribers, but also to those in underfunded neighbourhoods. As London notes, 'the will to diversity' is one of the main factors that builds 'a professional, activist, community theatre of place', and thus, one of the central ingredients in regional theatre.[3] Reparations grow in part out of a regional theatre's 'will to diversity', as informed by the demographics of the region. An examination of regional Shakespeare therefore must be an examination of the region itself. Allison Machlis Meyer's essay about all-femme and non-binary productions of Shakespeare in Seattle provides an example, asking 'What does it mean for these productions to raise the right questions, in the right moment, in a particular place?'[4] Meyer situates her examination of regional Shakespeare at the nexus of locality, topicality and temporality. Any attempt to chart regional Shakespeare's ability to offer reparations should begin from this intersection.

A regional company's attempt to provide reparations to the local community requires acknowledging and privileging local experiences of identity. The region is not simply geographic; it is personal and epistemological. Recently, Marissa Greenberg theorised 'critically regional Shakespeare', arguing 'The epistemologies located in regions are worthy of critical attention because they help to actualize the vision of inclusivity, equity, and recognition, both professional and personal, in Shakespeare studies.'[5] Importantly, as Greenberg acknowledges with her use of the plural 'epistemologies', regional identity is not a monolith, even at a localised scale. It is intersectional (per Crenshaw's definition), and multiple, as Meyer asserts: 'Regionality acknowledges the diversity of audiences with disparate identities, experiences, and political beliefs; it brings to reception studies a focus on audience pluralities, the social construction of spectator narratives, and the rhetorical patterns in reviews.'[6]

In defining the local engagement pillar of my methodology, I borrow Lauren Eriks Cline's concept of 'spectator narratives', a term which picks up on this notion of multiple epistemologies in a given region. Incorporating principles from performance studies, Eriks Cline urges scholars to think of spectators 'not only as *readers* of performance processes but also as *writers* of performance meanings' and acknowledge the role of spectator narratives as 'a medium for shaping performance meaning'.[7] This concept recalls Erika Fischer-Lichte's notion of the 'autopoietic feedback loop' by which spectator response shapes performer action and performer action shapes spectator response.[8] In regional theatre, this interaction is particularly significant, where the audience comprises a community of people who regularly patronise the same theatre, know the actors and artistic team, and engage with the theatre beyond one performance. Spectator narratives thus foreground regional epistemologies, writing performance meaning both in the moment of the production and in the ensuing days and weeks as those narratives become word-of-mouth recommendations, commentary or criticism, shaping understanding of the theatrical event even for those who haven't attended the production. These narratives can be tracked through audience surveys and local media coverage.

Of course, local engagement is not limited to how audiences respond to productions; it encompasses how regional theatre engages local concerns through educational programming, season planning, fundraising and charitable endeavours, etc. Additionally, regional theatres embed awareness of location in productions via regional accents, colloquialisms or place references; set or design features that allude to local history and culture; promotional or marketing materials that include local landmarks, local knowledge and local media outlets. This self-conscious emplacement of regional Shakespeare enhances what Katherine Steele Brokaw recognises as the mutually constitutive relationship between Shakespeare theatre and community: 'the social force of "Shakespeare" [is] something that transforms communities and is itself continually transformed by them'.[9] Not only does spectator response shape regional production; the region shapes the production.

Perhaps the greatest challenge to conducting scholarship on regional Shakespeare is the position of the scholar themselves. Yeo and I note, '[i]n the project to centre regional voices and productions, the researcher as participant is both a necessary and interfering presence' and performance analysis is accompanied by ethnography and embedded scholarship when we turn a critical eye to Shakespeare on our regional stages.[10] Brokaw advocates for 'performative ethnography': 'to approach theatrical productions with the awareness of one's own cultural performance as a spectator or participant'.[11] Scholars studying regional companies where they live must both acknowledge their cultural performance as scholar and distance themselves from the theatre in order to critique it, opening up worlds of scholarly inquiry where we live. We can see our work as scholars of regional Shakespeare as akin to the work of the theatremakers we study. Brokaw reminds us that performative ethnographers

> often focus on how performative practices 'produce, sustain, and transform' systems of power, which is a lens that should remain in view for all of those who study the way the work of a white, European, canonical playwright often perceived as symbolic of 'high culture' makes meaning in communities marginalised by economics, geography, or even and especially English colonialism.[12]

The scholar of regional Shakespeares can analyse how Shakespeare in the region might produce, sustain or transform systems of power at the local level, while the work of that scholarship might transform the power dynamics within the discipline of academic criticism itself.

In the above paragraphs, seeking to define the contours of a methodology that centres reparations, critical regionality, local engagement and scholarly position, I have found each of these elements relies upon and reinforces the others. Without a sense of critical regionality, one cannot calculate local engagement; without understanding the scholar's own position, one cannot honestly evaluate reparations while accounting for the cultural hegemony traditionally associated with Shakespeare. In what follows, I apply the methodology to the study of a professional theatre.[13] But first: my methodology calls me to acknowledge my own position relative to the Cincinnati Shakespeare Company. I am a subscriber and have served on the Board of Trustees since 2013, providing in-kind services through public engagement and education events. I deliver pre-show lectures and participate in round-table talkbacks, attend first reads, collaboratively brainstorm with performing artists and co-host a podcast for CSC with a founding member. I have been open with the staff and artists about writing scholarship about the company. I work hard to preserve my critical independence, but confess it is at times difficult to separate scholarly inquiry from my desire that CSC continue to thrive. Writing about CSC has opened my eyes as a citizen-scholar, and so as I consider the activist potential of regional Shakespeare to make reparations and engage with local communities in constructive ways, I seek to provide an honest exploration of an institution that is trying, and sometimes failing, to do better, while recognising that I am in fact implicated in the institution.

Shakespeare in Porkopolis

I begin with the region. In 1883, the Shakespearean Dramatic Festival took place in Cincinnati's new Music Hall, designed by architect Samuel Hannaford and completed in 1878. The Festival featured elaborate set pieces to celebrate the scale of the stage and the importance of Shakespeare in the city, including a 65-foot-square backdrop with a painted scene of an imagined Elsinore Castle. Attending *Hamlet* was A. G. Moore, superintendent of the Cincinnati Water Works who was working on a valve house near Eden Park. Inspired by the backdrop, he hired Hannaford's son, Charles, to design a castle-like arch. Elsinore Arch became a landmark in the city, and in 1980 was listed in the National Register of Historic Places.[14] Moore built this edifice, not as a recreation of a Danish castle, but as a revision of a set made both to illustrate Shakespeare and to showcase the dramatic potential of Cincinnati's own performance venue. In Cincinnati, Shakespeare is part of the landscape, present in a localising reference as Elsinore Arch's patron, an imposing structure that celebrates Cincinnati's own innovation in arts, architecture and engineering.

One hundred and ten years after the Shakespearean Dramatic Festival, the Fahrenheit Theatre Company was founded 'with the mission of producing Shakespeare and the classics for modern audiences'.[15] A few years later, FTC became the Cincinnati Shakespeare Company (CSC).

After eighteen years at their downtown location – a former movie theatre with a small proscenium stage, eighteen-inch trap, and no room for set storage – they began a capital campaign, raising money to build a new theatrical home. In 2017, CSC moved a few blocks north into the neighbourhood of Over-the-Rhine, opening the Otto M. Budig Theatre with a thrust stage and over 10,000 additional square feet. In theatrical and business terms, this was an excellent move for CSC. However, the Budig was built on the site formerly occupied by the Drop Inn Center, a homeless shelter founded by Buddy Gray, a beloved local social worker. Prior to that, it was a Teamsters' union hall. As one can imagine, a classical theatre company displacing these landmarks of labour and social service was tricky. Responses to the theatre have been generally, but not exclusively, positive. Throughout the Budig's first season, a protester stood outside the lobby, wearing a sign stating 'Buddy Gray rolls over in his grave.'

To understand CSC's local engagements and potential to offer reparations, we must know more about Over-the-Rhine and its complex history. Originally home to many of the city's German immigrants, in the twentieth century OTR was populated by poor white Appalachians, and then, as the close-by West End neighbourhood was torn down, a racially mixed population of poor residents. Beginning in the 1970s, the neighbourhood was locked in a battle of wills between two charismatic men: Buddy Gray, who advocated for existing residents; and Jim Tarbell, a wealthy restaurateur who advocated for neighbourhood development to bring the middle class into OTR. By 1990, the median household income in OTR had fallen to just $5,000 and '[a] quarter of the housing units sat empty; only three per cent were owner-occupied'.[16] In 2001, riots broke out when Timothy Thomas, an unarmed nineteen-year-old, was the fifteenth Black man to be killed by Cincinnati police in a five-year period. When the riots ended, a cooperative community plan helped make change, in part through the creation of a private non-profit, Cincinnati Center City Development Corporation (3CDC) to manage new development. Gentrification rapidly took hold. Today, OTR is the neighbourhood of choice for young professionals, featuring artisanal street food, donut shops and cocktail joints alongside elegant condos, music venues and the beautifully renovated Washington Park. A large mural of Jim Tarbell decorates the gateway to the district, clearly aligning this hip new OTR with Tarbell's mission of revitalisation. A vocal population has opposed gentrification, protesting what many have called the 're-white-ification' of the neighbourhood as the poor are moved north, further from the services available downtown. When Washington Park re-opened in 2012, this area which had served as a congregation spot for the city's unhoused population because of its proximity to the Drop Inn Center and the Salvation Army was suddenly made inhospitable. In an effort to 'clean up' OTR, 3CDC pushed the homeless population further away from its primary connection to health and wellness services.

Having moved into and thus partaken in the gentrification of this neighbourhood, what are CSC's obligations and opportunities? To engage the population of this city, CSC must reflect it in the stories it tells, the people involved in telling those stories, the patrons in the theatre, and the community members impacted by CSC's mission and outreach. According to Census.gov, as of 1 July 2019, Cincinnati's population was 42.3 per cent Black and African American.[17] Thus, reflecting the city means reflecting its substantial Black population and ensuring CSC's programmes, onstage and off, are available to that population. Over the last several years, as CSC prepared to move into OTR, opened its new theatre, and navigated a global pandemic, it has shown promising engagement with diversity and equity, though there is still much work to be done.

Shakespeare and Gentrification in Cincinnati: Artistic Reparations and Local Engagement

Given Cincinnati's history of anti-Black racism and racist housing policies,[18] I understand reparations as directed specifically towards the city's Black citizens. Despite the fact that Black Cincinnatians constitute almost half the city's total population, studies regularly point out the wealth gap between them and white citizens. Ta-Nehisi Coates explains the relationship between reparations and the wealth gap in 'The Case for Reparations':

> Perhaps no statistic better illustrates the enduring legacy of our country's shameful history of treating Black people as sub-citizens, sub-Americans, and sub-humans than the wealth gap. Reparations would seek to close this chasm. But as surely as the creation of the wealth gap required the cooperation of every aspect of the society, bridging it will require the same.[19]

The theatre community can work towards bridging the wealth gap by providing access to the theatre to all citizens of the city, inclusive of race and economic status. This access isn't just for audience members; it can also be accomplished through strategic hiring. CSC can hire Black staff and produce plays written by Black playwrights, featuring Black actors and telling stories of Black people. In doing so, the theatre would assert the artistic value of Black storytelling and invest financially in it, paying playwrights, actors and staff of colour.

CSC has made strides in this direction. The company prefaced its move to OTR by highlighting themes of space, borders and difference, producing *The Diary of Anne Frank*, *Elephant Man* and *A Raisin in the Sun*, calling attention to their impending move into the contentious new space while also making an implicit pledge to centre diversity and inclusion in their art. Significantly, CSC leadership intentionally built the company's diversity through several years of recruiting until they could cast Hansberry's play almost entirely from the resident ensemble.[20] They brought in a Black director, Christopher V. Edwards, the Artistic Director from Actors' Shakespeare Project in Massachusetts. Edwards returned to direct *Othello* the following season, and August Wilson's *Fences* the year after.[21] This shows three areas of growth: intentional recruiting of Black actors into the resident ensemble; regular collaboration with a Black director and providing Black artists from within the company with opportunities to direct; and emphasis on including in each season shows by Black playwrights that foreground Black experience.

Of course, bringing in a Black guest director to direct one show a season – particularly if that one show is a play like *Othello* – isn't a full-throated commitment to diversity, equity, inclusion and access. But as the diversity of the company increases, all shows – not just those by Black playwrights or featuring stories of Black characters – are cast with more actors of colour, and in recent years, it appears that CSC has become colour-conscious in its casting practices. As an illustrative example, we can compare the January 2016 *Henry VI* and the November 2019 *Merry Wives of Windsor*.

Part of a multi-year staging of Shakespeare's English history plays, CSC turned the three *Henry VI* plays into two productions starring Darnell Pierre Benjamin, the only Black actor to play a title role in the eight-play arc. Interestingly, Henry VI was also the first of Shakespeare's British kings to be played by a Black actor at the RSC (David Oyelowo in 2000).[22] Writing about the 2003 Chicago Shakespeare Theatre adaptation of *1–3 Henry VI* (in which the Asian American actor, Carman Lacivita, portrayed the king), Francesca Royster claimed that production 'asks us to think about whiteness in particular as an often unmarked privileged location of social belonging' (221).[23] Henry VI's outsider status, the extent to which he is manipulated and abused by those around him, is evocative of the damages of white supremacy. Notably, in CSC's production, Benjamin wasn't the only Black actor: Geoffrey Warren Barnes II played the dauphin and Tia Davis played the Duchess of Gloucester. All three characters suffer in the play: the manipulated king, the despised French prince, and the punished scheming woman. In a theatrical world where a Black petulant dauphin is mocked, a Black anxious monarch is cheated on by his white wife with her white lover, and a white lord's Black wife is humiliated and punished for threatening the white queen, it is easy to argue social belonging and privilege were allotted to the white actors on stage. While director Brian Isaac Phillips cast the three Black actors in positions of power as monarch, prince and noblewoman, that power was relentlessly appropriated or denied by the white actors/characters who surround them. It is troubling to consider this colour-conscious casting, as it so firmly undermines the authority and power of its Black actors' characters. According to Benjamin, race was 'never part of the conversation' when he was cast, and yet race absolutely informed his performance: he says he saw in Henry a recognisable anxiety and loneliness: 'He was a man not of that world, as I often feel in America.'[24]

Production reviews provide the best record of spectator narratives about *Henry VI*, but demonstrate little awareness of any racial meaning in CSC's production. While local reviewers praised Benjamin's performance, none acknowledged his race, the impact of the Black actors' presence on stage, or named the other Black actors.[25] If, as Meyer argues, spectator narratives can 'render visible or invisible actors' embodied identities', these reviews suggest that, at least in local media outlets, CSC's Black actors' embodied identities were invisible in 2016.[26] Perhaps such judgement is unfair. Ayanna Thompson reminds us, '[t]here is a clear need for companies, directors, and producers to explain their own philosophies with regards to race and performance'.[27] It cannot be exclusively the province of reviewers to note race within a production; if it matters to companies, their programme notes, promotional materials and more should advertise this fact. The programme notes for both parts of CSC's *Henry VI* did not include any language about race.

Change is slow and difficult, but CSC is making steps to change the company's culture, and those steps can be observed in the more conscious engagement with race and community in their production of *Merry Wives of Windsor* in 2019. This production partook in the city's celebration of the 19th Amendment's centenary: it was set in 1919 and the characters toted 'Votes for Women' signs. Anne Page, Master Page, Sir Hugh Evans, Master Ford, Fenton, Slender and Rugby were all performed by Black actors.[28]

Black actors thus spoke 40 per cent of the lines in the play, a proportion now normal for CSC productions as the company has a diverse talent pool to cast from. Unlike *Henry VI*, in which Black actors only played characters undermined in the text, Black actors in *Merry Wives* were in similar positions to their white peers. Masters Ford and Page are no greater fools than Falstaff; Sir Evans no more ridiculous than Dr Caius; Rugby and Slender no more laughable than Robin, Shallow and Mistress Quickly. Brokaw notes, 'in community performance, actor identities can matter as much as character choices or directorial interpretation, and the effects of the mere presence of production might reach far beyond the stage'.[29] The fact that the two central marriages – the Pages and the Fords – were interracial was itself a noteworthy visual for many. I took a (95 per cent white) class of twenty students to see this production, and they commented in reflections on enjoying the diversity of the cast, both being struck by their own surprise to find so many Black actors in a Shakespeare play, and rethinking their expectations based on this surprise. From this small sample set of spectator narratives, I can begin to extrapolate that the diversity was likewise legible and hopefully, positively impactful for much of the audience who viewed *Merry Wives*.

The political theming of the play rendered the actors' race more visible. At a post-show talkback, audience members discussed the disjuncture between the diverse cast and the reality that Black women were not welcome in the suffragette movement. The racial homogeneity of the talkback audience (almost entirely white, as CSC's audiences generally are) was disheartening, but their awareness of the complex racial politics of the suffragette movement was encouraging. However, the talkback panel was also almost entirely white and, just as was the case with *Henry VI*, the director's note for *Merry Wives* didn't mention race. CSC called its 2019–20 season 'Season of the Woman' – a year-long celebration of women, aligned with the city's celebration of the 19th amendment's centenary. The company scheduled woman-centred productions (such as Christopher M. Walsh's *Miss Holmes*, Tracy Letts' *August, Osage County* and Kate Hamill's adaptation of *Pride and Prejudice*), brought in women guest directors (though no BIPOC directors) and planned a *Hamlet* starring a (white) woman in the title role (delayed by theatre closures during the COVID-19 pandemic). However, not one of the season's plays was by a Black playwright, centred on a Black woman or directed by a Black director. This gap was immediately troubling to company members, and one responded by forming a year-long, free-access play reading group, inviting the public to engage in readings and discussions of plays written by Black women. This activism, coming from within the company, is another hopeful sign of the company's work to offer reparations to the city. It responds to a weakness in the company's approach to diversity: CSC has shown progressive instincts in terms of race and of gender, but not in intersectional terms. The programming hasn't demonstrated a rich understanding of how race and gender identities intersect to compound the challenges, harm and potential invisibility experienced by many. But members of the company are pushing the theatre to think more richly and responsibly.

Local reviews of *Merry Wives*, similar to those of *Henry VI*, generally did not comment on the diversity of the cast or the actors' embodied identities. Of the six reviews available, only Marissa Staples commented on '[t]he beautiful, diverse cast'. Notably, Staples is a Black woman affiliated with *The Voice of Black Cincinnati*, an organisation 'designed to educate, recognize and create opportunities for African Americans in the region'.[30] Other reviews didn't directly comment on race or diversity. Eriks Cline argues we should look to spectator narratives, not to reproduce in mirror-like fashion the meaning of a performance, but to shape it through indirection or redirection and to '[use] incoherence, opacity, and indirection to construct racial meanings'.[31] I find such indirection in two reviews. One, praising Sylvester Little, Jr's turn as Master Page, calls him 'a fine actor who plays the role like a wannabe gangster patterning himself on Denzel Washington in *American Gangster*'.[32] Another noted, 'Sylvester Little, Jr. plays George Page with the boyish charm of vintage Billy Dee Williams and newcomer David Everette Moore's Frank Ford is surprisingly multilayered and sympathetic.'[33] The first is troubling as it reads the performance in ways that seem unconnected to Little's actual performance choices. Little played Page as an energetic, enthusiastic man about town, all smiles and charm. There was nothing shady or criminal about his characterisation of Page, and as such, the connection to *American Gangster* seems a flawed attempt to liken him to a great Black film star when the only connection is the actors' Blackness. The second review similarly connects Little with Black film legend, but does so in a way that is at least recognisably connected with his performance. It further praises other Black performances in the production, which is a far cry from the review in *CityBeat*, which only names white actors when praising the talented cast.[34] Taken together, these reviews suggest some of the indirection Eriks Cline writes about, noting that spectator narratives '[allow] scholars to read audiences not as failing to see race, but as *using* incoherence, opacity, and indirection to construct racial meanings'.[35] It's possible to read these reviews as struggling to comment on the cast's diversity in ways that engage Shakespeare; instead, reaching for contemporary references drawn from Black presence in popular media. In Cincinnati, there is a regional desire for Shakespearean authenticity and 'classical' theatre that sits cheek by jowl with a diverse city's ongoing struggle to reckon with its own racist past and present. That tension is often reflected in the spectator narratives we have access to. And CSC is perhaps more vulnerable to audience failure to note racial meaning in productions, as it is aligned with the more 'classical' theatre companies in town. Two other theatres are known for contemporary productions, and their engagements with diversity in their productions – explicit or implicit – are more likely to be immediately recognisable to audience members who *expect* such engagement from them.[36]

And yet, in the years since the 2015–16 season's *Henry VI*, changes can be observed: a more diverse company; diverse casting and representation that isn't limited to the marginal or suffering characters; efforts to expand the diversity of the theatre's programming coming from within the ensemble; and a viewing and reviewing audience that is beginning to ask questions and make connections that suggest an awareness of the actors' embodied identities. CSC is beginning to make reparations to its local community. But to capitalise on the potential for productions of Shakespeare to work towards reparations, CSC's artistic language needs to reflect this intentionality. In particular, directors' notes should acknowledge how race matters within their Shakespeare productions, and not just in those plays that are explicitly about race. This, too, is beginning to shift: in fall 2021, the theatre reopened after COVID-19 closure with a production of *Romeo and Juliet* directed by Darnell Pierre Benjamin and featuring a racially diverse cast. In his programme note, Benjamin commented: 'By embracing the intersectionality of gender, race, class, sexuality, and physical appearance, [with] this production of *Romeo and Juliet*, CSC will build a Verona where audience members from all backgrounds will see themselves and their relationships depicted onstage.'[37] Despite this very encouraging start, reviewers nonetheless often missed this intention in Benjamin's production, picking up instead on his comment that the production 'imagines the Capulets and Montagues as underclass families in Verona and examines the overt presence of violence and discontent within their community', and reading the racial diversity of the production as reflective of violence and economic strife. Mackenzie Manley, writing for *CityBeat*, claims 'This concept is realised through a diverse cast in which actors often play roles that they may have been traditionally excluded from. Overall, this choice makes for a more accessible *Romeo and Juliet*, one in which a broader audience is more likely to see themselves reflected.'[38] Manley's narrative here betrays a problematic assumption of Black representation as synonymous with economic oppression and violence. I hope, in future years, to see our critics demonstrate greater insight in their narratives about increasingly diverse productions.

Of course, this will be aided by both a more diverse pool of critics, and a more diverse audience. To get diverse spectator narratives, you need diverse spectators. As stated, CSC's audience is fairly racially homogenous. An arts community, no matter how well intentioned, is beholden to the market. Thus, CSC's progress towards greater inclusion and access has been slowed by its need to raise ticket prices since its move to the Budig theatre, covering both increased facilities costs and production values. This change makes the theatre less accessible to new audience members. Recognising this shortcoming, in December 2020 CSC's Board approved a Diversity, Equity, Inclusion and Access plan [DEIA]. The plan outlines as its central goal:

> We will become *Cincinnati's* Shakespeare Company. We will do this through fostering a community of theater makers, patrons, supporters, and stakeholders who are representative of our City, united in their desire for artistic excellence, and unabashedly welcoming to all who wish to be a part of it. We will become Cincinnati's Shakespeare Company, because a world in which theatre matters to more people is one we want to live in, and one we commit to help build.[39]

The plan names five pillars: 'Outreach, Education, Engagement; People: Ensemble, Staff & Board; Audience; Art Programming; and Organization/ Culture'.[40] This plan centres BIPOC citizens and articulates specific year-over-year goals to increase engagement with under-represented minority groups as patrons and as staff/leadership/board members. They name their target as 'to reach 12% of the mainstage audience identifying as Black' within five years of reopening after pandemic closures.[41] While 12 per cent is a far cry from the 43 per cent of the city's population who identify as Black, it's a dramatic increase from current attendance trends. The plan enshrines a DEIA committee on the Board; sets goals for tracking company and audience demographics and for collecting 'feedback from underrepresented community groups to identify barriers to interest and opportunities for inclusion in classical theatre'; articulates plans to 'commission one play per year by an underrepresented artist', and to provide access to performances for low-income audiences.[42] The ambitious plan evidences both awareness of a need for change and the momentum to create that change.

One further way CSC contributes to the region must be taken into account. Begun in 1997, CSC's educational programming is its most significant local engagement and means of reparations. Each August, the acting interns prepare scaled-down, eight-person, two-hour Shakespeare in the Park productions offered for free within a three-hour radius of downtown Cincinnati. These same productions enter schools 'reaching students in 100 zip codes' in Ohio, Kentucky and Indiana.[43] In 2013, CSC developed its landmark PROJECT38 to produce performances from all thirty-eight of Shakespeare's plays with students in the greater Cincinnati area. These performances included recorded scenes or monologues, photography, painted masks or live staged scenes. PROJECT38 is now an annual, multi-day, free theatre festival showcasing the work of hundreds of area students who study with CSC Teaching Artists over several months. Between the park performances and PROJECT38, CSC engages with thousands of students over the course of each school year. In addition, CSC offers educational matinees of its mainstage shows and hosts a number of educational camps and theatre courses. The demographic data demonstrates that the theatre's educational programming reaches a wide and diverse swath of the region's population:

> [R]oughly 60% of participating students are Caucasian, 25% African-American, and 15% other races, including several Appalachian communities. A variety of neighborhoods and socio-economic backgrounds comprise the student audiences from rural groups in South Dearborn, Indiana to the rural Appalachian in Greenup, Kentucky. Schools also include a range of public (53%), parochial (24%), and private (23%) schools with administrators and teachers working within a wide spectrum of economic resources. 40% of parks served by the outreach tour are located in severely distressed census tracts, as are 26% of schools.[44]

These data argue that CSC is, in fact, making reparations, at least to the students of the region and to those who attend the free park productions.

In its privileged position in the Budig theatre, CSC is obligated not merely to benefit from the gentrification of the neighbourhood. It must intentionally engage with the region in a way that makes classical theatre accessible *and relevant* to all the city's citizens. If, as I argue above, Shakespeare has been made Cincinnatian through centuries of performance, art and architectural tradition, then the Cincinnatian Shakespeare must reflect the Cincinnati population. And it is getting closer. During the pandemic, CSC ensemble member Candice Handy formed the Cincinnati Black Theatre Artist Collective. The first of its kind in the city, this organisation is closely connected with CSC, as Handy has been named CSC's new Director of Creative Education. Putting a Black artist with an explicit commitment to Black theatre in the city in this position promises that Shakespeare may, in time, be less of a dead white man, less of a cold, historical stone structure, and more of a living, changing, active citizen in Cincinnati.

I have outlined a methodology for studying regional Shakespeares that focuses on critical regionality, local engagement, reparations and scholarly position. This study can be applied to professional or amateur theatre, to adaptations or 'traditional' productions. It must embrace not just the Shakespeare on display, but the emplacement of that Shakespeare. Finding Shakespeare where we live is an invitation to consider not only Shakespeare, but also place. That consideration can engage public humanities initiatives, shift scholarly investments into the community, and bring our academic work directly into the public sphere where we can contribute to the growth of our own neighbourhoods. A true scholarship of regional Shakespeare is wary of the siren song of gentrification, focusing not on drawing communities to Shakespeare as though he were an amenity we can offer, but on drawing Shakespeare into our communities, because there we will find the most exciting and enriching ideas.

Notes

1. Niamh J. O'Leary and Jayme M. Yeo, 'Our Neighbor Shakespeare', *Shakespeare Bulletin* 39, no. 3 (2021): 330–2, http://doi.org/10.1353/shb.2021.0029. Accessed 10 August 2023.
2. Todd London, 'Off the Map: Charting an American Theatre of Place', *Contemporary Theatre Review* 16, no. 3 (2006): 297–8, https://doi.org/10.1080/10486800600818517. Accessed 10 August 2023.
3. Ibid. 297.
4. Allison Machlis Meyer, 'Women's Shakespeare in Seattle: Regional Performance and Spectatorship', *Shakespeare Bulletin* 39, no. 3 (2021): 413, http://doi.org/10.1353/shb.2021.0041. Accessed 10 August 2023.
5. Marissa Greenberg, 'Critically Regional Shakespeare', *Shakespeare Bulletin* 37, no. 3 (2019): 357, http://doi.org/10.1353/shb.2019.0039. Accessed 10 August 2023.
6. Meyer, 'Women's Shakespeare in Seattle', 214.

7. Lauren Eriks Cline, 'Shakespeare, Spectators, and the Meaning of Race on Stage', in *Shakespeare On Stage and Off*, ed. Kenneth Graham and Alysia Kolentsis (Montreal: McGill-Queens University Press, 2019), 39.

8. Erika Fischer-Lichte, *The Transformative Power of Performance: A New Aesthetic* (London: Routledge, 2008), 38.

9. Katherine Steele Brokaw, 'Shakespeare as Community Practice', *Shakespeare Bulletin* 35, no. 3 (2017): 447, http://doi.org/10.1353/shb.2017.0034. Accessed 10 August 2023.

10. O'Leary and Yeo, 'Our Neighbor Shakespeare', 330.

11. Brokaw, 'Shakespeare as Community Practice', 447.

12. Ibid. 448.

13. I believe it could equally be applied to amateur companies as well, and thus, I don't address the definition of 'theatre' in my methodology. Others have done excellent work at this, such as Brokaw and London.

14. Kevin Grace, *Cincinnati's Literary Heritage: A History for Booklovers* (Charleston: The History Press, 2021), 102–6.

15. Cincinnati Shakespeare Company, 'Production History', *Cincinnati Shakespeare Company*, https://www.cincyshakes.com/production-history/. Accessed 8 May 2022.

16. Sarah Wesseler, 'Over-the-Rhine', in *The Cincinnati Anthology*, ed. Zan McQuade (Cleveland: The Rust Belt Chic Press, 2014), 49.

17. US Census Bureau, 'QuickFacts: Cincinnati, Ohio', *US Census Bureau*, 2022, https://www.census.gov/quickfacts/cincinnaticityohio. Accessed 8 May 2022.

18. University of Cincinnati Department of History, 'Going Home: The Struggle for Fair Housing in Cincinnati 1900 to 2017' (Cincinnati: University of Cincinnati Department of History, 2008), http://homecincy.org/wp-content/uploads/2018/02/Going-Home-2008.pdf. Accessed 10 August 2023.

19. Ta-Nehisi Coates, 'The Case for Reparations', *The Atlantic*, 15 June 2014, https://www.theatlantic.com/magazine/archive/2014/06/the-case-for-reparations/361631/. Accessed 10 August 2023.

20. The actor cast as Beneatha left the production, and so another actor was contracted in. And the actor cast as Lena, though not a member of the company, is a local Cincinnati actor.

21. Before the COVID-19 pandemic closed theatres, Edwards was slated to direct *Ma Rainey's Black Bottom* in the 2020–1 season. The show finally opened in the 2021–2 season, and was directed by a company member, Candice Handy, as her mainstage directorial debut. While *Othello* may be a tokenist choice for a Black guest director, it was balanced by the fact that the producing artistic director of CSC, Brian Isaac Philips, was simultaneously directing a production of Lolita Chakrabarti's play about Ira Aldridge, *Red Velvet*, at another professional theatre in town. The two productions were cross promoted as in conversation with each other, a concerted citywide

effort to stage these two stories in rep and generate conversation about race and performance.

22. Fiachra Gibbons, 'RSC Casts Black Actor as English King for First Time', *The Guardian*, 18 September 2000, https://www.theguardian.com/uk/2000/sep/19/fiachragibbons. Accessed 10 August 2023.

23. Francesa Royster, 'The Chicago Shakespeare Theater's Rose Rage: Whiteness, Terror, and the Fleshwork of Theatre in a Post-Colorblind Age', in *Colorblind Shakespeare: New Perspectives on Race and Performance*, ed. Ayanna Thompson (New York: Routledge, 2006), 221.

24. Darnell Pierre Benjamin, Personal interview, 9 January 2017.

25. Of the five local reviews I've been able to locate, only one mentioned Barnes's Dauphin, and didn't evaluate his performance. None mentioned Davis.

26. Meyer, 'Women's Shakespeare in Seattle', 426. Meyer noted a similar lack of attention to racial diversity in reviews of the Seattle productions she studies, stating 'reviewers in Seattle attend to gender over race'.

27. Ayanna Thompson, 'To Notice or Not To Notice: Shakespeare, Black Actors, and Performance Reviews', *Borrowers and Lenders: A Journal of Shakespeare and Appropriation* 4, no. 1 (2008): 13, https://borrowers-ojs-azsu.tdl.org/borrowers/issue/view/14. Accessed 26 February 2023.

28. Of these characters, Anne Page (Kahla Tisdale) and Rugby (Ernaijsa Curry) were played by women. The rest were men.

29. Brokaw, 'Shakespeare as Community Practice', 449.

30. Marissa Staples, '"Merry Wives" is a Hilarious Shakespearean Sitcom', *Arts Wave Guide*, 18 November 2019, https://guide.artswave.org/blog/cincinnati-shakespeare-co/merry-wives-is-a-hilarious-shakespearean-sitcom/. Accessed 10 August 2023. For more on the organisation, visit The Voice of Black Cincinnati's 'About' page: https://thevoiceofblackcincinnati.com/about/. Accessed 10 August 2023.

31. Eriks Cline, 'Shakespeare, Spectators', 39–40.

32. David Lyman, 'Review: "Merry Wives" Over-The-Top But Not All Together', *Cincinnati Enquirer*, 16 November 2019, https://www.cincinnati.com/story/entertainment/2019/11/16/review-cincinnati-shakespeare-merry-wives-over-top-but-not-all-together/4213950002/. Accessed 10 August 2023.

33. Sheldon Polonsky, 'CSC's "Merry Wives of Windsor": Shakes in the City', *League of Cincinnati Theatre*, 16 November 2019, http://leagueofcincytheatres.info/cscs-merry-wives-of-windsor-shakes-in-the-city/. Accessed 10 August 2023.

34. Jackie Mulay, 'Shakespeare Company's "Merry Wives of Windsor" is Enjoyable, but Unfocused', *City Beat*, 20 November 2019, https://www.citybeat.com/arts/cincy-shakespeare-companys-merry-wives-of-windsor-is-enjoyable-but-unfocused-12214890. Accessed 10 August 2023.

35. Eriks Cline, 'Shakespeare, Spectators', 39.

36. I refer here to the Ensemble Theatre, which is known for new works and regional premiers, and Know Theatre Cincinnati, which is known for hosting Cincinnati's Fringe Festival every year and promoting work by local playwrights, as well as more experimental or edgy theatre.

37. From Darnell Pierre Benjamin 'Closer Look: R&J Today', Director's Notes in the CSC's digital programme for their fall 2021 production of *Romeo and Juliet*.

38. Mackenzie Manley, 'REVIEW: Cincinnati Shakespeare Company's "Romeo and Juliet" is an Uproarious and Lusty Romantic Tragedy', *CityBeat*, 12 October 2021, https://www.citybeat.com/arts/cincinnati-shakespeare-companys-romeo-and-juliet-is-an-uproarious-and-lusty-romantic-tragedy-12265910. Accessed 10 August 2023.

39. Cincinnati Shakespeare Company, 'Diversity, Equity, Inclusion, and Access Plan, 2021–2026, Approved December 2020', email attachment (November 2020), 2.

40. Ibid. 3.

41. Ibid. 7.

42. Ibid. 4, 8.

43. Sara Clark, email interview, 9 February 2021.

44. Ibid. n.p.

8

Page and Stage Appropriations of
Two Gentlemen of Verona

Matt Kozusko

This chapter looks at some early rewrites of *Two Gentlemen of Verona*, Benjamin Victor and J. P. Kemble around the turn of the eighteenth century, and at records of three productions: William Macready and Charles Kean, in the nineteenth century, and the 2014 RSC staging in Stratford, directed by Simon Godwin. It identifies a tension in each case between fidelity to the Shakespearean text[1] and the attempts to manage the difficult or problematic moments in that text. In so doing, the chapter sketches the case for a tentative sense of continuity in how performance texts and productions deal with the play's so-called problem moments and argues that what Victor and Kemble do with alterations to the text, later productions do with staging choices. And while Macready and Kean appear at points to *un*do the Victor and Kemble rewrites, their project is best understood, I argue, as a fundamentally similar attempt at the recovery and presentation of an ideal Shakespeare. Like Simon Godwin's RSC production, Macready and Kean could be said to be presenting the 'original' play, but that understanding leans too heavily on simple textual fidelity as a guarantor. In distinction from a 'real' or originary Shakespeare, the 'ideal' these productions offer is effected through lightly curated versions of the play that attend or respond to identifiable or inferrable demands of the moment of production. My general thesis is that these productions – like most productions of Shakespeare generally – work in a space characterised by a kind of uneasiness with the implications of specific moments in the Shakespearean text, which they manage with limited, localised and specific instances of appropriation.[2]

Bringing Shakespeare into line with a preferred understanding of Shakespeare – itself evolving, always provisional – is perhaps the first and original impetus of appropriation, and it accounts for everything from editorial commentary to editorial practice to textual revision, to whatever it is we do in performance today when we manage our anxieties about a play's politics by shackling ourselves to a text, with its perceived authority, while acting away or acting around the awkward moments. I build here on some fairly well-established arguments: Daniel Fischlin and Mark Fortier for example on editorial practices that 'literally adapt Shakespeare, making him conform to a particular editorial vision',[3] or Margaret Jane Kidnie, whose wide-ranging *Shakespeare and the Problem of Adaptation* elegantly synthesises editorial practice, theatre production and various theories of appropriation while acknowledging the untidy components of critical assessment in the field of adaptation or appropriation studies.[4] I suggest that the use of staging choices – costumes and props and stage business and all manner of action unaccompanied by words – to banish Shakespeare's indecencies is merely a form of rewriting that doesn't disturb the 'original' text by adding to it (subtraction has never presented as significant a problem). Productions that restore early printed texts thus are not necessarily more faithful than others: they simply substitute one altered-but-authorised version of 'Shakespeare' for another. Like the light revisions we see in Victor and Kemble, they comprise a subset of appropriation that happens inside the mainstream of Shakespeare in production, where makers and consumers typically want to presume to be doing straight or unadapted Shakespeare, rather than transforming his work. Instead of speaking back to Shakespeare, that is, all the productions discussed here give the effect of attempting to speak for him.

Performance, I argue, always marks the difference between what is needed from a Shakespearean text and what is perceived to be available in that text. Performance compulsively highlights which moments in Shakespeare are understood to call for intervention. In this sense, performance is not synonymous with appropriation, but all performance inevitably slips into appropriation from moment to moment, or from instance to instance. And while I argue below for a sense of continuity in both the perception and the resolution of problems in the stage history of *Two Gentlemen of Verona*, I do not suggest that the same moments will always be seen to be problematic, or in the same way. One goal of this chapter, then, is to call attention to the critical value of appropriation studies for thinking about Shakespeare in production, even diachronically. Without reducing all productions to the simple status of appropriations, we can use the concept to frame some specific, identifiable actions a production takes to address what it perceives to be deficiencies in Shakespeare. And we can avoid some of the critical problems that have troubled the fidelity/appropriation binary by thinking of appropriation not as a fixed phenomenon, but as an articulation of a relationship among several other terms that we already understand to be provisional or unfixed: because 'Shakespeare' and 'text' and even 'performance' are always circumstantial, what counts as appropriation shifts from circumstance to circumstance; its contents and its boundaries can evolve in response to changes in what counts in any given production as 'Shakespeare'. To think of performance choices as small-scale, individual instances of appropriation is to refuse the essentialism that underpins authoritative readings of Shakespeare – particularly those bent towards the end logic of subjugation – without suggesting that Shakespeare can mean whatever users want it to mean.

Page

The end of *The Two Gentlemen* is famously broken, leaving us far from Verona, with no gentlemen to speak of and a silenced comic heroine. Silvia's formal function in the play is to articulate a redemptive vision for the wayward Proteus and the stumbling Valentine, and to embody, together with Julia, the play's feminine critique of the repressive customs of courtship and masculine privilege. The women cannot write love letters or be seen to take an interest in them; they are instead compelled to employ elaborate devices in order to pursue romantic relationships, which requires them to exercise the resourcefulness, wit and defiance typical of female characters in Shakespearean comedy. Starting in Act 2, however, Silvia's wit and beauty malfunction, generating only a series of faulty or misdirected arousals: first Thurio, and then Proteus, joins Valentine in pursuing her as a love object, with the horrifying result of the attempted rape in Act 5. This is followed by Valentine's awkwardly generous and ready forgiveness of Proteus, and then his ungenerous and improbable gift, of Silvia, to Proteus. All of this discomfort, for modern audiences, is compounded further by Silvia's utter silence in the aftermath. The gift, which pushes to an absurd conclusion the logic of *philia* as superior to *eros* – and of the distinction between them as the animating difference between male-male friendship, on the one hand, and female-male companionship, on the other – is then followed by a jarring reversion on Valentine's part to aggressive posturing. Suddenly solicitous of Silvia's well-being, and with renewed assertion of his possessive right to her, Valentine threatens to kill Thurio: 'Thurio, give back, or else embrace thy death . . . I dare thee but to breathe upon my love!' (5.4.124–9).

Thus, Silvia and Julia move from protagonists to victims to silence, while Valentine and Proteus move from a posturing (but amiable) cluelessness, to violence, and back to a kind of cluelessness that never quite resolves as a lesson learned. The confident, smart and capable women serve as paragons of fidelity and self-knowledge, while the men struggle and ultimately fail fully to recognise what has happened to their relationships with each other, and with Julia and Silvia. This is evident in their jarring and unsatisfying embrace of the principal of *philia* in Act 5.

This quick and dense summary of the play's principal problematic moments corresponds to a long and quite fascinating performance history. While that history is of course ongoing, the 2014 Royal Shakespeare Company production in Stratford, directed by Simon Godwin, serves here as a useful contemporary reference point: this production handily registers all of these problems and indexes contemporary reservations about them. But modern audiences are not the first to find these moments distasteful or problematic. The Benjamin Victor 1763 and J. P. Kemble 1808 rewrites of *Two Gentlemen of Verona* register early on all the unease with the play's ending that we are familiar with even today. This chapter begins with an overview of Victor's and of Kemble's versions, followed by a discussion of two early productions of Kemble as represented in prompt books.[5] It then traces similar moves in the 2014 RSC production. It concludes by considering some theoretical problems, and then making a brief case for understanding the rewrites and the productions as appropriations.

To begin with, both Victor and Kemble soften Proteus's rape attempt slightly. He still threatens to 'woo [Silvia], like a soldier, at arms end', but his ensuing lines, 'And love you 'gainst the nature of love – force ye', and 'I'll force thee yield to my desire', are cut.[6] Valentine intercedes, and he directs the outlaws to 'lay hold' of Proteus. He then turns his attention instead to the wronged Silvia in these non-Shakespearean lines, which are added in Victor and in Kemble:

Victor	Kemble
Val. My dearest Silvia,	*Val.* My dearest Silvia!
Kind heav'n has heard my fervent prayer!	Indulgent heaven at length has heard my prayer,
And brought again my Silvia to my arms!	And brought again my Silvia to my arms;
There is no rhetorick can express my joy!	No power on earth shall ever part us more
Sil. It is delusion all! Alas! we dream!	*Sil.* It is delusion all, – Alas, we dream,
And must awake to wretchedness again!	And must awake to wretchedness again.
O, Valentine! we are beset with dangers!	O, Valentine, we are beset with dangers.
Val. Dismiss those fears, my love; here I command!	*Val.* Dismiss those fears, my love; here I command:
No power on earth shall ever part us more.	Thou common friend, – that's without faith or love – [. . .]
Thou common friend! [. . .]	

Instead of addressing Proteus, Valentine talks to Silvia and articulates his joy at the reunion and his resolution never to be separated from her again. Silvia's new lines give her a voice in the aftermath of the attempted rape, and while it is one of despair ('we are beset with dangers!'), it also prompts Valentine's confident assertion that all will be well and defines the play's resolution in terms of their connection. The alterations thereby shift the focus of the moment to the Valentine-Silvia relationship and away from the Valentine-Proteus relationship that in Shakespeare dominates so much of Act 5.

The additions also develop Valentine as radically more aggressive in his initial response to Proteus. In Shakespeare's text, Valentine dismisses Proteus with a lament whose only threat is never to trust him again:

I am sorry I must never trust thee more
But count the world a stranger for thy sake
The private wound is deepest. O time accurst,
'Mongst all foes that a friend should be the worst! (5.4.69–72)

To these lines Victor adds a single stark one: 'prepare for death'. Kemble actually cuts the lines and replaces them with 'to die, but lightly expiates thy offence', giving us a Valentine whose response to Proteus's actions is less about foregoing friendship and more about violent retribution. Both make corresponding adjustments to Proteus's response. Here is Shakespeare's version, followed by the Victor and Kemble rewrites:

> *Pro.* My shame and guilt confounds me.
> Forgive me, Valentine. If hearty sorrow
> Be a sufficient ransom for offence,
> I tender't here. I do as truly suffer
> As e'er I did commit (5.4.73–7)

Victor	**Kemble**
Pro. My shame and guilt confound me------	*Pro.* My shame and guilt confound me.--
If to repent------if hearty sorrow	Thy wrath is just; and I as freely suffer,
Be a sufficient ransom for offence,	As e'er I did commit: I merit death.
I tender't here: I do as freely suffer,	
As e'er I did commit------I merit death.	

Extended dashes in Victor suggest the starts and stops of a great emotional strain. Kemble eschews those marks and offers an even shorter penance than Shakespeare's original Proteus, but mirroring Victor, his Proteus *freely* suffers, as opposed to *truly* suffering. This substitution of words gives us a Proteus who embraces the proposed punishment: in place of a comment about anguish, or perhaps penance, he instead accepts retributive justice, which is confirmed in both Victor and Kemble with the new final words 'I merit death.' The effect of a Valentine whose resolution to the conflict is the death of Proteus (rather than a turn away from friendship towards a life of solitude), coupled with a Proteus who accepts the proposed punishment as just and deserved, is a substantive revision to the play's treatment of *philia*. Shakespeare's treatment may or may not be sarcastic, but it does seem to confront the audience or reader with the absurdity of the principle of *philia* followed to its logical end. And while these modifications aren't exactly ennobling for Valentine and Proteus, both characters are moved some distance away from their position in Shakespeare, where their friendship jostles back into centre stage as the play's dramatic focus, crowding out the love relationships. In Shakespeare, the relationship between the two men refigures the two women – indeed, all the other characters – as supporting cast in a secondary drama: whatever the interpersonal dynamics among the others, to Valentine and Proteus, they are ultimately just a register of the shifts in their own lifelong mutual devotion. Victor and Kemble – and Kean and Macready, as we will see – try to manage this Shakespearean dynamic with textual revisions and staging choices that erase the awkwardness.

Other added lines in Kemble, for instance, give Valentine and Silvia further comment on Proteus's reaction once Julia reveals her identity and tells her story: '*Val.* He's touch'd to the very soul', and '*Sil.* Mine pities them.' Silvia is also given lines in which she enjoins Valentine not to 'hold out enmity forever' (61). Proteus's repentance is amplified with additions and revisions to the final two lines of the original:

Shakespeare / F	Kemble
Than men their minds? 'Tis true. O heaven, were man	Than men their minds! 'tis true: O heaven! Were man
But constant, he were perfect! That one error	But constant, he were perfect; that one blemish
Fills him with faults, makes him run through all th' sins.	Fills him with faults, makes him run through all errors:
Inconstancy falls off ere it begins.	Inconstancy falls off ere it begins:
	The magic spell dissolves that dimm'd my sight,
	And my true day-spring dawns to me again:
What is in Silvia's face but I may spy	All Silvia boasts of beauty I may see
More fresh in Julia's with a constant eye?	More fresh in Julia with a constant eye.

Silvia follows with more added lines in Kemble, and a stage direction during which she, not Valentine, joins Julia's and Proteus's hands. Victor adds no lines but does give Valentine's lines to Silvia. In both revisions, then, the speaking part and the actions are thereby transferred from Valentine to Silvia, restoring voice and agency where Shakespeare infamously leaves Silvia silent.

Finally, Kemble gives Proteus seven new lines to close the play:

Pro. Thanks, generous Valentine: – and I myself
Will be the trumpet of my Julia's worth,
Her steadfast faith, her still-enduring love,
And of my own misdoings. – Pardon me,
Ye who have ever known what 'tis to err! –
And be this truth by all the world confess'd,
That lovers must be faithful to be bless'd!

Only the final couplet appears in Victor, who also brings Lance and Speed back into the closing moments for some forty lines, adding levity, but the effect in both is further to rehabilitate Proteus. The lines elaborate on Proteus's two preceding speeches of penance: he recognises Julia's worth again and acknowledges his own mistakes, asks for general pardon and reminds us all that nobody is without fault. The lines also address a common contemporary complaint: if Proteus really is sorry, why does he have so few lines in Shakespeare in which to express that sorrow?

Most notable among all the changes, however, both in Victor and in Kemble, is that Valentine's offer to give Silvia to Proteus is cut altogether. Kemble replaces it with a command from Valentine for the outlaws to take Proteus to Valentine's cave, which in turn serves as the new occasion in the text for Julia's faint. The change effectively cleanses Valentine's character, erasing his troubling behaviour. Where Shakespeare deliberately compromises him by having him reaffirm the superiority of male-male friendship not only over male-female love matches, but precisely at their expense, Kemble and Victor confine all of the unwholesome behaviour in Proteus and refigure the affirmation of friendship as a matter purely of repentance and communal forgiveness. Valentine does embrace Proteus, but he does so at the behest of Silvia, and with the added incentive of an augmented apology from Proteus. Proteus's 'misdoings' (Kemble) are limited, at least somewhat, by the circumscription of his threat to Silvia, and Valentine's devotion to Silvia is no longer undercut by the gift.

These changes work to eliminate the same problems to which audiences, readers and editors tend to object today, suggesting that theatregoers, and by extension the theatremakers who sought to engage and please them, have never been comfortable with the attempted rape, with Valentine's conciliatory gestures in its wake, or with Silvia's silence. In other words, as appropriations go, these adjustments to the early Shakespearean text are effectively parallel with the revisions often – even typically – made to the play's ending in performance today. The difference is that contemporary productions use staging choices, rather than alteration or additions to spoken lines, to manage the difficulties.[7]

Stage

I return to the question of appropriation below, but just as noteworthy as the aversion of early audiences to *Two Gents* is the willingness, as early as 1841, not only to return to Shakespeare's problematic text, but to embrace and even play up the problems. William Macready's 1841 production and Charles Kean's 1846 production[8] use Shakespeare's text, not Kemble's or Victor's, and while they make some cuts and transpositions, they appear explicitly to reject the shaping fixes introduced in the early rewrites.

Macready, 1841

At the outset of Act 5, scene 4 (which in Macready is renumbered V, iii; see Figure 8.1), Valentine is 'discovered seated on [a] bank'. One line is cut, and several blocking notes for Valentine are added, along with cues

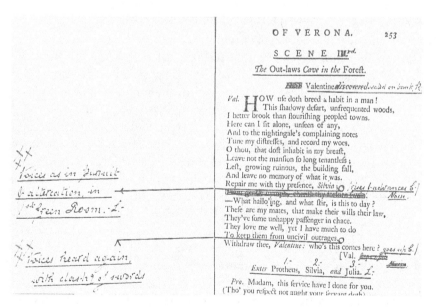

Figure 8.1 Folger *2 Gent 11* (1841)

for offstage noises. There are no significant alterations in these changes, however, and even the three lines cut from Silvia's 'when *Protheus* cannot love, where he's belov'd' speech could be cuts for time just as easily as they could be cuts for substance. The stage direction describing the action at Valentine's line 'Ruffian, let go that rude uncivil touch' reads thus: 'Drawing sword & rushing down C[enter] between them, Prot, also, draws his sword, & is about to attack him but recognizing Val, drops sword, & staggers back to R[right].' Other directions move Julia, Valentine and Proteus around: 'Julia X'es over, behd – to R'; Proteus 'goes to him [Valentine] and kneels'; Valentine 'X behd Prot to Julia' who 'falls, on stage R', and so forth. But there is nothing particularly surprising, and certainly nothing that indicates an attempt to work actively against Shakespeare's text. The closest the prompt book appears to offer on that front is the absence of any stage directions for the line 'All, that was mine in *Silvia*, I give thee.' There *are* editorial footnotes, one from Pope and one from Hanmer, complaining about the gift and attempting to explain it away as something required by the source material (Pope) or as written by someone else (Hanmer):

> this passage either hath been much sophisticated, or is one great proof that the main parts of this play did not proceed from *Shakespear*, for it is impossible he could make *Valentine* act and speak so much out of character, or give to *Silvia* so unnatural a behaviour as to take no notice of this strange concession if it had been made.[9]

These editorial footnotes predate even Victor, but the juxtaposition in this text of the notes, which articulate the familiar anxieties about the offer, and the unaltered line suggests a balance. Macready restores Valentine's offer / gift – this is our earliest record of the play performed with the line – but apparently without any accompanying stage business. There is no directed action here, no specified blocking, to indicate how the moment is to be staged; there is nothing that anticipates or attempts to shape the audience's reception or understanding of the offer the way the editorial notes shape the moment for the reader. This is notable in part because stage directions that follow are quite specific about which character does what: Valentine 'Joins their hands, & puts Prot across to Jul R' at 'long be foes'; as the outlaws enter shouting 'A prize!', he 'puts Sylvia quickly across to R C. & goes to L, putting Outlaws away from the Duke', etc. suggesting that any action accompanying the offer would also be specified. Were Macready aiming to make a point, in

other words, or even a pointed reading of the moment – were he looking to achieve anything in particular with the offer of Silvia to Proteus as
a conciliatory gift and marker of the value of male-male friendship – the
generally heavily annotated prompt book is oddly silent at precisely the
point it should speak most loudly.

Kean, 1846

The promptbook for Kean's New York staging in 1846 is more lively and
much more detailed. It describes scenery, costumes and even the disposition of props. Valentine is 'disc[overe]d seated on [a] bank', as in Macready,
but with further instructions: 'his hat & weapons / – crop – bow – quiver
& c / lying on it' (see Figure 8.2). And these properties appear later, too,
as when Valentine 'takes up his hat, &' followed by '*Steps aside*', a printed
stage direction, to which is added the handwritten elaboration 'into Cave,
R–3C.' The direction at the attempted rape reads:

> He [Proteus] seizes Silv by the waist – they change places – when Val
> speaks, he [Proteus] quits her instantly, goes a little to R – draws his
> sword, and, is rushing forward, again, to strike him, when recognizing
> his friend Valentine, he staggers back to R, – and drops his sword from
> his hand /–/ All done very rapidly! /

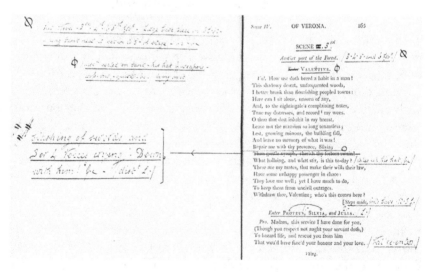

Figure 8.2 Folger *2 Gent 10* (1846), page 165

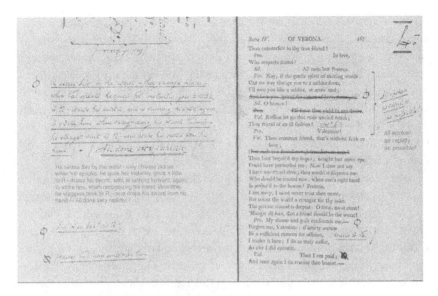

Figure 8.3 Folger *2 Gent 10* (1846), page 167

with this added injunction in the right margin: '<u>all spoken as rapidly as possible!</u>':

While the Kean book follows the Macready book for the most part, and while the repeated instruction calling for rapid delivery might read like a device to avoid emphasising the assault, there is a striking departure from Macready here in the addition of directions for the offer of Silvia to Proteus. Those directions make the moment clear and specific. At '. . . I give thee', the handwritten SD is 'takes the hands of Silv and Prot, and puts Prot a X to Silv, on his L – as Julia faints, Val catches her in his arms'. While Julia's 'disposition' is sketched obliquely in the next SD (the line after she faints is annotated 'very faintly – but reviving gradually'), Silvia is given no instructions or attention. Some seventeen lines later, she is directed to cross to Valentine: 'Silv passes behd to Val – and they both retire up a little way.' Kean evidently stages the gift aggressively.

William Carroll's excellent Arden 3 introduction reads this record oddly: 'In Kean's production, the text was softened even more than in Victor's adaptation. The lines were to be "All spoken as rapidly as possible!", but the stage action left no doubt about what was happening.'[10] Carroll goes on to quote from the Valentine-Proteus SD, but he does not mention the added SD for the offer itself. My sense is rather that Victor and Kean articulate two quite different, even opposed, choices in a range of approaches to this play's troubling ending. Both break with the late eighteenth-century trend of staging 'corrected' Shakespeare – that is, Shakespeare in which the perceived deficiencies and atrocities have been remedied – but Kean, despite trimming the lines in which Proteus threatens force, is far more aggressive and direct in staging the play's difficulties than any of his predecessors who left records. As noted above, the early aversion to the ending is not surprising, but the relatively early embrace of those moments, especially in Kean (1845), is remarkable, no matter what historical context we choose for it.

The more recent (2014) Royal Shakespeare Company production evinces both the implied reverence for the 'original' Shakespearean text and the urge to fix it. Like Macready and Kean (to an extent), director Simon Godwin avoids altering Shakespeare's text, but like Victor and Kemble, he makes staging choices that register a familiar unease. Godwin's Silvia and Julia are generally played as quite strong, and staging choices during the assault struggle recall moves made in Victor and Kemble to invest the women with voice and agency. Other choices have the effect of blurring Shakespeare's focus on a Valentine whose first impulse in the wake of Proteus's actions is dejection and whose second is full forgiveness and solicitous indulgence of the *philia* principle. The description below follows a full video production of the staged performance, available from the RSC on DVD and from library video databases.[11]

Silvia at one point chokes Proteus, on the ground, and uses his own knife to threaten him during their exchange early in Act 5, scene 4. Proteus disarms her at the line 'I'll force ye', but Valentine intervenes and puts Proteus in a headlock. Valentine then repeatedly submerges Proteus's head in a barrel of water during the 'friend of an ill fashion' speech, and Silvia apparently stops him from actually drowning Proteus at 'count the world a stranger for thy sake'. Valentine produces a handgun at the conclusion of the speech, however, and points it at the kneeling Proteus's head. The staged threats to Proteus's life do work in a similar way to added lines in Victor and Kemble, in which Valentine invokes death as a suitable punishment and resolution. Proteus delivers the first lines of his apology speech in drawn-out segments, directing some words to Valentine, some to Silvia, and some to an unfixed point between them (not at the camera, which in this production has no fixed location and, as is typical with filmed performances, is not visible or material to the characters). Proteus directs 'forgive me' specifically to Silvia, before looking back at Valentine, and at the gun, and then closing his eyes in acceptance of his fate. Thus, in moves neatly parallel with the general sense of Victor and

Pro. My fhame and guilt confound me.——
If to repent———if hearty forrow
Be a fufficient ranfom for offence,
I tender't here : I do as freely fuffer,
As e'er I did commit———I merit death.
   Jul. Ah me, unhappy———   [*fwoons.*]
   Silvia. Look to the youth.
   Val. Why boy ! how now ? what's the matter ? look up —
fpeak.———

Figure 8.4 Proteus's apology in Benjamin Victor's 1763 rewrite of
The Two Gentlemen of Verona

of Kemble, the RSC production empowers Silvia, ennobles Valentine
and lends earnestness to Proteus's first line and a half: his acquiescence
performs the same function as 'I merit death', and his halting delivery
strikingly suggests the punctuation we see in Victor's rewrite, with its
several elongated dashes.

'Ennobling' is debatable here, but like the earlier textual revisions, the
staging choice moves the character Valentine away from the pacifism or
indifference to sexual assault that is coupled, in Shakespeare, with a gift
of the neglected Silvia as a token to reaffirm a newly mended friendship.
Valentine's resolve to commit murder as punishment reads in all three
instances – Victor, Kemble and Godwin/RSC – as a kind of masculine
virtue, replacing a perverse (masculine) investment in a camaraderie that
outweighs all other human relationships and obligations.

A long silence follows Valentine's drawing the gun, during which Silvia
slowly walks over and joins him. She places her right hand around his, on
the gun, still aimed at Proteus. Silvia's intention to join Valentine in murder again empowers her, by giving her some agency and perhaps by linking her to the masculine 'virtue' of anger. But her resolve is short-lived,
and she pulls the gun away after a moment and falls to her knees, covering
her face. Proteus, realising he is likely to live, delivers the remainder of his
speech still on his knees, facing down, and Valentine, looking at Silvia,
the handgun and then Proteus, accepts the apology. This Valentine seems
to happen on the line 'by penitence th'Eternal's wrath's appeased' in the
moment, and quite earnestly; it appears to be the catalyst that leads him
to a realisation and to the act of forgiveness. The production retains the
line 'all that was mine in Silvia, I give thee'. Valentine kneels as he delivers it and joins his forehead to Proteus's. The line's potential force – and

its dark semantic content – is thereby blunted, but not dulled entirely. While the camera does not catch Silvia's reaction, Julia's delivery of 'o me unhappy!' both refocuses the scene and suggests the urgency she feels is needed in drawing attention away from the moment. The effect of these staging choices is debatable, but the production clearly avoids making a specific choice here about what Valentine means by 'all that was mine in Silvia, I give thee'.[12] It allows the ensuing wonder and the reconciliation of Proteus to Julia to shut down any further consideration of Valentine's gift. From there, the scene proceeds without any apparent interplay between text and staging choices until after Valentine delivers the closing couplet. The production's concluding moment is a sombre acknowledgement of the enormity of Proteus's betrayal of Julia: they are alone on stage, and although they step towards each other after a silence, they do not exit together. Instead, the lights go out.

Appropriation

This overview of early changes to the text of *Two Gentlemen of Verona*, next to snapshots of Act 5 in two nineteenth-century productions and a twenty-first-century production, suggests a range of practices in the play's stage history but also a provisional sense of continuity. The early rewrites track with early editorial unease about troubling moments, particularly in Act 5, as well as with staging practices today: anxieties about the play on stage that were initially managed with textual emendation are now managed with staging choices, often to strikingly similar ends. We can also see, however, that those early interventions barely preceded production choices that restored and even appeared to embrace the troubling moments in the Folio text. Victor and Kemble read pretty clearly as rewrites, that is, whereas Macready and Kean seem to return to the Shakespearean text in a corrective move. In this sense, these versions and productions of the play appear to be heading in different directions. To focus on what they have in common, however, rather than on what appears to separate them, all the productions and production records discussed here present a *Two Gentlemen of Verona* that could be said to meet a need. What they have in common as productions (or production texts) of the play puts them in the same critical category. While recognising the apparent distinctions, then, between Victor and Kemble and Godwin on the one hand, and Macready and Kean on the other, I want to advance the fairly innocuous observation that they are all doing the same thing by straining to manage the play's unruly moments on stage. Victor and Kemble do so with alterations to the text, and Macready and Kean and Godwin, with staging choices that supplement or overwrite the text. One approach privileges the text, even if only implicitly, while the other seems to acknowledge its inadequacy for meeting the needs of the moment. But all are best understood as attempts to bring Shakespeare into line with perceptions about what is desirable or viable at any given moment.

This back-and-forth in performance, between fidelity to Shakespeare's text and revisions to that text, effected in rewriting or in staging choices that eke out or even overwrite the text, recalls categories that have figured prominently in academic work on Shakespeare's afterlives: fidelity and appropriation. It is a dynamic we can see throughout the play's stage history, as well as in the popular reception of Shakespeare productions and adaptations. While long out of fashion in academic critique, the tenacity of the fidelity-vs-appropriation dynamic is still evident especially in popular responses to Shakespeare in performance, where productions are frequently understood either as cleaving to or departing from Shakespeare. That tenacity also suggests the futility of trying to do away with these categories in academic work. Despite decades of critique, that is, and decades of compelling alternative models that work to reconfigure the relationship between an instance of Shakespeare and its Shakespearean reference point – Douglas Lanier's rhizome model has dominated for some time now – fidelity and appropriation persist as a conceptual polarity. So while it is important to continue to critique the easy certainty of the related terms that are central to this line of thinking – terms such as 'original' or 'appropriation' or (especially) 'Shakespeare' – and the frequency with which they are deployed in critical and popular responses alike to Shakespeare in production, the impulse to dismiss them altogether is both needlessly limiting and doomed. If these terms will always be unstable, even untenable, they will just as certainly continue to circulate, and perhaps to be useful.

Indeed, even within academic discourse about Shakespeare in performance, the spectre of fidelity can often be found lurking. For example, the notion of fidelity continues to drive stage histories of Shakespeare – the preceding two sections of this chapter are a good example, in fact – where changes or revisions or notable staging choices tend to register as departures from, or returns to, Shakespeare's early texts. Textual fidelity, in other words, is actually not uncommon in academic writing when 'appropriation' is itself not explicitly part of the conversation. As long we avoid textual essentialism and certain other critical problems (such as fixing the relationship between text and performance, which I'll discuss below), critical traffic in 'fidelity' is not particularly objectionable among academics. The concept seems to acquire its sinister connotations only in proximity to 'appropriation', which always threatens to introduce value or hierarchy into the assessment, indexed to one or another model of derivation. 'Shake-speare' becomes the source and governing centre of meaning and value, around which derived objects situate themselves in a subservient relation-ship. Such an understanding quickly becomes unpalatable and confining, and the menacing potential of 'Shakespeare' emerges as most troubling: the power assigned to that entity has a long history of subjugation.

The threat can be resisted, and even neutralised, however, and we can make the case for the critical value of fidelity and appropriation – not as a regression, but as a way of articulating a relationship between and among the various contingencies we invoke when we talk about Shakespeare circulating in the spaces of production and consumption. And especially about Shakespeare in performance. The essence of my argument for applying the term 'appropriation' to the productions dis-cussed above – and for thinking of all productions as peppered at least by isolated instances of appropriation – comes down to the use value of 'appropriation' in identifying and theorising the difference in any given instance between what is needed from Shakespeare and what is perceived to be available in the play at hand.

The productions discussed in this chapter, I think, are trying to be 'Shakespearean'. The records that describe them give the effect of being troubled by certain components in the received text of Shakespeare, and they address themselves to altering those components with light revision and deliberate staging. They seem silently to agree with Hanmer's gloss or with Pope's blaming of the source material. They thus offer themselves as Shakespeare, with the tweaks and fixes necessary to recover, or produce, the noble poet imagined by early editors and commentators. The revisions and alterations that these productions make are not wholesale transfor-mations of the Shakespearean text: as appropriations go, they are modest revisions and elaborations whose aim is to remain 'Shakespearean'. Indeed, if we adopt the Hanmer logic – that 'it is impossible [Shakespeare] could make *Valentine* act and speak so much out of character, or give to *Silvia* so unnatural a behaviour as to make no notice of this strange concession if it had been made' – these appropriations are best understood as attempts to restore a fundamentally decent *Shakespeareaness*, or perhaps a fundamen-tally Shakespearean decency, to moments in the play where it has unac-countably gone missing.

This argument does raise some critical challenges that I want to con-sider in the remainder of this section. First, to pin down what constitutes an appropriation requires defining any number of entities and boundaries, from what counts as a playtext to what we mean by appropriation, adaptation, and so forth. Thankfully, there is an abundance of critical work that has set itself to that task. While yet another full review of terms is not necessary, I do want to borrow a specific observation from Kidnie's *Shakespeare and the Problem of Adaptation*, one of a dozen-odd really good recent studies that address themselves to the question of definition. Kidnie points out that by finding adaptations everywhere, we just end up reducing the term 'adaptation' to an effective equivalence with the term 'production'.[13] Such a reduction is theoretically tenable and even intriguing, but as Kidnie and others have noted, it merely moves the problem of defining 'adaptation' elsewhere, and it leaves unaddressed a fairly obvious, if fraught, distinction between productions that are trying to be 'Shakespearean' and productions that are actively trying to do something else, or something different, or something more. The texts and productions discussed above fall in the former category, and yet, thinking of them as appropriations, at least in this context, keeps the focus on the acts of intervention that mark the attempt, in each case, to present a version of the play that solves problems that surface in performance. Appropriation can be 'local' even within a production, a kind of performance choice that slips into a corrective or ameliorative mode for a delimited, identifiable span.

Second, assessing performance in terms of appropriation is tricky because it draws on the relationship between text and performance. Most appropriation theory follows performance theory here by acknowledging the many problems involved in identifying a stable source text and by debating whether performance is the *telos* or completion of a process in which the text (or any given text) is an antecedent or earlier part. Does performance transmit text, which contains the essence of the play, or does text merely point towards performance, where we can find full expression? Or, to use the terms Andrew Hartley has suggested, is performance 'interpretive' vs 'constructive'? Hartley focuses on the aspects of performance that are constructive, noting the 'essential incompleteness of the script' and pointing out that a playtext 'does not contain all possible performance choices, nor can it circumscribe the limits of staging because their respective modes of signification are different'.[14] The productions discussed here also draw attention to the sense in which stage choices construct a Shakespeare play, but without necessarily nominating performance as the realisation of playtext: there is semantic movement back towards text in rewrites like Victor's or Kemble's, which can function as objects of inquiry even apart from their status as records. In any case, the relationship between text and performance constitutes a significant and often exciting theoretical challenge, for academics and for theatre practitioners alike. It makes some sense to think that the stakes are quite different for theatre practitioners, however, whose process is understood to culminate in public performance and who are perceived, by critics and audiences alike, to be doing something with Shakespeare. If that perception is reductive (and how could it not be?), it is nonetheless both common and excusable, and the productions discussed here are best understood, I think, as trying both to idealise and then to realise Shakespeare's project by resolving tensions and problems that arise in the course of staging the play. They all submit to an impulse to fix whatever isn't working, with performance as the circumstance in which the idealised Shakespeare is presented and consumed.

It is in this sense that performance tends most readily to highlight moments of appropriation.[15] As a mode of engaging with Shakespeare, that is, performance tends to foreground the most troubling or problematic moments in Shakespeare. It draws the focus to what is most topical from moment to moment or from context to context, and therefore to those aspects of a play that are perceived to be most fertile (or perhaps most barren) for cultivating a topical interest or imperative. Like a kind of cultural bubble test, performance reveals the points in the play where what is perceived to be the integrity of the Shakespearean text fails to hold: holes and fissures leak, thinner stretches of the membrane warp and bulge, marking areas inadequate for containing the cultural pressures of a given circumstance. Fill a Shakespeare text with the pressure of any given moment's particular needs and fears, and the text will spring a series of little leaks. Accordingly, what is most interesting about *Two Gents* in performance is that it highlights the moments in Shakespeare that are perceived to be broken at any given historical moment. It thereby calls attention to the sense in which all performance is appropriation – not because stage productions are supposed to be 'ministerial' to a text and can never manage fully and properly to actualise the vision encoded in and governed by the text.[16] Not because performance takes its cues from the text – the metaphor immediately suggests the absurdity of trying to establish either term in the text / performance binary as primary. Rather, it is because performance articulates a relationship with a text, and like all other kinds of relationships we have with texts, performance always marks the distance between what we see in the texts and what we want to see in them.

Despite all of these caveats, the fidelity / appropriation binary always seems to mystify 'the text' and invest it with some kind of unknowable and unchallengable authority. I return to the suggestion above that this threat can be neutralised by recognising that any given text is a historically situated material production, not a self-evident and self-perpetuating noumenon. Kidnie urges us to understand the text – the 'Shakespeare' to which productions are understood to have a relationship of fidelity or appropriation (or adaptation, etc.) – as 'work' or as 'ongoing process' in the textual theory sense.[17] The 'Shakespeare as "work"' model emphasises how Shakespeare 'modifies over time and from one reception space to another', and the model is, at least for now, the most satisfying and sensible and critically accommodating option we have.[18] But once it is understood that 'Shakespeare' is an evolving and provisional reference point, and that all of the other terms in the mix are themselves similarly evolving and provisional – circumstantial – it makes some sense to retain the notion of fidelity and appropriation as a way of characterising the relationships among those terms. To reiterate, a compelling reason for thinking of Shakespeare productions as appropriation is that performance always marks the difference, in any given instance, between what is perceived to be 'the text' and what is perceived to be appropriate to the instant or instance.

Third, and finally, the stage history I have offered above has dealt extensively with prompt books as records of staged productions. Thus, joining the early printed Shakespeare text, a *second* text, itself with a history of revision or evolution, complicates matters further, as does the absence of a single particular performance to be nominated as the critical object. Whereas we might easily problematise the idea of 'performance' by pointing to the impossibility of identifying and delimiting what that idea involves (Which particular performance of a production? And from whose perspective? What about changes in the cast?, etc.), those problems are compounded in this discussion because the Macready and Kean productions are even more unrecoverable than is typically the case with modern productions. The prompt books are second, intermediary texts that become performance texts, adaptations and 'original' texts, all at once, depending on who is using them and for what purpose.

Take the 2014 RSC production of *Two Gentlemen of Verona* as a point of contrast. We can agree, despite the challenges of identifying and delimiting the 2014 RSC *Two Gents*, that it was directed by Simon Godwin; that it featured specific actors in specific roles; that it ran until 4 September of that year, etc. The production is in some sense circumscribed and defined by these data points. We can, of course, trouble this agreement endlessly: is the DVD version of the production a record of the production, or is it something slightly or even significantly different, with credit given, in some records but not others, to a different director, Robin Lough? Is the video a paratext? Is it not an incomplete text of the performance, in that the recording apparatus has a limited scope and focus, relative even to any given audience perspective? Is it not also a *more* complete text, since it allows for repeated viewing; since its record, though limited, is more thorough, more iterable? Such questions may be the stuff of minutiae, but they are not idle. Recent inquiry into the relationship between staged theatre and streaming broadcasts or video recordings of staged theatre has raised these and other issues and suggested the many ways in which remediation here introduces difference and even, arguably, absolute distinction.[19] The relationship between what is presented and what is seen on stage is itself far from fixed and inevitable, of course, and even in cases where video strives to recreate theatrical experience, full representation is not possible. There is nonetheless a sense in which filmed versions of live productions, despite the interventions of whole teams of additional artists, give us a better record of a stage production than a prompt book can provide. We can know – objectively, even – quite a lot more about this RSC production than we can about the Kean or Macready productions discussed here, for which we have instructions that are different, in important ways, from records, from reviews, from video versions.

To treat the decisions recorded in the Kean and Macready prompt books in easy equivalence with the decisions visible in the RSC video, then, is to allow a number of unsteady assumptions to stand unchallenged. And in proposing that the staging decisions animating the 2014 RSC *Two Gents* are similarly motivated as the additions and changes made by Victor and Kemble, and later unmade by Kean and Macready, I admittedly pass over these problems and a good many more. In the interest of sketching out some examples of performance as a mode of doing Shakespeare that highlights instances and moments of appropriation, however, my aim has been to find resonances and echoes across time periods and performance media, and I hope those links remain valid despite the challenges. I have also tried to think through the use value of an outmoded binary. If we separate the notion of 'fidelity' from the ideological baggage that has tended to accompany it, and if we think about 'appropriation' as a concept we can use selectively, to understand specific choices in any given production, we can see the value and the appeal of these troublesome terms. Viewed as a register of anxiety about Shakespeare, rather than as a measure of fidelity to an idealised original source, appropriation and fidelity can still help us think about staging choices that manage perceived deficiencies while also trying to operate under the imprimatur of 'Shakespeare'.

Notes

1. All references to the 'Shakespeare' version of *Two Gentlemen of Verona* pertain to the 1623 Folio, the earliest printed text. Parenthetical citations are keyed to the New Kittredge Shakespeare edition, ed. Matt Kozusko, (Newburyport, MA, 2014).

2. I am deeply indebted to the editors of this volume for their care, their feedback, and their patience through many rounds of revision.

3. Daniel Fischlin and Mark Fortier, 'General Introduction', in *Adaptations of Shakespeare: A critical anthology of plays from the seventeenth century to the present*, ed. Daniel Fischlin and Mark Fortier (New York: Routledge, 2000), 17.

4. Margaret Jane Kidnie, *Shakespeare and the Problem of Adaptation* (New York: Routledge, 2009).

5. Kemble's revision of Shakespeare (and of Victor) evidently took place in multiple rounds. He first revised the play for a 1790 performance, and an 1808 prompt book (Folger, 2 GENT 15) not only differs from Victor's 1763 text but also indicates on the title page that it is revised by Kemble. But this 1808 printed book also contains additional handwritten annotations, attributed to Kemble, that are themselves subsequently incorporated into later printed editions of the Kemble revision.

6. 2 GENT 7, 59. Passages reproduced here come from an undated copy of Kemble's revision. It is the Folger's 'rehearsal copy' (Folger call number 2 GENT 7), described in the Folger catalogue as 'a copy of Kemble's text, annotated by Owen Stanley Fawcett in 1879'. There is no lineation, so I cite page numbers. This text prints annotations and line alterations Kemble makes by hand to the 1808 prompt book (Folger, 2 GENT 15) and is therefore easier to cite. For Victor, I cite a digital edition of the 1763 printing (London: J. and R. Tonson).

7. For another recent account of Victor's and Kemble's alterations to *Two Gents*, see Lisanna Calvi, 'Of Flowers and Weeds. Veering Towards Comedy in Benjamin Victor's Adaptation of *The Two Gentlemen of Verona* (1762)', *Il Castello di Elsinore*, 13 May 2020, doi:10.13135/2036-5624/216.

8. The productions are related. Kean's prompt book for a New York production in 1846 (Folger 2 GENT 10) was prepared by George Ellis from the prompt book for Macready's 1841 Drury Lane production (Folger 2 GENT 11). Kurt Schlueter discusses both at length in the 2012 update to his 1990 Cambridge edition of the play, noting that Macready's production ran for thirteen performances with solid reviews before Kean, 'with the help of a copy of Macready's prompt-book', took the production to New York and eventually back to London, at the Haymarket Theatre, in 1846.

Schlueter's account of the 1841 Macready production paraphrases extensively from the prompt book for the Kean 1846 New York production,
possibly attributing to Macready some stage decisions that appear to be
unique to Kean. It is unclear whether specifics unique to the Kean production, that is, should be understood to reproduce the earlier Macready
staging, since the Kean prompt book makes different cuts and is considerably more verbose in its descriptions of stage action. See Schlueter, *The
Two Gentlemen of Verona*, ed. Kurt Schlueter, updated edition (Cambridge:
Cambridge University Press, 2012), 34–8; Folger 2 GENT 10, 164–71;
and Folger 2 GENT 11, 251–9.

9. Folger, 2 GENT 11, 255 n2. Hanmer's note first appeared in 1745, in his
    The Works of Shakespear: In Six Volumes. London: J. and P. Knapton.

10. William Carroll, 'Introduction' to *The Two Gentlemen of Verona*, ed. William
    Carroll. *The Arden Shakespeare*, Third Series (London: Thomson Learning,
    2004), 97.

11. I discuss below some of the problems that come with drawing an equiva-
    lence between a production in performance and version of that production
    remediated in video. The video I discuss here does function well as a record
    of staging choices, regardless of whether those staging choices appeared dif-
    ferently on video or were reformulated for, or even shaped in anticipation
    of, a live broadcast or video record.

12. At least one reviewer read the offer as a response to Silvia's decision not
    to help Valentine murder Proteus: 'When Proteus spoke what seemed like
    heartfelt words of regret, the disgusted Valentine grimaced as if to suggest
    that since Sylvia was not angry enough with Proteus to want to kill him,
    she could not truly love Valentine himself . . . It was clear that Valentine
    offered Sylvia to Proteus impulsively, intending to wound Sylvia's feelings
    and to express his own fury rather than to sever the relationship or to insist
    upon the superiority of his friendship for Proteus over his love for Sylvia.'
    See Sujata Iyengar, Review of *The Two Gentlemen of Verona*, by Royal
    Shakespeare Company. *Shakespeare Bulletin* 33, no. 1 (2015): 145.

13. Kidnie, *Shakespeare and the Problem of Adaptation*, 5.

14. Andrew James Hartley, 'Page and Stage Again: Rethinking Renaissance
    Character Phenomenologically', in *New Directions in Renaissance Drama and
    Performance Studies*, ed. Sarah Werner (New York: Palgrave, 2010), 80–1.

15. I am indebted to Kathryn Vomero Santos for the formulation and for the
    argument developed in this paragraph.

16. For more, see W. B. Worthen, *Shakespeare and the Authority of Performance*
    (Cambridge: Cambridge University Press, 1997), especially Chapter 1.

17. Kidnie, *Shakespeare and Problem of Adaptation*, 5–6.

18. Ibid. 5.

19. The absence of a standard citation format for video version of the 2014 RSC
    production itself raises questions about oversight, direction, design, and so

forth, all the way to the shaping influence a live broadcast can have on staging and performance choices. For more on this, see Erin Sullivan, '"The forms of things unknown": Shakespeare and the Rise of the Live Broadcast', *Shakespeare Bulletin* 35, no. 4 (2017): 627–62. Many other strains and angles of critical inquiry are relevant here as well, however, including questions about what constitutes 'liveness'. See Geoffrey Way, 'Together, Apart: Liveness, Eventness, and Streaming Shakespearean Performance', *Shakespeare Bulletin* 35, no. 3 (2017): 389–406. See also Pascale Aebischer, Susanne Greenhalgh and Laurie E. Osborne, eds, *Shakespeare and the 'Live' Theatre Broadcast Experience* (London: The Arden Shakespeare, 2018).

9

(Un)Veiling Isabella in *Measure for Measure*

Nora J. Williams

Nicholas Hytner's 1987 production of *Measure for Measure* for the Royal Shakespeare Company, starring Josette Simon as Isabella and Sean Baker as Angelo, offers an early example of a staging choice that has since become commonplace. According to Penny Gay, Baker's Angelo 'attempted to rape Isabella, ripping her veil off' in Act 2, scene 4.[1] Hytner may have been among the first modern directors to include an extra-textual unveiling of Isabella, but he certainly was not the last. Other more recent examples of Isabellas who unveil themselves or are forcibly unveiled onstage include Mariah Gale in Dominic Dromgoole's 2015 production for Shakespeare's Globe; Hayley Atwell in Josie Rourke's 2018 Donmar Warehouse production; Lucy Phelps in Gregory Doran's 2019 production for the Royal Shakespeare Company; and Anna Khalilulina in the Cheek by Jowl and Pushkin Theatre collaborative production, which toured from 2013 to 2019. Indeed, in a majority of prominent productions of *Measure for Measure* in England and North America since the mid-eighties, directors have veiled and unveiled Isabella on stage.[2]

In this chapter, I propose that the veiled figure of Isabella activates patriarchal anxieties about visibility, legibility and control that are already present in *Measure for Measure* and are often played out in production through her costume and its use. I argue that the play's misogyny combines with the veil's instability and overdetermination as a semiotic signifier to make Isabella's veil particularly vulnerable to appropriation by audiences during performance. As I will argue in more detail below, Isabella's veil continuously comes into being through acts of spectatorship: through the palimpsests, contexts and cognitive links that an audience brings with them into the theatre. With this semiotic vulnerability in mind, I also read Isabella's

veil against the politics attached to Muslim women's veiling to demonstrate the real-life stakes of its appropriation. In the context of the War
on Terror, escalating Islamophobia in the West from 2001 has often been
gendered: 'Muslim women face the consequences', Lola Olufemi says,
for the entrenchment of '[t]he image of the black and brown terrorist' in
'media coverage of the last decade'.[3] The veil, as a visible symbol of faith,
becomes a particular target, 'refracted through a prism that sees Islamic
beliefs as regressive, constituting oppression and violence'.[4] As Mona Eltahawy puts it, 'Muslim women are especially vulnerable to [. . .] a trifecta
of oppressions: misogyny (faced by all women), racism (faced by women
of colour), and Islamophobia (faced by Muslims).'[5] As a result, Muslim
women's 'bodies – which parts of them are covered or uncovered, for
example – become proxy battlefields'.[6] While Isabella is an explicitly (and
emphatically) Christian character, in the context of the post-9/11 West
her particular veil becomes one piece of a complex network of potential
semiotic significations attached to the concept 'veil'. As a symbol of 'both
power and provocation', the veil's overdetermination opens the door to
audience appropriation, where existing associations an audience member
may hold within a network of significations determine the boundaries of
this costume piece's reception in performance.[7]

I do not at all mean to suggest that anyone goes into a theatre to see a
production of *Measure for Measure* and consciously links Isabella's Christian
veil to hijab or codes Isabella as Muslim – particularly if the actor is white
or white-passing. The connections I draw out in this chapter between
Isabella and Muslim women are neither essential nor totalising, but rather
pieces of a complex semiotic and cognitive web that contemporary productions of *Measure for Measure* must navigate. I aim to show that the same
media landscape that insists on replicating the 'erotic trope of the unveiled
woman' resonates with unveiled Isabellas in the theatre and produces a set
of potential valences that the veil might carry when it is appropriated by
audiences.[8] As Ambereen Dadabhoy argued in her keynote address for the
Globe's 2021 symposium Empowerment to Disempowerment: Intersectional Voices, Islamicate cultures are 'over-determined' in the 'American
imagination' by Orientalist interpretations of the Middle East, and the
West's perception that Islam is fundamentally misogynist has been a driving factor in the War on Terror, with Muslim women always constructed
as in need of 'rescuing'.[9] Veiling becomes part of this narrative and mixes
with existing Western associations with veils and veiling – influenced by
misogyny and Orientalism – to frame veiled Muslim women as necessarily
oppressed and submissive. Tied to this framing is the trope of unveiling in

Western media, which plays out a fantasy of removing Muslim women's veils, specifically, as a narrative of sexual awakening and social freedom.[10]

Isabella's Christian veil is itself laden with assumptions about her submissiveness and subjugation – particularly in the play's final scene, when she is famously silent in response to the Duke's proposal of marriage. That proposal becomes possible, in many productions, as a result of her unveiling: the act of baring her head signifies her availability as a sexual partner for the Duke, and – especially given the removal of the Duke's friar disguise in the same scene – implies that religious conviction might be put on and off as easily as a garment. Isabella thereby forces a reckoning for patriarchal attempts to control women who veil but do not withdraw from society, as nuns typically do: by suggesting that the faith implied in the veil might be merely a costume, the garment is brought back under patriarchal control, to some extent.[11] As Ashley Denham Busse shows, the veil in the Western imagination is 'the quintessential representative of the violent regime of sight-as-knowledge' and participates in narratives which suggest that to unveil is to reveal the truth.[12] As Busse acknowledges, however, this revelation is always 'violent', bound up in the assumption that concealment via veiling is always against one's own desire or will. However, as Rafia Zakaria argues, the relative invisibility provided by the veil might be considered subversive to the patriarchal and imperial powers in our highly surveilled society, which seek always to know, to uncover and to penetrate.[13] The idea that a woman might choose to veil of her own volition, for her own peace, faith or even empowerment, disrupts that patriarchal 'regime of sight-as-knowledge'. Isabella's veil, then, becomes a signifier vulnerable to appropriation, or co-option, into a narrative that links veiling with subjugation in general, and with the assumed oppression of veiled Muslims in particular.

The veil's current semiotic vulnerability is part and parcel of a media landscape that altered profoundly and rapidly in the first two decades of the new millennium. Making a case for the power of 'unthought', N. Katherine Hayles lays out the ways in which 'the embodied subject is embedded and immersed in environments that function as distributed cognitive systems'; these systems 'are always in transition, constantly adding components and rearranging connections'.[14] As a result, she argues, it is ever-more important to attend to 'unthought: a mode of interacting with the world enmeshed in the "eternal present" that forever eludes the belated grasp of consciousness'.[15] In her previous book, *How We Think*, Hayles contends that digital technologies 'operate on vastly different time scales, and in significantly different cognitive models, than human understanding', with the result that 'objects are not seen as static entities that, once created, remain the same throughout time, but rather are understood as constantly-changing assemblages'.[16] 'Objects in this view', Hayles says, 'are more technical individuals enmeshed in networks of social, economic, and technological relations'.[17] Applying this theory to a non-digital object, I consider the concept 'veil' at the centre of such a network, with nodes spiralling out in multiple directions, some of which connect to each other at various degrees of separation – and many of which connect in the realm of 'unthought', without one's conscious awareness. The saturation of tropes about the veil in the post-2001 media landscape I outline above influences, to some extent, the parameters of this nodal network.

Theatre creates potential for any of these nodes to be activated, either by the performers or in the minds of spectators, who – perhaps unthoughtfully – will make connections between their own experiences and contexts and what they see on stage. 'Embodied practice', as Diana Taylor reminds us, represents a particular 'way of knowing'.[18] As a protracted act of embodiment that collapses history, contemporary culture and performance conventions, theatre creates opportunities for seemingly disparate nodes to touch, and spark, together. These unexpected connections can lead to new knowledge – or, at the very least, reconfigurations of that which we think we know, and reactivations of associations that might be latent but unconsciously held, operating in the realm of Hayles's unthought. The instability of Isabella's veil as a signifier makes it particularly available for such reconfigurations and reactivations, leaving it potentially vulnerable to links with Islamophobic tropes.

Readings of Isabella and her faith are therefore complicated by performance: on stage, she is simultaneously four hundred years old and our immediate contemporary; of the past and of the present moment (and all the moments in between) all at once. She operates across overlapping networks, becoming, in some senses, her own assemblage, or palimpsest. In his work on *Untimely Matter*, Jonathan Gil Harris suggests that Shakespeare's *Othello*, in particular, is 'palimpsested', functioning as 'a dynamic field whose contours keep shifting, bringing into startling and anachronistic proximity supposedly distant and disparate moments'.[19] Harris's metaphor of palimpsested time also accurately describes what happens in the theatre when old plays are staged for present-day audiences with present-day actors. The theatre is always 'palimpsested' both by the histories of the play in question and by the cultural contexts of any given production. This idea is perhaps most familiar to theatre scholars as 'haunting', in Marvin Carlson's sense; as Carlson puts it, theatre is 'the repository of culture memory, but, like the memory of each individual, it is also subject to continual adjustment and modification as the memory is recalled in new circumstances and contexts'.[20] At the same time, as Hayles argues, '[m]ateriality, like the object itself, is not a pre-given entity but rather a dynamic process that changes as the focus of attention shifts'.[21] Audience members' individual acts of looking and perceiving – two already-fraught concepts in relation to the veil – produce a range of nodal connections that might activate during any given performance.

One way to unpack the veil's vulnerability to appropriation via these cognitive networks is by considering it as a dramaturgical object. By 'dramaturgy' here, I mean the organising structures and principles of a play, which are both concrete and abstract; this makes a stable, singular definition of 'dramaturgy' challenging. Acknowledging the slipperiness of the term, Cathy Turner and Synne Behrndt define dramaturgy as 'the composition of a work, whether read as a script or viewed in performance', but also, crucially, 'the *discussion* of that composition' (emphasis original).[22] Dramaturgy, then, is both something a play *has* and something that scholars and practitioners might *do* in relation to the work. It is both a theory and a praxis that is concerned with systems, assumptions and structures: the logics that hold a play together. And while dramaturgy has often been 'associated with literary aspects of pre-production work', particularly in anglophone contexts, it can also be expanded to encompass 'a kinesthetic and embodied understanding of the impact of a theatrical production'.[23] Here, I take this expanded definition – considering simultaneously the work done by the text of *Measure for Measure*, the links between particular production decisions and the world in which the production takes place, and the pressures or valences that these external contexts might bring to the work – in order to suggest that Isabella's veil has dramaturgical agency in the context of theatrical production.

Dramaturgy's focus on systems of knowing and communicating links with Kate Manne's definition of misogyny as a system whose end is the subjugation of women (inclusively defined) and the maintenance of patriarchy through a system of moral debt.[24] While single actions or production choices may be misogynist, the root problem is systemic rather than individual. As a result, productions of Shakespeare's plays may continue to promote a misogynist world view even when everyone involved would self-identify as feminist or avow a desire to resist the misogyny that attaches to Shakespeare. This happens because his plays both reproduce and reinforce what Manne calls 'patriarchal norms and expectations' *through* their dramaturgies – through the structures and logics that hold them together.[25] And, as Sarah Grochala argues, there can be 'discord between the ostensible political content of a play and the political character of the dramaturgy through which it is articulated'; in other words, 'a play operates politically through its form, as well as through its content'.[26] When I say that *Measure for Measure*'s dramaturgy is misogynist, I mean that its organising structures are set up towards the maintenance of patriarchy, such that a feminist or resistant reading of the play becomes very difficult to achieve, even within the appropriative space of performance.[27]

If Isabella's veil is a dramaturgical object, then it has some agency relative to the production within which it is situated, operating as what Robin Bernstein calls a 'scriptive thing'.[28] Bernstein argues that objects themselves have the power to inform, direct and delimit responses to and interactions with them.[29] A 'scriptive thing', then, 'like a play script, broadly structures a performance while simultaneously allowing for resistance and unleashing original, live variations that may not be individually predictable'.[30] Bernstein is careful to note that this approach to the material object does not erase human agency; rather, she suggests that 'agency, intention, and racial subjectivation' take place 'in the processual interaction' between human and thing.[31] Still, as Ian Bogost puts it, objects 'do things, and the manner by which they do them matters'.[32]

On Western stages, then, Isabella's Christian veil is scripted, to some extent, by the existing scripts for 'veil' operative within the wider culture, which frame the veiled woman as *both* dangerously fanatical *and* oppressed and in need of saving. Although hijab or niqab is not explicitly staged in most Western productions of *Measure for Measure*, it is part of the script of religious devotion that a veiled Isabella presents. The play frames Isabella herself as a zealot – her first appearance presents her as desirous of a cloistered life, perhaps even excessively so: 'I speak not as desiring more [privileges], / But rather wishing a more strict restraint' (1.4.4–5). Lucio's entrance immediately following prevents an in-depth discussion of Isabella's reasons for entering the sisterhood, and she does not bring up the subject again. Still, her faith manifests throughout the play in other ways. In her first scene with Angelo, for example, she offers to 'bribe' him 'with true prayers / That shall be up at heaven and enter there / Ere sunrise' (2.2.154–6), and she asserts to Claudio that had Angelo demanded her life rather than her virginity, she would 'throw it down for [his] deliverance / As frankly as a pin' (3.1.107–8). Isabella's veil underscores the character's tangible belief in the peril to her eternal soul that Angelo would engender:

And 'twere the cheaper way:
Better it were a brother died at once,
Than that a sister by redeeming him
Should die forever. (2.4.105–8)

Although she comments on Angelo's hypocrisy, too – 'Seeming, seeming!'
(2.4.150) – her decision to reject his attempt at coercion has a religious
basis. As I examine in more detail below, there are long-standing associations between Isabella's refusal of Angelo and twentieth- and twenty-first-
century readings of her as frigid, selfish and manipulative: the strength of
her faith, and its representation in her veiling, is dangerous to the misogynist order of things.

The play's obsession with legibility, visibility and accessibility – issues
also crucial to the dramaturgy of the veil – shows itself in three unveilings
called for in the text, all of which take place in Act 5, scene 1. As Mariana,
the Duke and Claudio are unveiled in turn, the veil's overdetermination
as a semiotic signifier becomes clear: its burden increases throughout this
long scene, in which it is asked to carry valences of hidden and forbidden
knowledge, truth and reconciliation, disguise and deceit, and more. It
also, however, becomes ground zero of the play's misogynist dramaturgy,
as shown by Mariana's unveiling. Confronted with the veiled Mariana,
who presents herself as a witness to contradict Isabella's testimony against
Angelo, the Duke at first insists that she should 'show her face and after
speak' (5.1.167), activating a misogynist narrative that haunts depictions
of veiled women: while her face is covered, Mariana reads as an unreliable
witness to the men around her. And yet, she counters the Duke's reading by constructing her veil as a form of submission to a particular man:
her husband, without whose permission, she says, she will not unmask
(5.1.169–70). Picking up the invocation of her 'husband', the Duke asks,
'What, are you married?' (5.1.170). Mariana replies, 'No, my lord' – a
paradox that perhaps confirms the men's suspicions that a veiled woman
will not present plain truth (5.1.171). Mariana further denies being either
'a maid' or 'a widow', after which the Duke proclaims that she must be
'nothing then: neither maid, widow, nor wife' (5.1.172, 174, 176–7).
Her veil renders Mariana illegible in reference to these various patriarchal
categories, each of which denotes her status relative to a man. Lucio offers
one further category, into which she also does not fit: 'she may be a punk,
for many of them are neither maid, widow, nor wife' (5.1.178–9). The
desire of the men on stage to identify Mariana under one of these head-
ings – to make her body both literally visible and metaphorically legible in

patriarchal terms – is an important context for this chapter and exemplifies some of the problems that attach to Isabella's extra-textual veil.

I call Isabella's veil 'extra-textual' because she is, strictly speaking, a novitiate: not quite a nun. Situated within the play's historical context, one 'yet unsworn', like Isabella, would not have worn a veil (1.4.9). This status allows her to speak with Lucio and, subsequently, leave the convent to plead her brother's case before Angelo. Francisca, a full sister of the Order of St Clare, discusses veiling with Isabella explicitly upon Lucio's arrival to the convent in Act 1:

> It is a man's voice. Gentle Isabella,
> Turn you the key and know his business of him;
> You may; I may not. You are yet unsworn.
> When you have vowed, you must not speak with men
> But in the presence of the prioress.
> Then if you speak, you must not show your face;
> Or if you show your face, you must not speak. (1.4.7–14)

This is the only mention of veiling in the playtext. Additionally, as Brinda Charry points out, while 'it was customary for all married women to veil themselves' during the Middle Ages in Europe, by the fifteenth century veils had become 'associated less with modesty than with decoration'; by the Elizabethan period in England, veils were moving out of fashion entirely, with 'younger married women expos[ing] their hair'.[33] It is therefore unlikely that the boy actor playing Isabella would have been veiled in the earliest performances of *Measure for Measure*.

In the twentieth and twenty-first centuries, however, Isabella consistently appears veiled onstage. Robert N. Watson reduces the semiotic possibilities of this costuming to a choice that merely 'strengthen[s] the signals of moral conflict', but Isabella's veil actually carries a multiplicity of possible interpretations on the contemporary stage. It participates in several overlapping semiotic networks, echoing Busse's understanding of the veil in early modern literature as a 'supremely over-determined symbol'.[34] It takes part in the action onstage, as it functions scriptively (in Bernstein's sense) to shape and delimit interpretations of Isabella's character, her relationships with other characters, and her actions and choices within the drama. In particular, Isabella's veil picks up the play's interest in legibility and knowability, for the veil, according to Busse, 'exists always as paradox: it is an item both of concealment *and* revelation'.[35] As the example of Mariana's unveiling in Act 5 shows, the veil is also 'a *metonymy* for woman': 'both representative part and that which forms a network of associations, from hair to veil to dishabille to wanton coyness and amorous delay'; 'both an affirmative symbol of modesty and a negative sign of shame'.[36] The men of Vienna do not know what to do with the veiled Mariana, 'neither maid, widow, nor wife' – they can neither parse her testimony, nor place her in the realm of possible affiliations to masculine power.

Similarly, Isabella's veil marks her as other within the hypersexualised Viennese culture to which Claudio and Lucio belong, while simultaneously activating a fetishisation of virginity in Angelo, who 'desire[s] her foully for those things / That make her good' (2.2.176–7). This contradiction – embodied in her veiling – inflects both readings of the play and their interpretation of her in performance. Isabella's refusal to be coerced by Angelo, embedded always within the play's misogynist dramaturgy, has attracted a number of problematic scholarly readings. She is variously interpreted as a selfish prude (Watson suggests that she is 'unhelpfully self-involved' in her pleas for Claudio's life, for example);[37] sexually repressed and in need of 'awakening' (Anne Barton argues that her attachment to purity 'conceals an hysterical fear of sex');[38] and sexually powerful and knowing (see, for example, Watson's comment that '[e]veryone seems to have a sense of her sexual power, except maybe Isabella herself – and perhaps she does, too').[39] These scholarly readings echo staging choices and performance reviews: responses to John Barton's watershed 1970 production for the Royal Shakespeare Company cast Isabella as 'wholly selfish' (*Sunday Times*) and 'an impossible prig suffering some sort of frigidity complex', who is nonetheless, simultaneously, 'both tolerable and touching' (*Evening Standard*).[40] Dymkowski suggests that Isabella's refusal of Angelo was read more sympathetically in the UK in the 1980s, however, in light of the creeping authoritarianism and moral hypocrisy of Margaret Thatcher's government. Isabella's choice, in this context, 'no longer surfaced as an anachronistic problem for reviewers' because it threw focus onto 'the corrupt political system that could engender the deputy's behaviour' – although, of course, Thatcher's was hardly the first corrupt government in England's modern history.[41] I note that the majority of these reviews were written by cisgender white men.

This range of interpretations of Isabella's quite straightforward refusal of Angelo is, in some ways, unsurprising: patriarchy routinely punishes women who are seen as either excessively or insufficiently sexual (or sometimes, both at once – the elusive perfect balance is a moving goalpost). As the play itself demonstrates, this punishment particularly targets women who report instances of sexual harassment and violence. Manne understands this problem in terms of the system of 'asymmetrical moral support relations' that patriarchy both engenders and enforces: 'We can think of a more or less diverse set of women on whom such a man [i.e. white, cis, straight, Christian, middle class, non-disabled] is tacitly deemed entitled to rely for nurturing, comfort, care, and sexual, emotional, and reproductive labor'.[42] This asymmetrical relationship can lead to the type of victim-blaming narratives that were active in the early modern period and still attach to Isabella.[43] As Katherine Angel notes in *Tomorrow Sex Will Be Good Again*, '[w]omen know that their sexual desire can remove protection from them and can be invoked as proof that violence wasn't, in fact, violence'.[44] Framing Isabella as simultaneously repressed and sexually knowing erases the violence that Angelo, the Duke and even Claudio would enact on her, by virtue of their feeling of entitlement to her 'distinctly human services and capacities';[45] such readings entertain the possibility that she might, after all, 'want it'.

Isabella's veil, in this context, becomes overloaded with potential significations, its script stretched and challenged. As Aoife Monks argues, 'costume does far more than decorate the surface of the body'; 'rather', she says, 'it comes with risks and possibilities for the bodies and psyches of the audience and actor alike'.[46] As a piece of the actor's costume, Isabella's veil implicates her in the development and leveraging of each of these possibilities. Which of the veil's potential significations are activated through performance is determined by the alchemy that takes place between the play, the actor and the audience – informed, of course, by the 'script' that the thing itself offers.[47] In other words, interpreting the onstage veil is itself an act of appropriation: the complexity and weight of this overburdened signifier make it a vulnerable sign on stage, one whose signifieds are especially in flux. As a piece of a production's overall dramaturgy, the veil-as-costume also situates itself 'within a wider set of social power relations', and 'anchors and produces the social body within a web of social and economic relations'.[48] More specifically, the veil onstage becomes part of a 'Western tradition that favors visibility/presence over invisibility/absence and truth/light over concealment/darkness'.[49] Far from a mere symbol of moral conflict in the play – to rebut Watson's configuration – Isabella's veil speaks to her situation relative to the patriarchal structures within the fictional world of the play *and* within the society of which the production team and audience are part.

If wearing a veil in performance activates this much potential anxiety around Western Isabellas, removing her veil complicates the issue further.

Monks suggests that costuming always creates 'multiple, contradictory, uncanny bodies', which audiences parse in real-time through the course of a performance.[50] The interruption and redirection of this relationship through onstage undressing highlights the processual nature of the network connecting actor, costume, character and audience: when the costume changes, so does an audience's relationship to the body wearing it. The precise nature of that change depends upon the contexts and significations that the veil has accrued up to that point in the performance, as well as on the Haylesian nodal connections that each individual audience member might make between what they see on stage and what associations they've brought into the theatre with them.

To illustrate this point, I turn to Cheek by Jowl and Pushkin Theatre's Russian-language production of *Measure for Measure*, which premiered in Moscow in 2013 before completing various tours around the world, including a visit to the UK in 2015, where it streamed from the Barbican in London. Cheek by Jowl's is a particularly relevant production for my purposes because its geographic instability (British, Russian and global; situated and streamed) highlights the difficulty of reading Isabella's veil. In the production, Anna Khalilulina as Isabella wore a white, knee-length dress with a high neckline and long sleeves, pull-up stockings, white shoes and a white veil. Her costume presented a stark contrast to the red and black of the rest of the cast and echoed in the set and lighting designs, signifying simultaneously her difference from the 'dark corners' of Vienna, her sexual and moral purity, and her religious conviction (4.3.154). She wore her veil throughout the performance, including during a graphic sexual assault by Angelo (Andrei Kuzichev) in Act 2, scene 4, in which he removed her shoe and stocking in order to kiss up her leg. At the end of Act 5, however, when the Duke (Alexander Arsentyev) revealed that Claudio (Peter Rykov) was still alive, Khalilulina threw herself at Rykov's feet, pulling off her own veil to reveal her dark hair, cut in a short, modern bob. A few moments later, Arsentyev attempted to take the veil – still in her hands – as he made his marriage proposal. Khalilulina snatched it back, stepping away for a moment, before moving into position to waltz with him – reluctantly, the veil still hanging from the hand clasped in his. The Duke and Isabella, Claudio and Juliet, and Angelo and Mariana slowly waltzing together presented a final picture of tentative resolution: the tension between Isabella's removal of her veil – a symbol, simultaneously, of her chastity, faith and subjugation – and her insistence on holding onto it as she danced registered as an ambivalence to the play's supposedly comic ending.

The timing of this veil removal, coinciding with the revelation that Claudio had not been executed, evoked one of the valences that Busse ascribes to the veil in early modern English literature. In this reading, the veil activates particular anxieties for a culture that persists in constructing 'truth as already "there" but reliant on our penetration and liberation of it'.[51] As the truth of Claudio's redemption has been revealed to Isabella, so must she reveal herself and make herself available to 'penetration' – metaphorical and literal – by the Duke. Khalilulina's Isabella, without her veil, is both knowing and knowable, clued in at last to the extent of the Duke's machinations, and available to him as a potential wife and sexual partner. That Angelo does not remove her veil in the otherwise violent and invasive coercion scene (2.4) suggests, in the same vein, her ultimate inaccessibility to him: although he behaves violently towards her, she remains veiled both literally and metaphorically. The bed trick cements the veil's power as a dramaturgical object, keeping Isabella (who tells Angelo she will meet him only in darkness, '[u]pon the heavy middle of the night' (4.1.33)) unreachable. Mariana, Isabella and the Duke – all of whom are veiled at various points in the production – take advantage of the veil of darkness to hide the truth from Angelo, '[w]ho thinks he knows that he ne'er knew [Mariana's] body, / But knows, he thinks, that he knows Isabel's' (5.1.200–1).

Khalilulina's portrayal of Isabella also activates another of the veil's potential valences. Although white-presenting to a Western European (and more specifically, an anglophone) audience, Khalilulina's name is Turkic and, 'in combination with her appearance, identifies her as non-Slavic, thus complicating her assumed whiteness' and 'suggest[ing] the possibility of Islamic roots in her family'.[52] As M. L. Roman argues, during a 'five-year period between 1992–97', '"black" became defined [in Russia] not only as African but also as Caucasian and Central Asian', meaning that Russians with 'non-Slavic' heritage were racialised and marginalised from this point in time.[53] While Khalilulina's unveiling as Isabella is framed as voluntary in Cheek by Jowl's production, the node of her heritage links her to the violent unveiling of veiled Muslims in the West, whether through discriminatory laws and regulations or through physical violence. As recently as the Spring of 2021, the French Senate voted in support of an 'anti-separatism bill' that bans girls under the age of eighteen from veiling in public.[54] Racist hate crimes directed at women wearing hijab and other garments such as niqab have spiked periodically in North America and Europe since 11 September 2001, notably around the 'Unite the Right' rally in Charlottesville, Virginia in August 2017, and following the attack of two New Zealand mosques that killed fifty worshippers in 2019. In the latter case, Tell MAMA data shows that reports rose from an average of thirty or thirty-five per week to ninety-five reports in the week between 15 and 21 March 2019.[55]

Linking Isabella's veil and Islamic veiling creates a case study for the veil's potential appropriative power: although Shakespeare's Isabella is explicitly Christian, her appearance in twenty-first-century (and more particularly post-9/11) performances generates friction between the dramaturgy of the play and production, the actor's performance, and 'the wider set of social power relations', crystallised in the veil, within which the production takes place.[56] The post-9/11 and War on Terror sociopolitical landscape is therefore a relevant piece of the social power relations that affect how Isabella's veil can be appropriated through performance. In Bernstein's terms, the veil scripts particular readings on twenty-first-century Western stages, as its broader media portrayal tells audiences that it is a symbol of dissidence, otherness, concealment and mistrust. This script delimits, in part, the manner in which Isabella's veil can 'do things', to paraphrase Bogost.

The stakes of the 'unthought' connections I draw here between Isabella's veil and hijab have interpretive consequences beyond the theatre, too. Busse works through the implications of the veil as 'the quintessential representative of the violent regime of sight-as-knowledge in Western culture', through which the veil also becomes 'the natural metaphor for encounters with the Orient'.[57] As Edward Said notes, 'Orientalism depends for its strategy on [a] flexible *positional* superiority, which puts the Westerner in a whole series of possible relationships with the Orient without ever losing him the relative upper hand' (emphasis original).[58] This problem has recently reactivated as women in the West lamented the plight of Afghan women following the United States' withdrawal from Afghanistan and the Taliban's return to power in August 2021. As Dadabhoy puts it: '[m]ost of these folks wouldn't be able to tell you the difference between hadith, fiqh, and sharia, but they are all experts on "Islamic extremism." This positioning is Orientalist and Islamophobic.'[59] Muslim women are continually framed as universally helpless, desperate for the saving hand of the white, Christian West to 'liberate' them.

This framing of Muslim women also implies its converse: a perverse desire on the part of Western imperial patriarchy to play the part of the white saviour, uncovering and thereby rescuing the helpless hijabi. Busse places that desire in a theatrical context, noting that 'there is something about attending a play which incites a desire to see and experience *fully* the action onstage'.[60] The Duke's triumphant series of revelations at the end of *Measure for Measure* construct him as a patriarchal saviour in the same vein. His final flourish, the marriage proposal to Isabella, 'rescues' her from a cloistered and celibate life in the Order of St. Clare – never mind that she talks explicitly about her desire for such a life in Act 1, scene 4. The Duke's machinations at the end of the play highlight the extent to which the removal of Isabella's veil is always violent: it wrenches both character and performance into a misogynist dramaturgical frame, which insists that she must be married (or, at the very least, marriageable) by the end. Real-life violence towards veiled Muslims and the larger context of Islamophobia that enables it trade upon similar associations between the veil and illegibility and inaccessibility, which activate a patriarchal, extractive desire to uncover and claim.

Notes

I am grateful to the volume editors, the peer reviewers, and Nedda Mehdizadeh, Vanessa Corredera, Natalia Khomenko and Katharine Cockin for their valuable feedback. Particularly given the subject matter of this chapter, I wish to acknowledge at the outset the revolution currently taking place in Iran, sparked by the murder of Mahsa Jina Amini by the so-called 'morality police' in September 2022. I join the cry for regime change and for a new Iran. Zan, Zendegi, Azadi!

1. Penny Gay, *As She Likes It: Shakespeare's Unruly Women* (London: Routledge, 1994), 142. The *Black and British Asian Shakespeare Database* records that Simon was only the second Black woman to play Isabella in a major professional production in the UK (she was preceded by Cleo Sylvestre in 1973). 'Isabella in Measure for Measure', *Black and British Asian Shakespeare Database*, https://bbashakespeare.warwick.ac.uk/roles/play/Measure%20for%20Measure/role/Isabella. Accessed 26 February 2023.

2. For detailed production histories of *Measure for Measure* in the twentieth century, see Penny Gay, '*Measure for Measure*: Sex and Power and a Patriarchal Society', in *As She Likes It: Shakespeare's Unruly Women*, 120–42, and Christine Dymkowski, '*Measure for Measure*: Shakespeare's Twentieth-Century Play', in *Shakespeare in Stages: New Performance Histories*, ed. Christine Dymkowski and Christie Carson (Cambridge: Cambridge University Press, 2010), 164–84.

3. Lola Olufemi, *Feminism Interrupted: Disrupting Power* (London: Pluto Press, 2020), 69. See, for example, Tell MAMA's 2018 interim report, which notes that 'Muslim women, where gender data is available, account for 58% (n=233) of incidents. The targeting of Muslim women due to their overt religious identity demonstrates how the hijab (headscarf) has become

an "essentialist" way to see "Muslimness", which, in turn, "others" Muslim women through a process where their Islamic identity is perceived to embody ma[n]y of the things that are "wrong, problematic and threatening about Islam and Muslims in the West."' Faith Matters, 'Gendered Anti-Muslim Hatred and Islamophobia: Interim Report January – June 2018', *Tell MAMA: Measuring Anti-Muslim Attacks*, 29 November 2018, 3.

4. Afia Ahmed, 'The Clothes of My Faith', in *It's Not About the Burqa: Muslim Women on Faith, Feminism, Sexuality, and Race*, ed. Mariam Khan (London: Picador, 2019), 66.

5. Mona Eltahawy, 'Too Loud, Swears Too Much and Goes Too Far', in *It's Not About the Burqa: Muslim Women on Faith, Feminism, Sexuality, and Race*, ed. Mariam Khan (London: Picador, 2019), 4.

6. Ibid.

7. Rafia Zakaria, *Veil. Object Lessons* series (London: Bloomsbury Arden, 2017), 8.

8. Ambereen Dadabhoy, 'Going Global with *Measure for Measure* and Muslim #MeToo'. Keynote address. *Empowerment to Disempowerment: Intersectional Voices* symposium, Shakespeare's Globe, 10 December 2021, n.p.

9. Ibid.

10. Ibid.

11. See Theodora A. Jankowski, *Pure Resistance: Queer Virginity in Early Modern English Drama* (Philadelphia: University of Pennsylvania Press, 2000). As Jankowski argues, the nun's withdrawal is not necessarily punitive, as in Hamlet's infamous framing, but rather potentially liberatory in a society that insists upon 'male economic and social control of her physical body'; she goes so far as to suggest that women who choose virginity as an alternative 'are essentially opting out of patriarchy' (5–6).

12. Ashley Denham Busse, 'Dangerous Ornament: The Figure of the Veil in Early Modern English Literature'. Unpublished doctoral dissertation, The George Washington University, 2010, 12.

13. Zakaria, *Veil*, 8.

14. N. Katherine Hayles, *Unthought: The Power of the Cognitive Unconscious* (Chicago: University of Chicago Press, 2017), 2.

15. Ibid. 1.

16. N. Katherine Hayles, *How We Think: Digital Media and Contemporary Technogenesis* (Chicago: University of Chicago Press, 2012), 13.

17. Ibid.

18. Diana Taylor, *The Archive and the Repertoire: Performing Cultural Memory in the Americas* (Durham, NC: Duke University Press, 2003), 3.

19. Jonathan Gil Harris, *Untimely Matter in the Time of Shakespeare* (Philadelphia: University of Pennsylvania Press, 2009), 169.

20. Marvin Carlson, *The Haunted Stage: Theatre as Memory Machine* (Ann Arbor: University of Michigan Press, 2003), 2.

21. Hayles, *How We Think*, 2012.

22. Cathy Turner and Synne Behrndt, *Dramaturgy and Performance*, revised edition (London: Bloomsbury, 2016), 5.

23. Rachel Bowditch, Jeff Casazza and Annette Thornton, 'Introduction', in *Physical Dramaturgy: Perspectives from the Field*, ed. Rachel Bowditch, Jeff Casazza and Annette Thornton (London: Routledge, 2018), 1–12.

24. Kate Manne, *Down Girl: The Logic of Misogyny* (London: Penguin, 2018).

25. Ibid. 19.

26. Sarah Grochala, *The Contemporary Political Play: Rethinking Dramaturgical Structure* (London: Bloomsbury Methuen, 2017), 10, 4.

27. See Nora J. Williams, 'Incomplete Dramaturgies', *Shakespeare Bulletin* 40, no. 1 (2022): 1–22.

28. Robin Bernstein, 'Dances with Things: Material Culture and the Performance of Race', *Social Text* 27, no. 4 (2009): 67–94.

29. Although I use 'object' and 'thing' interchangeably in this chapter, Bernstein draws a distinction between them, on the basis that a 'thing forces a person into an awareness of the self in material relation to the thing'; in other words, 'an object becomes a thing when it invites a person to dance'. Bernstein, 'Dances with Things', 69–70.

30. Ibid. 69.

31. Ibid. 68–9, 86.

32. Ian Bogost, *How to Talk About Video Games* (Minneapolis: University of Minnesota Press, 2015), ix.

33. Brinda Charry, '"[T]he Beauteous Scarf": Shakespeare and the "Veil Question"', *Shakespeare* 4, no. 2 (2008): 114.

34. Robert N. Watson, 'Introduction', *Measure for Measure* by William Shakespeare, ed. A. R. Braunmuller and Robert N. Watson. Arden Shakespeare Third Series (London: Bloomsbury Arden, 2020), 69. Busse, 'Dangerous Ornament', 4.

35. Ibid. Emphasis original.

36. Ibid. 3–4. Emphasis original.

37. Watson, 'Introduction', 75.

38. Anna Kamaralli, 'Writing about Motive: Isabella, the Duke and Moral Authority', *Shakespeare Survey* 58 (2005): 48–59.

39. Watson, 'Introduction', 78.

40. Quoted in Dymkowski, '*Measure for Measure*', 166.

41. Ibid. 173.

42. Manne, *Down Girl*, xiii.

43. For more on victim-blaming in the early modern period, see Kim Solga, *Violence Against Women in Early Modern Performance: Invisible Acts* (New York: Palgrave, 2009) and Frances Dolan, *Marriage and Violence: The Early Modern Legacy* (Philadelphia: University of Pennsylvania Press, 2008).

44. Katherine Angel, *Tomorrow Sex Will Be Good Again: Women and Desire in the Age of Consent* (New York: Verso, 2021), 5.

45. Manne, *Down Girl*, xiii.

46. Aoife Monks, *The Actor in Costume* (Basingstoke: Palgrave, 2010), 3.

47. Bernstein, 'Dances with Things'.

48. Monks, *The Actor in Costume*, 7, 10.

49. Lamia Ben Youssef Zayzafoon, *The Production of the Muslim Woman: Negotiating Text, History, and Ideology* (Oxford: Lexington Books, 2005), 66.

50. Monks, *The Actor in Costume*, 12.

51. Busse, 'Dangerous Ornament', 27.

52. I am grateful to Natalia Khomenko, who provided feedback to this effect on a version of this chapter presented to the 'Embodying Difference in Global Shakespeare Performance' seminar group at the 2021 Annual Meeting of the Shakespeare Association of America. Natalia Khomenko, Personal Correspondence, 1 April 2021, n.p.

53. M. L. Roman, 'Making Caucasians Black: Moscow Since the Fall of Communism and the Racialization of Non Russians', *The Journal of Communist Studies and Transition Politics* 18, no. 2 (2002): 3. See also Nikolay Zakharov, *Race and Racism in Russia: Mapping Global Racisms* (Basingstoke: Palgrave, 2015).

54. 'French MPs approve controversial "anti-separatism" bill', *Al Jazeera*, 16 February 2021, https://www.aljazeera.com/news/2021/2/16/french-mps-approve-controversial-anti-separatism-bill. Accessed 24 August 2023.

55. See, for example, Nicola Slawson, 'Police Are Investigating After A Muslim Woman Has Her Hijab "Ripped Off Her" in London', *HuffPost*, 1 April 2019, https://www.huffingtonpost.co.uk/entry/hijab-attack-turn-pike-lane-london_uk_5ca1f954e4b0474c08d1b163. Accessed 24 August 2023; David K. Li, 'Hate Crimes in America spiked 17 percent last year, FBI says', *NBC News*, 13 November 2018, https://www.nbcnews.com/news/us-news/hate-crimes-america-spiked-17-percent-last-year-fbi-says-n935711. Accessed 24 August 2023; Chiara Giordano, 'Man arrested after Muslim woman's hijab "ripped off" on London Tube platform', *The Independent*, 2 April 2019, https://www.independent.co.uk/news/uk/crime/hijab-tube-attack-arrest-muslim-woman-turnpike-lane-london-a8850601.html. Accessed 24 August 2023; Stephanie Babych, 'Hijab torn and woman beaten in racially motivated attack in Prince's Island Park: Calgary Police', *Calgary Herald*, 22 March 2021, https://calgaryherald.com/news/crime/hijab-torn-and-woman-beaten-in-racially-motivated-attack-in-princes-island-park-calgary-police. Accessed 24 August 2023.

56. Monks, *The Actor in Costume*, 7.

57. Busse, 'Dangerous Ornament', 12.

58. Edward Said, *Orientalism* (New York: Penguin, [1978] 2003), 7.

59. Ambereen Dadabhoy, 'Islamophobic White Saviors' [blog post], *Ambereen Dadabhoy*, 29 August 2021, n.p. https://ambereendadabhoy.com/2021/08/29/islamophobic-white-saviors/. Accessed 26 February 2023.

60. Busse, 'Dangerous Ornament', 133.

10

'I have perused her well': The Hypersexualisation of Anne Boleyn in Shakespeare and Fletcher's *Henry VIII* and Showtime's *The Tudors*

Yasmine Hachimi

Anne Boleyn, the woman for whom King Henry VIII annulled his first marriage and broke with the Roman Catholic Church, has become the most famous of Henry's six wives.[1] Part of Anne's appeal are the questions still surrounding her life and death. The historical evidence available to us is heavily weighted by the religious and political biases that shaped who went on the record at the time. In addition to biased records, there is scant surviving textual evidence where she speaks for herself or in her own words.[2] Despite the lack of surviving documents in Anne's own words and perhaps because of it, Anne persists as a flashpoint of discussions about female sexuality, power and vulnerability. The questions that generally circulate around Anne are linked to her sexual agency. Arguably, several of these questions remain at the forefront of conversations about Anne and her relationship with Henry. She continues to be an occasion of speculation about female sexuality.

Popular representations of Anne explore the allure that she has held within the cultural imagination since she first made her debut at the Henrician court.[3] Extensive studies, like those by Susan Bordo and Stephanie Russo, consider the different versions or fictions of Anne created in each century, but we have not yet considered fictional representations of Anne *as* appropriations. Considering fictional representations of Anne as appropriations encourages us to recognise what happens when 'what is being "taken over" for fictional purposes really exists or existed' and draws attention to the ways in which Anne, once taken over, has become an ideal figure upon which people, and men in particular, can play out their fantasies.[4] Seeing this process as appropriation helps me to highlight its violence. This chapter focuses on Anne Boleyn's early courtship with Henry and explores the ways in which William Shakespeare and John Fletcher's *Henry VIII, or All Is True*[5] and Showtime's *The Tudors* fictionalise and appropriate Anne Boleyn as a sexual object to contain female sexual ambiguity and perform it in accordance with the misogynist male gaze of popular culture. I argue that male appropriations of Anne represent her pornographically, a tendency that culminates in *The Tudors* but can be seen in the earliest historical fiction about Anne as well. Although these historically distant appropriations use socially relevant tropes active at the time of production to highlight the erotics of passivity and agency, they accomplish the same end. *The Tudors* series exploits its visual medium – television – to make explicit and confirm what is latent in Shakespeare and Fletcher's play. Recognising how these directorial and appropriative choices operate both within the text and with the text to direct Anne perpetuates conversations about her body and sexuality and limits Anne's agency by denying her the right to perform her own identity.

All Eyes on Anne in *All Is True*

Shakespeare and Fletcher's *All Is True* (1613) invites audiences to understand the play, and by extension the archival documents on which it is based, as fictionalisations of the historical record. Allison Machlis Meyer has helped us to see how Shakespeare and Fletcher's appropriation of intertextual sources privileges multiple perspectives that remind readers and audiences of the contrasting histories in the public imaginary.[6] I suggest that *All Is True*, beginning with the prologue, invites us to overlay the fictions that we find most compelling onto the real-life characters, essentially fictionalising them 'as they were living' (Prologue 27). Like many of Shakespeare's history plays, *All Is True* relies heavily on historical sources such as Holinshed's *Chronicles* and the play asks us to fictionalise history by blurring these boundaries. For example, Shakespeare and Fletcher versify almost the entirety of Holinshed's account of Katherine[7] of Aragon's speech to Henry, which took place during a special legatine court that was convened to determine the fate of Henry and Katherine's marriage.[8] By replicating historical chronicles onstage while simultaneously calling the truth into question with the alternate title, *All Is True*, the play encourages audiences to consider how historical documents shape popular interpretations of historical figures and calls on readers as the interpreters of truth.[9] So the audience is tasked with interpreting the truth about Anne and whether or not she actively pursued Henry. While contrasting histories depict Anne as either a homewrecker or a martyr, *All Is True* presents an appropriation of Anne whose desirability and utility is predicated solely on her ability to sexually satisfy the king and reproduce.

The directorial status of men who attempt to shape how we see Anne Boleyn is written into her first scene in the play. Anne first appears onstage with a bevy of female courtiers, all of whom have congregated for his majesty's pleasure. As the Chamberlain approaches the group, he begins to direct them:

> Sweet ladies, will it please you sit? Sir Harry,
> Place you that side; I'll take charge of this:
> His grace is entering. Nay, you must not freeze;
> Two women placed together makes cold weather:
> My Lord Sands, you are one will keep 'em waking;
> Pray, sit between these ladies. (1.4.19–24)

The Chamberlain manages the entire scene, providing Lord Sands with an opportunity to flirt and gain the favours of the women surrounding him.[10] Anne, like the rest of the ladies, is an ornamental figure that can easily be moved around to suit the whims of the court and create a pleasing picture for Henry to see upon his entrance. Kim H. Noling suggests that Anne's visibility 'comes not from positions that she assumed according to her own will, but from positions determined for her by other characters'.[11] Compared to other Shakespeare plays in which stage directions are rather sparse,[12] *All Is True* is noteworthy for its robust use of descriptive stage directions, many of which coalesce around Anne, thus highlighting the directive and appropriative behaviours of men.[13] Women are directed into positions that leave them physically vulnerable to the advances of male courtiers, like Sands, who inserts himself between Anne and another lady under the guise of providing body heat. But it is Henry, who comes into the scene later, who will single Anne out from the crowd and place her body at the centre of the stage, making her the object of his and the audience's gaze.[14]

Throughout the play both men and women sexualise Anne and in doing so, appropriate her and deny her the right to perform her own identity. Henry's desire to take Anne as his wife is revealed in a private scene between Anne and the Old Lady when Anne insists by her 'troth and maidenhead' that she will not be queen (2.3.24). The Old Lady responds, 'Beshrew me, I would, / And venture maidenhead for't; and so would you, / For all this spice of your hypocrisy' (2.3.25–6). The

Old Lady calls into question Anne's disinterest in becoming queen and
presents the possibility that Anne does not have a maidenhead to risk
losing. Anne, as the object of appropriation, is constantly vulnerable to
people overwriting her voice, which is evident when they call her a liar or
hypocrite. The blend of history and fiction already marks Anne as wanton
and underpins the assumption that she is probably not a virgin. The Old
Lady quickly moves on to assess Anne's attributes, including her 'fair parts
of woman', and 'woman's heart', and assures Anne that 'the capacity /
of your soft cheveril conscience would receive, / If you might please
to stretch it' (1.4.31–3).[15] Each of Anne's parts will pave her way to the
king's bed and to a position of power, if she would only make herself
sexually available to the king. The Old Lady is mistaken perhaps in thinking that Anne's sexualisation affords her some degree of agency, however.
In making these assumptions, the Old Lady makes similar appropriations
to men, but for completely different purposes and implies Anne's complicity in her objectification. The Old Lady's bawdy jokes not only set
Anne 'in a sexual light', as Micheli points out in her work on the play,
but also pose a potential threat to Anne's reputation because the Old
Lady would be privy to her secrets.[16] Additionally, the Old Lady's words
invite the possibility that she knows things about Anne that we do not
know and invites speculation about Anne's sexual history, which has the
effect of reinforcing the archival material that implicates her as a whore.
Ultimately, the Old Lady's insinuations suggest that it isn't only men who
sexualise Anne and shows us that she is vulnerable to everyone: women
as well as men, from aristocrats like Lord Sands to the lowliest servant.
There is no safe space outside of surveillance and judgement for Anne.

The assumptions that are overlaid onto Anne are because of her
attractiveness and this is the dominant theme of the play. We see another
example of this when Henry sends a servant to Anne's chamber. After
delivering a present to Anne on behalf of the king, the Chamberlain takes
a moment to tell the audience:

> I have perused her well;
> Beauty and honour in her are so mingled
> That they have caught the king: and who knows yet
> But from this lady may proceed a gem
> To lighten all this isle? (2.3.75–9)

It seems fitting that as the household manager, the Chamberlain is playing
the part of a pander sent to peruse and evaluate the goods before the king

takes Anne to his bedchamber.[17] As an extension of the king, the Chamberlain maximises Anne's display potential in this scene by speaking in an aside, so that Anne remains on stage and within the scope of the audience's vision. The Chamberlain admits that Henry's attraction to Anne is primarily based on his attraction to her beauty and honour, although the sexualised appropriations of Anne suggest that it was her beauty and not her honour that first caught the king's eye. The idea of honour, however, is applied to Anne by men and is another way of directing her. The combination of sexual desirability and honour is unstable because of the implicit assumptions, evinced by the Old Lady, that sexual attractiveness means agency and ambition. Ultimately, the Chamberlain's perusal of Anne is driven by sexual anxiety because the safety of the country relies on the king having a living son.[18] But while Anne's attractiveness is what draws men to her and makes her a prime candidate for the king's bed, she does not invite the attention she receives.

Anne's character is indiscernible primarily because we do not hear from her very often. Although Anne is a major character in the play, she rarely speaks, and has only 58 lines compared to Katherine's 357.[19] Micheli expertly notes the many points of contrast between Katherine and Anne: age vs youth, royalty vs petty nobility, assertiveness vs compliance, moral virtue vs sexual appeal, everyday vs holiday virtues and falling vs rising fortunes.[20] This juxtaposition is further emphasised by the way Katherine and Anne speak. While Katherine gives speeches and is respected by those around her, Anne's lines are limited and she struggles to maintain her autonomy. Rebecca Quoss-Moore argues that Anne's representation is subject to the audience as much as to Henry and while I agree, I would also suggest that the audience filters their perspective through what characters say because Anne does not speak for herself.[21] According to All Is True, Anne Boleyn was an ornament, a beautiful woman to be adored, a vessel for the king's heir, a woman reduced to her reproductive potential, a supplicant, a figure of male fantasies and desires. By reducing her this way, Shakespeare and Fletcher conflate fiction with history like they do in the prologue, because history is defined by lineage. Anne is contained here by her silence and her sexuality is conflated with the body politic. Speaking would mean that the appropriators (whether it be Henry, a servant, or Shakespeare and Fletcher) would have to deal with her as a real person, rather than a symbol onto which they can project their fantasies. In the early twenty-first century, this agency is articulated but in a more covertly misogynistic way, as Anne is reimagined as a more active seductress, complete with her own sultry voice.

Sex without Liberation in Showtime's *The Tudors*

From 2007 to 2010, Showtime's *The Tudors* captivated audiences with
its titillating and erotic depiction of King Henry VIII and his court.[22]
Considering its relation to previous historical dramas, Jerome De Groot
notes how 'The show's confidence in foregrounding sex demonstrates its
self-consciousness in rejecting the norms of historical drama and also its
historiographic investment in suggesting that Henry was not that different
from a modern celebrity.'[23] Viewers are introduced to Henry in the opening sequence of the show as the commanding voice of Jonathan Rhys
Meyers says, 'You think you know a story, but you only know how it
ends. To get to the heart of the story, you have to go back to the beginning.'[24] Like Shakespeare and Fletcher's *All Is True*, *The Tudors* begins
with claims about historical truth, but creator and showrunner Michael
Hirst insists that 'Just like Shakespeare's history plays, they [*The Tudors*
and *Vikings*] only start with some historical facts, then the drama takes
over. You can't have both.'[25] The show's opening sequence assumes that
viewers might have previous knowledge about Henry VIII and invites us
to reconsider what we think we know about England's most notorious
king and his court.[26]

Much like Shakespeare and Fletcher's play, Showtime's *The Tudors*
sexualises Anne, but it exceeds its early modern predecessor by painting her as an enchanting seductress.[27] Part of the seduction is, of course,
Natalie Dormer, the attractive actress playing the role of Anne Boleyn.[28]
The other part of Anne's seduction is made possible by Showtime, a network known for suggestive and explicit content, which exploits Anne's
sexuality even more. On *The Tudors*, we see the sexual fantasies characters have of Anne in *All Is True* play out on screen. Whereas in seventeenth-century stagings of *All Is True* desire is mapped onto the body of
a boy actor playing Anne, on *The Tudors*, desire is mapped onto Natalie
Dormer's body, which directly links the fantasy to an actual female body.
Desire is also written into Anne's character because the show emphasises
Dormer's attractiveness, which is a classic misogynistic tactic that claims
she 'wanted it' because of how she looks. As we have seen, the Old
Lady in *All Is True* expresses the notion that Anne's attractiveness invites
and warrants male attention. Ultimately, on the screen, Dormer's body
becomes a kind of shorthand for the misogynistic logic that appropriates Anne. Elena Woodacre argues that 'Anne's increasingly ambitious
and hypersexualized portrayal can be seen as a reflection of modernised
society, reframing Anne as a sexually liberated, proto-feminist figure that

twenty-first century women might be able to relate to.'[29] But this isn't progress. Anne is repurposed to fit the needs of modern storytellers and audiences, who want a more active, vibrant and feisty modern woman, but in giving Anne autonomy, the show paradoxically reveals that it is still profoundly uncomfortable with that level of sexual assertiveness. The only way they can imagine Anne to be in control is to portray her as devious. *The Tudors* echoes Shakespeare and Fletcher's play in how it sits in the middle ground of performing and appropriating history. The television medium takes Anne's silence as an invitation to look and designs her as something to be looked at. *The Tudors* perpetuates and expands the hypersexualisation of Anne, using the culture of the time to make this explicit and titillating to the contemporary viewer.

One of the first glimpses of Anne Boleyn at the English court is during the historic Field of the Cloth of Gold meeting, where Mary Boleyn (Perdita Weeks) searches for Anne in a crowded tent and finds her in a corner, surrounded by admirers ('Simply Henry'). Anne turns her head towards her sister and offers the camera a tantalising grin.[30] The next time we see Anne, the camera is focused on a black falcon with a blurry female figure approaching.[31] As the figure draws closer and the camera focuses, we see Anne walking towards and kneeling before her father, Thomas Boleyn (Nick Dunning),[32] in what Laura Mulvey refers to as the feminine position of 'to-be-looked-at-ness'.[33] With the king's interest in Mary dwindling, Boleyn suggests that Anne supplant her as the king's mistress and asks, 'Perhaps you could imagine a way to keep his interest more prolonged? I daresay you learned things in France. How to play his passions?'[34] There's something deep and dangerous in you, Anne. *Those eyes of yours are like dark hooks for the soul*' ('Simply Henry').[35] Recognising Anne's beauty as foreign and dangerous, Boleyn demonises his daughter's attractiveness and equates male inability to resist it to something dangerous and inherent in women.[36] This is similar to the way in which the Old Lady ascribes agency to Anne based on assumptions about her sexual availability in *All Is True*. When Anne hesitates to take up this task, Boleyn strokes her cheek the same way he stroked the glistening dark feathers of the falcon. The falcon is a predator, but she is also a common figure for a wife – tamed, obedient and intimate with her master.[37] Like the falcon, Anne is a predator who is being primed for the hunt in her master's service.[38] She is also directed by men, much like Anne in *All Is True*, but because *The Tudors* is a modern appropriation, the ways that men direct Anne are more overtly weaponised. On the show, Anne's objective is to seduce the king of England for her family's advancement, and her father or the family urges her to achieve this objective by using her sexuality, but only in ways that accord to the standards and expectations of established 'sexual scripts'.[39] This image – Anne as the subject of men who wish to control her sexuality according to their own desires – consistently appears in Tudor adaptations and suggests that her family's interest in her is limited to her ability to manipulate the king.[40]

The Tudors may have changed the way audiences think about historical dramas, but it didn't really change how they think about Anne. Like previous depictions, it focuses on how men appropriate Anne's body for political uses. Anne's father and uncle, the Duke of Norfolk (Henry Czerny), regularly share the screen while plotting and planning how best to use Anne to their family's advantage.[41] In one such scene, Norfolk asks Boleyn if he has found a way to arrange for Anne to meet Henry. Boleyn confirms the arrangement has been made and that Anne will 'find a way to draw his attention' to which Norfolk responds, 'Good. Once she opens her legs for him, she can open her mouth and denounce Wolsey' ('Simply Henry'). This is an example of how speech is not always self-expression or power and how men place their speech in Anne's mouth while they look at her body. Norfolk goes on to say that 'the sharpest blades are sheathed in the softest pouches'. Boleyn and Norfolk anticipate using Anne's desirability and sexuality as a weapon that will enable her to influence Henry's political decisions. Ramona Wray argues that the show explores 'previously uncharted representational territory' and is a 'radical revision' of the Tudors in the popular imaginary,[42] and while I agree that The Tudors was a departure from previous historical dramas,[43] the overall depiction of Anne as a sexual object is strikingly familiar.[44] Whether it's referred to as a 'soft pouch' in The Tudors or 'soft cheveril' in Shakespeare and Fletcher's All Is True, Anne's body and her vagina, in particular, get a lot of attention because of the 'strain' they are expected to endure and the work they are supposed to perform.[45] They are what define her; their attractiveness and function, sexually and reproductively. Anne is the sum of her parts, particularly the parts that serve the king's pleasure.

Anne exists as much as a fantasy as she does a real woman in the show, and this blending of fiction and reality echoes Shakespeare and Fletcher's appropriation. As Henry's attraction for Anne grows, he has a particularly poignant fantasy where he walks into the Great Hall and sees Anne standing in a burnished gold dress ('Wolsey, Wolsey, Wolsey!'). He smirks and Anne seems to silently accept the unspoken challenge and begins running away from him in a game of cat and mouse. Henry's desire for Anne is written on his face and when he approaches a wall that separates him from Anne, his hand slowly grazes the wall's surface as though he was running his hungry hands across the soft contours of Anne's body. Henry finds Anne lying across the royal dais and as he puts his hand up her skirt she says, 'no, not like this . . . seduce me. Write letters to me, and poems, I love poems . . . Ravish me with your words. Seduce me' and disappears behind a closed door. The fantasy that Anne is an object of pleasure is extended to courtiers, servants and audiences of Shakespeare and Fletcher's *All Is True* and comes full circle in *The Tudors*, when Henry dreams that Anne will not only sate his pleasure but that she desires him too. Anne is a fantasy – both for good and ill – of desirability and agency. Henry fantasises about Anne's agency, then panics and lashes out when he thinks she is empowered to want other men.

Henry's fantasy effortlessly moves from Anne's desire to be seduced by Henry's words, to the possibility of the long-hoped-for ravishment when an out-of-breath Henry opens the door to find Anne undressed and completely naked, in the Venus pudica pose.[46] He smiles and the scene cuts to a sweat-drenched Henry violently waking from a dream. Henry's fantasies are a visual reality for viewers who see Anne's naked body, presenting her as an object of desire in a way that was unavailable for staged theatrical performances in the early seventeenth century. We are invited to share his fantasy and it is reminiscent of *All Is True* by making a private moment of sexual activity a public activity, which echoes the general male gaze of contemporary media. Robert Schultz notes how Mulvey's work considers the ways in which 'a film's gaze overcomes male sexual anxiety, bringing female characters under a controlling surveillance or rendering them as pleasure-giving fetish objects'.[47] Using the dream sequence, *The Tudors* submits Anne to the male gaze and presents her as an object of fetishisation for both Henry and viewers at home. Anne's Venus pose is a visual cue to audiences of this fetishisation, particularly for those who are aware that Venus is the Roman goddess of love, beauty, desire, sex and fertility.[48] It also hints at the possibility that Anne will fulfil Henry's desire to have a son since Venus was the mother of Rome through her son, Aeneas. Anne's actions in the dream sequence can easily be interpreted as a reflection of her reciprocated sexual desire for the king, making her complicit in his fantasies. This, however, is not the case since Anne has yet to voice any personal attraction towards Henry even though the voice she is given in Henry's fantasy expresses longing for Henry. Casting the young and handsome Jonathan Rhys Meyers as Henry VIII empowers Anne sexually and makes the assumption that he's attractive enough for her to want him, which ultimately writes Anne's sexual desire onto her. This taps into deeply misogynistic assumptions about women and suggests that the advances of attractive men are always welcome. Furthermore, it conflates contemporary media hotness (specifically white men) with the political authority that is presumed to make powerful men desirable in Shakespeare and Fletcher's play.[49]

Henry's dream becomes a reality in the following episode when he meets Anne in the Great Hall late one evening ('His Majesty, The King') and we see a conflation of sex and violence that haunts Anne and has done so from the beginning. Because of his power, Henry realises his fantasies, which affirms the supremacy of the powerful male gaze. As Anne's outstretched hand meets Henry's, he whispers, 'I've dreamt of this moment a long time. Anne, you must know that I desire you with all my heart.' Henry's hand runs up the length of her arm, skims her shoulder and lingers on her neck before gripping her throat. This gesture suggests that hostility is often built into the sexualisation of women, which underpins *All Is True*, and is made explicit and titillating in *The Tudors*. Rather than appearing shocked, Anne smirks, making it plain to viewers that she not only expected this hostile response, but most likely orchestrated the previous scene where Henry sees Anne engaged in an intense conversation with a young man. The audience has already been introduced to Anne's brother, George Boleyn (Pádraic Delaney), but Henry has not. Henry's misperception of the exchange between Anne and George foreshadows the incest accusations that will send the siblings to the Tower in season 2 and creates speculation about the nature of their close familial bond. It invites the audience to see her as Henry does – to share his appropriating gaze. Using her brother to make Henry jealous is one of the many unsavoury tactics that is imposed upon Anne by men, in this case Michael Hirst, as a way of suggesting that she ensnared Henry and shows us that sexualised women are dangerous. Tom Betteridge's work on Henry VIII and popular culture acknowledges the way '*The Tudors* depicts Henry as losing himself in a fantasy of female sexual promiscuity'.[50] I would also add violence to Betteridge's assessment. The threat of male competition combined with the possibility that Anne's affections might lie elsewhere arouse Henry's violent predilections.[51] With a smirk that suggests Anne expected and even provoked Henry's violence, the show portrays her as a promiscuous woman who traverses the boundaries of social propriety and on some level invites everything that happens to her. At this point, *The Tudors* does not care whether or not Anne is actually interested in Henry as a lover, because it subscribes to the idea that sexy women enjoy arousing and stringing men along. The show depicts Anne's manipulation of Henry as much more strategic than the courtship represented in

Shakespeare and Fletcher's *All Is True*, which suggests that regardless of how much agency she is shown to have, Anne always submits to Henry and his desires.

Conclusion

From an almost mute mannequin to a vibrant sexual seductress, Anne Boleyn continues to be a hypersexualised figure of male fantasies and desires within adaptations and appropriations. Examining Shakespeare and Fletcher's *Henry VIII, or All Is True* and Showtime's *The Tudors* side by side shows how male appropriations of Anne represent her pornographically, occlude her interiority and limit her agency. These appropriations of Anne, written almost 500 years apart, are an important reminder that however much has changed in our understanding of gender and sexuality, the depiction of Anne as a sexual seductress remains surprisingly consistent. After watching *The Tudors*, viewers come to other adaptations and appropriations of this history that they encounter with extra-textual knowledge of the actors' bodies and movements.[52] Indeed, the audiences of Tudor adaptations are primed, or pre-eroticised, having already seen Anne Boleyn's naked body on *The Tudors* from multiple vantage points and in multiple positions. The traces of Hirst/Dormer's Anne Boleyn exist in the popular imaginary and can easily influence a modern audience's experience of the early modern play and its interpretation of Anne's character, regardless of what is written on the page or performed on stage. As the entertainment industry produces more content written and directed by women, it will be interesting to see if historical dramas will move away from the male gaze and pornographic appropriations of Anne in favour of more feminist portrayals, or if the sexual objectification of Anne will continue to be a long-held tradition that shows no signs of stopping.

Notes

1. This research came out of a graduate seminar with Professor Frances Dolan, who has championed me and my endeavours throughout my graduate school journey and beyond. I would also like to thank Louise Geddes, Geoffrey Way and Kathryn Vomero Santos for shepherding this work into the chapter you are reading today and for the support, patience and care they showed me throughout the publication process. Lastly, to Rebecca L. Fall for helping me work through final revisions.

2. Aside from a handful of letters written to Thomas Boleyn and Cardinal Wolsey, and a couplet written in Anne's Book of Hours, few traces of her voice survive in the archive.

3. Anne Boleyn has provoked fantasy and speculation since the sixteenth century, including in the love letters Henry wrote to her, so the process was underway before her death and long before Shakespeare and Fletcher.

4. Julie Sanders, *Adaptation and Appropriation* (New York: Routledge, 2016), 176.

5. Henceforth I will be referring to the play as *All Is True*.

6. For more on this see Allison Machlis Meyer, 'Multiple Histories: Cultural Memory and Anne Boleyn in *Actes and Monuments* and *Henry VIII*', *Borrowers and Lenders: The Journal of Shakespeare and Appropriation* 9, no. 2 (2015).

7. Katherine's name is spelled differently in different places, but I've chosen to use the play's spelling since my emphasis is on the fictionalisation of Katherine and her status as a fantasy.

8. Julie Sanders notes how this is an instance in which 'we might wish to register how authors and directors are stretching history to ask important ethical questions about the everyday and about the here and now, as well as about our individual and collective engagements with the past(s)'. Sanders, *Adaptation and Appropriation*, 184.

9. Out of all of Shakespeare's history plays, *Henry VIII or All Is True* is the only play that has this subtitle and makes such claims. For more on the reception of Shakespeare's plays, see Nigel Wood's *Shakespeare and Reception Theory* (London: Bloomsbury Arden, 2020).

10. Although he is listed as Lord Sandys in the List of Rolls, I will be referring to him as Sands, as he is called in the actual play.

11. Kim H. Noling, 'Grubbing Up the Stock: Dramatizing Queens in *Henry VIII*', *Shakespeare Quarterly* 39, no. 3 (1988): 299.

12. There is, of course, the possibility of editors adding directions over time. For detailed studies and discussions of stage directions, see *Stage Directions and Shakespearean Theatre*, ed. Sarah Dustagheer and Gillian Woods (London: Arden Shakespeare, 2017).

13. While most of Shakespeare's stage directions are embedded in the dialogue, *All Is True* stages Anne Boleyn's coronation and includes detailed directions. The Arden Shakespeare cites this scene as one of the only onstage re-enactments of a royal coronation.

14. Linda Micheli cites this as the moment that visually establishes the attraction between Henry and Anne. Micheli, '"Sit By Us": Visual Imagery and the Two Queens in Henry VIII', *Shakespeare Quarterly* 38, no. 4 (1987): 457. This is also the only scene in the play that Henry and Anne share together.

15. This is a kind of blazon and the Old Lady's figuration links Anne's conscience and her vagina, so that even her physically intangible parts are genital.

16. Linda Micheli, '"Sit By Us"', 459.

17. The Lord Chamberlain was the head of the Chamber, which comprised the 'above-stairs' apartments where the king lived. From 1526, his department had two sections: the Privy Chamber, which looked after the king's personal needs; and the Great Chamber, comprising the outward chambers and the Privy Wardrobes. The role of Lord Chamberlain was both administrative and political because he often advised the king or spoke for him in the Council or Parliament (Weir 58).

18. Robert Schultz, 'When Men Look at Women: Sex in an Age of Theory', *The Hudson Review* 48, no. 3 (1995): 368.

19. Noling, 'Grubbing Up the Stock', 299. The list of roles includes an overwhelming number of men (thirty-seven) and four women (Katherine, Anne, Old Lady and Patience), with a list of other characters including courtiers, attendants, servants, musicians, etc.

20. Micheli, '"Sit By Us"', 454.

21. Rebecca Quoss-Moore, 'The Political Aesthetics of Anne Boleyn in *Henry VIII*', in *The Palgrave Handbook of Shakespeare's Queens*, ed. Kavita Mudan Finn and Valerie Schutte (New York: Palgrave Macmillan, 2018), 271.

22. *The Tudors* is an Emmy-award winning show created by English screenwriter and producer Michael Hirst, also known for History Channel's, *Vikings*, as well as for his films *Elizabeth* and *Elizabeth: Golden Age*.

23. Jerome De Groot, 'Slashing History: *The Tudors*', in *Tudorism: Historical Imagination and the Appropriation of the Sixteenth Century*, ed. Tatiana C. String and Marcus Graham Bull (Oxford: Oxford University Press, 2011), 251.

24. Michael Hirst, 'In Cold Blood', *The Tudors*, Season 1, episode 1. Showtime, 1 April 2007.

25. Quoted in Dalya Alberge, 'Martin Scorsese Teams up with British Writer for Epic Take on the Romans', *The Guardian*, 10 February 2018, http://www.theguardian.com/film/2018/feb/11/martin-scorsese-romans-tv-series-caesars-british-writer-michael-hirst. Accessed 25 August 2023. Hirst's open familiarity with *All Is True* suggests that it is one of the texts that informed and possibly inspired Hirst's depiction of the Tudor court. We can perhaps consider Hirst's appropriation of Anne Boleyn to also be an appropriation of Shakespeare and Fletcher's Anne.

26. For more on the opening sequence of *The Tudors*, see Ramona Wray, 'Henry's Desperate Housewives: *The Tudors*, the Politics of Historiography, and the Beautiful Body of Jonathan Rhys Meyers', in *The English Renaissance in Popular Culture: An Age for All Time*, ed. Greg Colón Semenza (New York: Palgrave Macmillan, 2010), 25–42.

27. *The Tudors* was filmed for and by Showtime, a premium television network, as opposed to more traditional venues for historical dramas.

28. Michael Hirst, the writer and creator of *The Tudors*, has been unabashedly vocal about the decision to cast attractive actors who do not necessarily fit

the mould of the historical characters they are portraying, in order to attract a wider audience to a historical drama. For more on Hirst's approach to the show and interviews from the cast, see Susan Bordo, *The Creation of Anne Boleyn*.

29. Elena Woodacre, 'Early Modern Queens on Screen: Victors, Victims, Villains, Virgins, and Viragoes', in *Premodern Rulers and Postmodern Viewers: Gender, Sex, and Power in Popular Culture*, ed. Janice North, Karl C. Alvestad and Elena Woodacre (Basingstoke: Palgrave Macmillan, 2018), 33.

30. Moments later Mary whispers to Anne that the king has asked to see Mary in his chambers, in private, which leads to the start of Mary and Henry's affair.

31. Anne's heraldic symbol was the white falcon. Eric Ives, *The Life and Death of Anne Boleyn* (Malden: Blackwell Publishing, 2005), 221.

32. For the rest of this chapter, I will be referring to Anne's father as 'Boleyn'.

33. Laura Mulvey, 'Visual Pleasure and Narrative Cinema', in *Issues in Feminist Film Criticism*, ed. Patricia Erens (Bloomington: Indiana University Press), 62.

34. In a conversation with Henry about the French Court, Thomas Boleyn tells him that 'it has a reputation for loose morals and licentiousness'. He assures the king that his daughters, who spent the past few years in the French court, have not been sullied by their surroundings because of their goodness. Hirst, 'In Cold Blood', *The Tudors*, Season 1, episode 1. Showtime, 1 April 2007.

35. My emphasis.

36. Lauren Mackay's recently published book, *Among the Wolves of Court*, dispels the narrative that Thomas Boleyn was a manipulative, uncaring man who pushed his daughters towards Henry VIII. Mackay, *Among the Wolves of Court: The Untold Story of Thomas and George Boleyn* (London: Bloomsbury, 2020).

37. Falcon imagery also appears in two other Shakespeare plays: *Othello* and *Taming of the Shrew*. Petruchio compares taming Kate to taming a hawk (which, like the falcon, is a bird of prey) and when Othello doubts Desdemona's fidelity, he refers to her as a hawk that is no longer tame.

38. Later in the series, Anne will criticise George Boleyn for drawing an image of Anne's falcon devouring a pomegranate, the sigil of Katherine of Aragon.

39. Carissa M. Harris discusses 'sexual scripts' in her book, *Obscene Pedagogies: Transgressive Talk and Sexual Education in Late Medieval Britain* (Ithaca, NY: Cornell University Press, 2018).

40. When Anne recovers from the sweating sickness in a later episode, her father says, 'Praise be to God. You know what you've done child? You've risen from the dead. Now you can see the king again. It can be just as before.' Hirst, 'Message to the Emperor', *The Tudors*, Season 1, episode 7. Showtime, 13 May 2007.

41. Henceforth, I will be referring to Thomas Howard as Norfolk.

42. Wray, 'Henry's Desperate Housewives'.

43. For more on how *The Tudors* undresses the costume drama, see De Groot's 'Slashing History: *The Tudors*'.

44. Anne Boleyn becomes a more fleshed out character in season 2, where we see her actively engaging in and influencing political and religious change. In interviews after her contract with Showtime was over, Natalie Dormer admitted that this change was the result of her insistence that Anne should not be portrayed as a tart, but rather a strong and intelligent woman. The character shift is most notable when comparing the final scene in season 1 where Henry and Anne have a half-naked romp in a forest ('The Death of Wolsey'), with the opening of season 2, where Anne is at prayer and conservatively dressed in black from the neck down ('Everything is Beautiful'). However, the character shift is reminiscent of the virgin/whore dichotomy and is therefore still limited in its portrayal of Anne.

45. The Latin meaning of vagina is a 'sheath' for a sword.

46. For more on the Venus pudica pose, see Valerie Traub, *The Renaissance of Lesbianism in Early Modern England* (Cambridge: Cambridge University, 2002), 117.

47. Robert Schultz, 'When Men Look at Women: Sex in an Age of Theory', *The Hudson Review* 48, no. 3 (1995): 368.

48. For more on Venus and her Greek counterpart Aphrodite, see *The Encyclopædia Britannica*, 'Venus', http://www.britannica.com/topic/Venus-goddess. Accessed 25 August 2023.

49. For more on masculinity in costume dramas, see Basil Glynn, 'The Conquests of Henry VIII: Masculinity, Sex and the National Past in *The Tudors*', in *Television, Sex and Society: Analyzing Contemporary Representations*, ed. Basil Glynn, James Aston and Beth Johnson (New York: Continuum 2012) 157–71 and Wray, 'Henry's Desperate Housewives'.

50. Tom Betteridge, 'Henry VIII and popular culture', in *Henry VIII and His Afterlives: Literature, Politics, and Art*, ed. Mark Rankin, Christopher Highley and John N. King (Cambridge: Cambridge University Press, 2009), 214–15.

51. For more on this see Mark Breitenberg, 'Anxious Masculinity: Sexual Jealousy in Early Modern England', *Feminist Studies* 19, no. 2 (1993): 377–98 and Frances E. Dolan, *Marriage and Violence: The Early Modern Legacy* (Philadelphia: University of Pennsylvania Press, 2008).

52. For example, viewers might recognise Natalie Dormer from her role as Margaery Tyrell from HBO's *Game of Thrones*. On both shows, Dormer plays a sly, cunning seductress, whose close relationship with her brother sparks suspicions of incest.

11

Trammelling up the Consequence: Making Shakespeare Fiction

Andrew James Hartley

This will not be an argument so much as a reflective narrative. It is also the first time I have tried to set down some thoughts on what became a milestone in my professionally hybrid identity, and as such it functions as a kind of literary therapy, a working out – or towards – a more fluid middle ground between the old binaries used to delineate what we think Shakespeare in performance is, or should be. The popular forms of those binaries include words like 'straight' and 'adaptation', 'original' as opposed to 'derived from'. Then there are the conceptually soft honorifics like 'true to' or 'in the spirit of', and a host of cautiously optimistic nouns for the thing itself: a 'retelling', a 'reimagining', an 'interrogation of', a 'take on', a 'response to'. They amass like fog making the objects at its heart ever harder to make out, though perhaps that is because the performative object is itself no more substantial than the fog, a shadow cast by something else, some 'original' we think we know to be firmer, more precise, while its adaptive, performative shadow distorts as the light shifts.

Rather than taking a macro theoretical approach, using specifics to illustrate the larger play of ideas, I'm going to take a less scholarly route and talk about how a particular pair of 'productions' (a term you may want to debate) came to be. What follows foregrounds not so much the scented smoke of 'the creative process' as it does the series of accidents, happy and otherwise, which are the stuff of all practical production, however much their consequences get retro-fitted as intent. It is a personal reflection, enmeshed, conflicted, unsure of itself, because that's how I feel about the productions themselves, though they were successful in the terms by which such things are usually measured. Some of that uncertainty is rooted in the form of the productions in question, a form which further falls between – or slithers through – the cracks of the old binaries, being a genre of performative adaptation which rarely gets much academic scrutiny: novelisations written expressly (and initially exclusively) for performance as audiobooks.

First, the back story. In 2009 I was asked by thriller writer Doug Preston to contribute an essay to a collection compiled by the International Thriller Writers organisation entitled *Thrillers: 100 Must Reads* edited by David Morrell (of *First Blood*, aka 'Rambo' fame) and Hank Wagner. The essays would be about significant thrillers from the past as experienced by contemporary thriller writers, but would include works not generally considered in that genre and would have a wide historical scope (I think the earliest title in the collection is *Theseus and the Minotaur*). Because the editors knew of my work as a Shakespearean, I was asked to write something on *Titus Andronicus*.[1] I asked if I could write about *Macbeth* instead, and did so, talking about the play not in terms of the issues that would undergird my usual teaching strategy, but in terms of how the story works, its pacing and its dramatic effects.

Fast forward to the New York release party/signing for the book in July 2010 when I was seated, by accident of alphabet, with a British mystery author called David Hewson. We got talking and he inquired if there had been many novels based on *Macbeth*. I found myself struggling to come up with many, and very few that were fairly 'straight' retellings of the play's core story rather than radical adaptations. Perhaps, we wondered, we might do one together. Earlier in the day, David had been approached by Steve Feldberg, the head of Audible (the audiobook publisher and distributor housed with Amazon) who was on the hunt for original content. When he dropped by our table, we pitched Steve the idea for a *Game of Thrones*-esque *Macbeth* written in contemporary prose but set more or less in the period of the original Scottish king. A deal was struck almost immediately.

My last use of Shakespeare in fiction (*What Time Devours* – an instance of the inevitable and ubiquitous 'lost manuscript' subgenre) had done my career as a novelist no great favours,[2] and I had a couple of other Shakespeare-y novels which I had never been able to sell. I found it extremely difficult not to slide into Lecture Mode when writing fiction about Shakespeare, burdening the reader with details, insights and pedantry which no one outside academia could be expected to care about. At best the books developed great chains of accumulated Shakespearean *stuff* that they dragged around like Marley's ghost, and at worst they killed the story deader than Banquo with twenty trenchèd gashes in its head. Though my agent occasionally pressed me to do something Shakespearean and main-stream (preferably YA), believing that my academic status would bring instant respectability to the project, I found that the stuff I wanted to do with Shakespeare immediately pushed the project out of the mainstream and still felt like work.

In short, I would not have written the *Macbeth* novel (or the *Hamlet* one which followed) alone. I couldn't have done it successfully and would have become quickly bored by the attempt. But I had gotten pretty good at collaboration through years of theatre work as a dramaturg and director, during which I had taken to heart W. B. Worthen's notions of the rela-tionship between text and performance and its implications for the nature of the meanings generated on stage through an essentially collaborative practice, premised on the assumption that all performance was adaptation.[3] So the appeal of David's proposal to construct a *Macbeth* novel for perfor-mance spoke to me not so much as a literary project, still less as a critical one, but resonated as a form of theatre.

David had encountered Shakespeare as a grammar school boy, but left school at sixteen to become a journalist, and his Shakespearean encoun-ters thereafter were largely theatrical, mainstream and unacademic. He was also a very different kind of novelist from me, and we have substan-tially contrasting interests, so that from the outset we were each supplying different insights and angles on the story. As I was the academic I became, in a sense, the dramaturg to the project, highlighting theoretical and his-torical issues, as I might in discussion with a theatre director, tossing stuff up for consideration like Hamlet's gravedigger. This meant that I could indulge my tendency to lecture and rely on my co-author to help sift the usable wheat from the chaff.

Let me clarify that 'usable'. The novel, like a theatre production, could have been anything. What ours became makes no claim to rightness, accu-racy or authenticity. What we decided was usable (what, in Worthen's theatrical sense 'worked') depended entirely on an internal logic of what seemed to fit a story which evolved as we made choices.

There's an idea (usually attributed to Michelangelo) that sculptors *find* their statues in the stone, removing the excess marble to reveal them to the world. While there may be some truth to this which has to do with natural striations of colour, say, in the rock, things which influence the way the work should go, I think it mostly mystificatory bollocks. The statue could be anything, and what comes out is the result of choice and accident at the hands of the sculptor, and the notion that the statue was somehow present in the rock before the artist showed up is merely a way of authorising the resultant work. It's a kind of creative *sprezzatura*, the stripping of the artist/performer of conscious agency in order to elevate the result according to whatever qualitative terms the audience likes best: natural, divine, Platonic, organic, spontaneous. Praising art in these terms, of course, effaces the work of the audience/viewer/reader as well as the artist, since terms like 'organic' minimise judgement or opinion in favour of something we are supposed to accept as self-evident and (in every sense) essential.

There are an infinite number of potential *Macbeths* when the director first chooses the play, but those infinities gradually get reduced as decisions get made – casting, period setting, costume, music, etc. – and are refined further in scene work. In a conventional production each line (which lines? More choices) will only be said once, but how they are said is minimally clued by the script (much of that OP 'the directions are all in the text' stuff is, I suspect, more mystificatory bollocks). Rehearsals whittle down possibilities until something which is, broadly speaking, *single* emerges like the statue out of the marble. The production which results, regardless of its attitude to the text which pre-existed it (kind of), is essentially both an adaptation of that text and a new art object. There is no ideal production of *Macbeth*, merely a range of choices, and as an audience member I go to a show not to have my sense of the play confirmed but in hope of being surprised.

Which is where art diverges from criticism, or from a lot of it. When we write essays for Shakespeare journals or train the students in our literature classes, we enact a similar honing of the infinite to the singular, but the rationale is different. We want our essays to be unified and thesis-driven, so they cannot easily be plural without seeming to fail as examples of the genre, but in their pursuit of singularity they commit (or seem to commit, or pretend to commit) the crime of absolutism. 'Shakespeare's representation of Lady Macbeth suggests X, not Y, about gender, and here is why anyone who says otherwise is wrong.' If the student makes a good case, cites their sources, writes compelling and grammatical prose, they attain the sweet fruition of that earthly crown, the A.

That's fine as an exercise, but the pursuit of correctness, the assumption that if we look really carefully we will discover The Answer to *Macbeth* before which all other answers fail (42, perhaps) doesn't work for creative adaptation, though actors and directors make similar arguments about the rightness of their productions, despite their process suggesting otherwise. All of this is to say that I went into the process of writing a novel not in pursuit of the true *Macbeth* but of *a Macbeth*, a distinct, possibly even unique iteration of an old story, one which was most clearly inspired by Shakespeare's telling of it, but which would draw on other sources (unused bits of the historical record, for instance) and would make interpretive and (like theatre practice) *constructive* choices which suited our purposes, our story.

Our version began with an assessment of what we could do in a novel which the play couldn't or hadn't. That included deciding to show some of what happened offstage in Shakespeare's version, like the initial battle which we restored, as in Holinshed, to two, one centring on MacDonwald, the other on Sueno. Drawing on the sources, we rendered those battles in significantly different terms, one as a castle siege, the other as a nocturnal raid on a camp. In the case of the latter, we used Holinshed's remarkable account of how Macbeth drugged the ale going to Sueno's army so as to take them unawares. We liked this because it made the two battles tonally quite different but also because it created a through line to other key moments of poison and potions, particularly Lady M's drugging of Duncan's guards (which in our version had tragic collateral consequences).

One of the sections of the story which had fallen to me was combat because I had done it before in my fantasy fiction. The decision to show the battles was in part to distance our telling of the story from the play but also because the project had been conceived as a thriller in contemporary terms. Macbeth and his wife would be our protagonists and would die at the end, but we wanted to escape the pall of tragedy at least in certain respects. When the play works on stage it is often because the audience feels drawn to the Macbeths, something which is largely extratextual and reliant on the charisma brought to the roles by the actors, because the play gives us so little of them before they turn, as my students say, to the Dark Side. It may have mattered less to Shakespeare (and less still to Aristotle) but modern audiences/readers want to *like* their heroes, and we resolved to use that as our starting point, so that the battles and the time around them were our opportunity to write large what Shakespeare only sketches, establishing Macbeth's patriotism, nobility and trustworthiness, while building into his virility a moral compass and a devotion to his wife.

We worked from that theatrical given – that the Macbeths are the happiest couple in Shakespeare – and followed a now common actorly solution to the conundrum of Lady M's childlessness, by deciding that they had lost a child and could not get another. Their pursuit of the crown was for us – as it has been for many actors – an attempt to fill the resulting void and, most importantly, a crucially flawed impulse for each of them to give the other what they *thought* they wanted, somewhat against both their natures. The result was gently critiqued by Bill Carroll as being one of several fictional iterations of the story which softened Lady M instead of embracing her glorious transgressiveness.[4] But in the wider (non-academic) culture for which we were writing, Lady Macbeth is not a figure of glorious transgressiveness so much as a murderous, evil bitch – Eve to Macbeth's Adam, and the root of everything bad which happens in the play. Lady M is a misogynist's fantasy, and whether you think that a nuanced reading of the play or not is neither here nor there; it's a widely held assumption, and as such it presented a serious challenge to our attempt to render the core couple likeable. Moreover, any engagement with the play which works in the realm of realist characterisation, as ours did and as most theatrical productions do, find the consequences of Lady M's actions rather more difficult to celebrate than do scholars working at the level of ideas, of symbolism and abstraction: we celebrate Lady Macbeth's glorious transgressiveness right up to the moment that we have to spend a night in her house.

After the initial idea, things moved very quickly, first to the contract and then to the book itself, constructed collaboratively by email (I was in the US, David in the UK). We wrote feverishly, the five-hour time difference meaning that I frequently woke to find several pages in my inbox which I then had to match. We each tracked certain elements or characters who especially appealed to us, constructing a first draft with minimal revision, then editing each other with the kind of dispassion that could only come from distance and the fact that we didn't know each other that well. If we were upset with each other's cuts, we never said so, and though it took us a few passes to settle on a consistent style we could both live with, it was all surprisingly painless.

And fast. Though we talked a lot about broad-stroke ideas, we wrote impulsively so that much of what emerged did so without much consideration or deliberation, following each other's lead without much second-guessing, accepting what went before as premise and building accordingly like improv actors. The play provided a shape for the whole, though we augmented, adapted and altered fairly freely. David supplied research on Scotland (taking a trip for the purpose and sending photos as well as his own richly evocative prose). I supplied stage history, textual glosses, etc. We discussed academic approaches to the play – especially concerned with gender, how the world of the story seems to define it, and what to do with the moments and characters which seem to slide between gendered categories (settling, for instance, on three very different witches, each one ambiguously gendered in various terms) – but we wrote what we considered a thriller. Two months after committing to the project, we had a first draft.

While several of my novels had been recorded for audio, none of them had been conceived with that format in mind, but David had been part of a book expressly written for delivery by an actor. His insight affected the form of the novel. For instance, since speech tags ('he said', 'Banquo asked', etc.) and those adverbial phrases tacked onto dialogue which screenwriters call 'wrylies' (i.e. 'he said wryly') tend to slow the scene down and become redundant when presented by a capable performer, we wrote the apparatus around speech sparingly, relying on the actor's voice to communicate which character was speaking and how. Sometimes we left the vocal equivalent of stage directions in square brackets to give the actor tacit pointers, but mostly we tried to let the content of the dialogue clue the performer in and left the execution to their judgement. As such I was constantly reminded that while I was writing what was formally still a novel, it wasn't precisely like anything I had written before, and was built to embrace – or at least to allow – what was theoretically unavoidable: that the final product would be shaped by someone other than the people writing it. Though the document we generated looked like a book, it would function as a script, and our delivery of the manuscript was therefore the beginning of a process as well as the end of one.[5]

Meanwhile, the producers sought a suitable performer. One of the things we had set out to do was to deliberately engage with the play's putative Scottishness, something which doesn't really manifest in the play other than in its place names and its (only partially comprehended?) notion of tanistry. David is a great writer of place, and we had sought to anchor our sense of the nation (regardless of that term's historically problematic nature when applied to medieval Scotland). Audible committed early to the idea that they wanted a Scottish voice for the narrator and they considered several high profile Scots (David Tennant, even Sean Connery) before selecting and contracting Alan Cumming. We had no real say in these dealings, but were delighted by the outcome.

The book was recorded and released in June 2011 as *Macbeth, a Novel*, and was – for the most part – well received, earning an Audie nomination and achieving bestseller status. A paperback of the text came out from Thomas and Mercer (also owned by Amazon) in May 2012, by which time we had been contracted to attempt *Hamlet*. That one was out by May 2014, voiced by Richard Armitage (*Hamlet, Prince of Denmark: a Novel*). It also sold very well, was named Audible's book of the year, was nominated for two Audies, and got a rave review in the (London) *Times*, for what any of that's worth. I should say that the audiobook market – though it has devoted fans – is considerably smaller than the regular book market and bestsellers are measured in the tens of thousands, not the hundreds of thousands or millions. The *Macbeth* has done well enough that in 2021 Audible paid (more than the original commission) to extend its original ten-year contract for another decade.

The appeal of the books, both to the publisher and, apparently, to 'readers' (or whatever the audio equivalent is) seems partly grounded in the idea that they are fun, immediate, even emotive adaptations of material that people assume to be foreign, dry and difficult. This clearly reductive binary has been the heart of the books' success and – I suspect – is a good part of the impulse behind the series of Shakespeare novels from Hogarth (penned by writers more famous than either me or David), though they have – thus far – been less successful on audio. As a novelist and a Shakespearean I find this both baffling and sad, even as I am delighted to have become part of the larger cultural story of these plays (Alan Cumming, for instance, cited recording our *Macbeth* as one of the influences which drove him to perform the play as a one-man show on Broadway). Such responses also indicate the difference between the expectations of general readers and those of academics, both of which are a long way from our guiding motivations. What has been clear from the reader/listener reviews (3,418 for *Macbeth* on Audible as I write this, which is a lot, almost 4,000 for *Hamlet*) is that our decision to render the core couple likeable, even admirable – particularly in the face of a Duncan who is both incompetent and despotic – worked for a lot of people. Our readers weren't appalled by the Macbeths so much as they were horrified and saddened to see them go increasingly off the rails as their misguided actions (more misguided than evil) take them to increasingly awful places. This was what we wanted.

But if a good deal of the positive response to the book was slightly surprised, almost all the negative response grew out of horror at what we had done to the play, the novel frequently being presented as a debasement of the hallowed original. This was to be expected, of course, but I confess to being surprised by how our (to my mind pretty tame) moments of sex and violence were singled out for particular outrage, despite their proximity to the play. We did not linger unduly over Macbeth's unseaming of MacDonwald from the nave to the chops, but we were called on the carpet for the moment nonetheless, a detail which made me think that many of those who professed themselves appalled by what we had done to the play didn't actually know said play anywhere near as well as they thought they did. Indeed, the play invoked by such reviews often seems to be another kind of abstraction, a poetic ideal unsullied by bodies or by the grim material and political realities it presents. Other negative responses said that we simply retold the story from the play, another assessment which seems not to remember the original at all. We created a major character out of the Porter, making him an agent of Macbeth's moral decline, as we later turned Hamlet's reflective soliloquies into snappy dialogue with the court dwarf, son of old Yorik, a figure which may be a figment of Hamlet's imagination, or might be another of Elsinore's ghosts. Some people loved these deviations from the originals, others hated them, others seemed not to notice them, even as they made pronouncements about how much we repeated/violated Shakespeare.

But the flipside is also true, of course. The Magic Bard whose holy ambience we may have sullied in our retelling according to some readers (listeners?) also bought us equally undeserved credibility and gravitas. The book offers the frisson of the Magic Bard, a brush with his sanctity, without readers actually having to deal with the difficulties of early seventeenth-century poetry, picking up its cultural references, or piecing out the imperfections of something whose natural end-form exists in performance. The audio-novel's semiotic apparatus makes semantic determinations which the play does not, closing off alternatives, but somehow feels more complete, more unified. The performers also brought a particular gravitas to the respective projects in ways benefiting us. Cumming made full use of his Scottish brogue in the *Macbeth* performance, in ways matching the book's grounding in a sweeping Highland landscape barely present in the play. He is also a Shakespearean actor, so the performance – as well as dignifying the prose in ways good actors always do – obliquely reconnected the story to its origins Shakespearean and Scottish. These things counter the charge of inauthentic Shakespeare which might be levelled at the project with other authorising means. Something similar happened with the *Hamlet*, whose narrative benefited not just from Armitage's RSC credentials but from his starring role in the three-year swords-and-sorcery extravaganza which was *The Hobbit*. In a small way my own credentials as an academic were seen to justify and dignify the project, the whole thing, enacting a curious negotiation or navigation of Shakespeare's own status. Similar responses – pro and con – began emerging in response to the Hogarth series long before any of the novels actually came out, so that one can't help feeling that for some readers their reaction is determined more by the fact of the books, than by their execution.

It is easy to dismiss the outraged reviewers who think the hallowed Bard has been violated by our adaptation and, for me, pretty easy to dismiss those who complain because our version doesn't enact the one reading they imagined as essential. Less easy to dismiss are the readers whose critique grows out of bafflement: 'Why do this?' they ask. We already had the plays. As a radio interviewer asked me, 'Did we need these?'[6] Beyond the multivalently hubristic 'Oh reason not the need!' (my actual response on air), I don't have a good answer, and I confess that if someone else had written them I probably wouldn't have read them. I co-wrote them as a sidebar, an adjunct to both my creative and academic endeavours, and as such they model both and neither. They are curiously liminal entities about which I was passionate during the writing, though I always felt I was performing an exercise, a high-wire act, perhaps, whose daring was more impressive than its beauty, and which I could only pull off so long as I didn't look down.

But then perhaps it's the academic in me which sees the attempt as courageous. There are plenty of Shakespeare-inspired novels floating around these days, the vast majority of them penned not by scholars but by people who, I assume, feel none of the low-grade anxieties I do about moving into Lecture Mode. Shakespeare the man has been usefully dead a long time, which means that his works are out of copyright and are therefore fair game (as well as 'fair use') for appropriation and adaptation, be the refashioning minimalist or radical. Shakespeare ethically, culturally and *legally*, belongs to all of us. As a theatre professor directing students performing Shakespeare, I often feel that the key is getting them to that moment where they feel – and the audience feels – that the language is theirs, that it's in their minds and hearts, their blood and bones, that they *own* it. This is ownership in the sense of both aesthetic mastery and the politically loaded question of who gets to claim Shakespeare's cultural legacy and impact in our more profoundly diverse present. It is expressly not the kind of ownership which denies others the right to possess the Shakespearean original and make it theirs, which is, perhaps, why that sense of ownership feels so much more elusive for me as a novelist, and not only because some people want to deny me that right. Because, the truth is that I'm not convinced of it myself.

There is something appealing about moving outside the conventionally dramatic genre in reimagining these stories, and I suppose there is a slightly anti-theatrical impulse there: the desire to stage a production in my head without having to deal with all those pesky actors and designers who insist on stamping the production with their own ideas and talents.

In that sense, authorship is a claim to ownership, that Shakespeare – or at least *this* Shakespeare – is mine. We did it and, when the first one was well received (if ignored by scholars – which I'll take over the inevitable sneering) we did another, better – I think – than the first, more confident, sparer, less overawed by the original and managing an occasional self-awareness which I rather liked. Both books suffer from a tendency to take themselves too seriously, and sometimes I think there are more opportunities missed than taken, but there are moments which work quite well and – as in the theatre – you can't hope for much more than that.

But it still doesn't feel like ownership, and all told my own response to the books remains conflicted. I'm glad a lot of people like them, but I haven't listened to either audio version in its entirety and the prospect of doing so wearies and unnerves me. The positive responses seem to me loaded with factors from outside the novel *qua* novel, be that adoration of the performer (some of it fanatical), or of 'history' or 'Shakespeare', and I'm doubly ambivalent about those who praise the book as a 'way in' to Shakespeare for struggling students, as a successful 'updating' (whatever the hell that means), as if the books were a kind of gateway drug designed to lure in Reluctant Shakespeareans. I find myself strangely invisible in the finished product, unable to read the text and identify which bits were originally mine without recourse to notes. David and I did a decent job rendering the voice of both books pretty seamless, I think (though the two novels read quite differently), but that doesn't begin to explain how little of me I find in the book compared to my other novels, books whose ownership is less in question. When David told me he was too busy to pursue a third and that he was happy for me to proceed alone or find another co-writer, I did not seriously consider doing either, despite Audible's continued interest.[7] Though I feel strongly that the books are innovative and inventive in response to the plays, I can't help feeling oddly subsumed by them, reduced to barbarian or scribe, engulfed by the grotesque and sprawling amoeba which is Shakespeare, his works, and their cultural legacy. No matter what we tried to do, it would always feel somehow pre-empted by the original, ours being a minor iteration of something richer and more amorphous, something which always – somehow – anticipates every idea, every tweak of phrase, character or plot point. I don't know why this is, and though I'm more inclined to assign it to a kind of cultural projection onto the original than read it as something essentially protean in Shakespeare's originating genius, I still feel like I'm standing on the shoulders of a giant so large that without a powerful lens and a great deal of patience I cannot be seen at all. But then that is, perhaps, for the best.

To return to the ideas I started with, I find myself asking what this thing is that we made, and by 'we' I include not just my co-author, but the editors, actors, engineers, directors, producers, marketers and everyone else who, in the broadest sense, contributed to the final product. That inclusivity, of course, implies the product's performative dimension, the ways in which the audiobook is as close to theatre as it is to a book designed for a more traditional form of 'reading'. The list of co-creators must necessarily include Shakespeare and, if we are to deal rightly with the matter, the innumerable editors, theatre/film practitioners and, perhaps most importantly, educators, who – over the last four centuries – have all made incremental contributions to the wider cultural sense of what plays like *Macbeth* and *Hamlet* are, were and might be. To include such a wide swath of history as collaborative authors might reduce the term to technicality, but it serves to problematise those simple binaries with which I began, indicating the extent to which subsequent creation and adaptation is less like a line drawing than it is a collage, made up of shreds and patches cut by many hands. As a scholar, I am acutely aware of how much of our stories pre-existed our project, but as a creative artist I insist upon the newness of our version, the extent to which it is a response to cultural and academic history as much as it is a retelling of the 'original' stories which were themselves adaptive recreations of existing texts. I say this not to fudge the primacy of Shakespeare's telling of those stories, but to acknowledge a sense that story always emerges from multiple origin points and always finally escapes its author, mutating not just as it is retold, but as it takes on different forms and meanings through interaction with the unavoidably loaded and constructive interpretations made by its audience. My struggle to spot the contribution I made to the final product is theoretically inevitable in ways reminiscent of the collaboration essential to theatrical production, a collaboration which is temporal as well as spatial, and which diffuses authorship across a wide body of contributors, however much the scale of those contributions may vary. The confusion arises out of the popular persistence of a heroic modernist valorisation of single authorship which reduces that collaborative collage to the either/or binaries with which I began, one which pits the modern 'adapter' against the 'original author' in an endless, tedious cage match over issues of authority and authenticity.

Retellings of *Macbeth* – contrary to that popular desire – cannot and should not be merely a persistent echo resembling Banquo's ghost, the undead thing stalking the adapter and brandishing the evidence of that adapter's transgression. They are more like the apparitions of his descendants which stretch out not just to King James, but to the crack of doom; each one spawns new genetically related scions, but each – by virtue of the mothers unidentified by the play – are informed by wholly unrelated genetic material making them unique. Our story contains some of Shakespeare's play, but it is radically reshaped by formative elements from outside the text, the author or his moment in history. Some of that genetic material, literally and metaphorically, comes from me and David, our accumulated experiences and interests and those of the period in which we live, but it also comes more generally from the legacy of an old play which has been bent into new shapes by four centuries of art, education and cultural evolution Shakespeare could not have imagined, and will be further reshaped by the future. Framed in these terms my quest for my own authorial presence in the books aligns me uneasily with some of their detractors who, like Macbeth gazing upon the apparitions of Fleance and his descendants, can only rage at the way they are subsumed by an unstoppable future.

Notes

1. My fiction is published mostly under the A. J. Hartley name, though I also use the pseudonym Andrew Hart. My academic work is generally published under Andrew James Hartley. The distinctions are slight but useful. Speaking as AJ, I don't like *Titus Andronicus* very much.
2. It was my third archaeologically inflected mystery/thriller published by Penguin-Berkley, but it performed poorly, and the publisher dropped the series.
3. Though he has published much which is excellent since, I still return most to *Shakespeare and the Authority of Performance* where these core ideas are laid out (Cambridge: Cambridge University Press, 1997).
4. William C. Carroll 'The Fiend-like Queen: Recuperating Lady Macbeth in Contemporary Adaptations of *Macbeth*', *Borrowers and Lenders* 8, no. 2 (2013), https://borrowers-ojs-azsu.tdl.org/borrowers/article/view/139/275. Accessed 26 February 2023.
5. When the book was taken by Thomas and Mercer and published as a novel some time after the audio release, we had to go back in and fill out some of the speech tags and tone, probably inflecting the text according to what the actor had done in the studio.
6. Mike Collins on 'Charlotte Talks', broadcast on the NPR affiliate WFAE, 14 July 2011.
7. As it turned out, David wound up doing a solo *Romeo and Juliet* audiobook a few years later.

Index

Page numbers with the suffix 'n' refer to notes while those in *italics* refer to figures.

Printed in the USA
CPSIA information can be obtained
at www.ICGtesting.com
JSHW061333050324
58627JS00004B/39